GETTING THE GREEN

FUNDRAISING CAMPAIGNS

for Community Colleges

GETTING THE GREEN

FUNDRAISING CAMPAIGNS

for Community Colleges

Stuart R. Grover

Published by

Community College Press®
a division of the American Association of Community Colleges
Washington, DC

in partnership with
Council for Advancement and Support of Education
and
Council for Resource Development

Community College Press
American Association of Community Colleges
One Dupont Circle, NW, Suite 410
Washington, DC 20036

Community College Press® is a division of the American Association of Community Colleges (AACC), the primary advocacy organization for the nation's community colleges. The association represents more than 1,200 two-year, associate degree–granting institutions and more than 11 million students. AACC promotes community colleges through five strategic action areas: recognition and advocacy for community colleges; student access, learning, and success; community college leadership development; economic and workforce development; and global and intercultural education. For more information, go to www.aacc.nche.edu.

This book was published in partnership with the Council for Advancement and Support of Education (CASE) and the Council for Resource Development (CRD). For more information, go to www.case.org and www.crdnet.org.

Publication of this book was made possible by generous support from Fintelo.™ Fintelo is a next-generation Internet-based learning software program that makes online teaching and learning for instructors and students engaging, immersive, enjoyable, and easy to use. For more information, go to www.fintelo.com.

Design: Brian Gallagher Design
Editor: Deanna D'Errico
Printer: Kirby Lithographic, Inc.

Library of Congress Cataloging-in-Publication Data

Grover, Stuart R.
Getting the green: fundraising campaigns for community colleges/Stuart R. Grover.
p. cm.
Summary: "Comprehensive guide to planning, carrying out, and following up fundraising campaigns for community colleges. Published by AACC in partnership with Council for Advancement and Support of Education and Council for Resource Development"—Provided by publisher.
Includes bibliographical references and index.
ISBN 978-0-87117-390-4
1. Community colleges—Finance. 2. Educational fund raising. I. American Association of Community Colleges. II. Council for Advancement and Support of Education. III. Title.

LB2328.G76 2009
378.1'06—dc22

2009030004

DEDICATION

This work is dedicated to my brother Warren, who has encouraged me in all my endeavors; to Pamela Transue, who is my life partner and provides a model for effective leadership; and to Griselda "Babe" Lehrer, who inspires everyone with her selfless dedication to volunteerism.

Contents

PART 2: THE CAMPAIGN

PART 3: AFTER THE CAMPAIGN

Foreword

I took a nontraditional path to the community college presidency, right through the development office. I wish I had had this book and its accompanying set of resources before I plunged, blindly, into an executive director position to launch a foundation for my hometown community college. At the time, I had no fundraising experience, but I had community connections, administrative experience in community colleges, and a passion for our mission with an eagerness to take on something new. This was in the late 1980s, when many community colleges moving into their second and third decades needed an independent vehicle to accept private gifts, primarily for scholarships. Few of our community colleges had comprehensive private fundraising programs or development offices. We were one- or two-person shops doing grants and special events, able to passively accept private gifts. Few of us had clear and systematic strategies for asking for gifts or for thoughtfully connecting with and thanking donors. We were, in many regards, leanly staffed operations doing fundraising without all the necessary ingredients and tools, ingredients and tools that are clearly described in this first-of-its-kind book.

I was fortunate that many of the key ingredients for success were in place at my first college. The president wanted to fundraise. The board of trustees was unanimous in forming the foundation and eager to supplement public funding with private giving. The foundation board members were not afraid to ask for money. And, as a novice development leader, I was not wed to special events fundraising and intuitively understood the importance of large, major gifts from individuals and corporations. We had large-scale institutional support. And I was eager to move into a new arena where I could translate my marketing, strategic planning, and writing skills into developing and telling a compelling story about the college's needs—its case for support.

It was during these early years that I learned the truth of this simple statement: The number-one reason people don't give is that they are not asked. Few of those we asked in these early years said "no," and most commented that they had never been asked to give. Now, as a president, having fielded a few "no" responses, I've learned to take these answers as questions (as is suggested by Webber, 2009, in *Rules of Thumb)*. A "no" could mean that the case for support is in need of refinement that can be discovered by asking questions. What some describe as the "no, not yet" rationale.

Over the years, I have relied on two professional development groups for fundraising advice and support: the Council for Resource Development (CRD), an affiliated council of the American Association of Community Colleges (AACC), and the Council for the Advancement and Support of Education (CASE). As a president, I'm still involved with CRD, and as a budding development professional, I took several of my foundation board chairs to the CRD training programs in the 1990s. During my time as a vice president for advancement, I was very involved with CASE, serving on the District II Board. And, now, as a president, I volunteer for and benefit from the work of AACC. So, I am thrilled and heartened by this first-time partnership between AACC, CASE, and CRD, which has led to this groundbreaking book on community college fundraising. This is an important partnership, on an imperative topic, at exactly the right time.

My background in fundraising is a primary reason that, as a president, I have made alternative resource development an institutional priority from my first year. We community college leaders have a responsibility to set up systems in our colleges that allow us to cultivate, ask for, and steward private gifts. It is clear, now more than ever, that public funding alone will not support us fully in reaching our institutional aspirations, nor will it ensure the viability and vitality of our colleges into the future. One of the first ways presidents set the foundation for successful fundraising is with the development of compelling visions and strategic plans for our colleges that map out ways for private donors to help us to reach our institutional goals.

As community colleges, we are uniquely positioned for great success in private fundraising. Our local connections greatly expand our donor universe, if we think and act creatively. Our corporate ties are tangible. We supply the local workforce of the future (95% of our graduates live and work in the immediate region). And, because we are late to the game of private fundraising compared to other sectors of higher education, our larger, community-based, donor universe is largely untapped. How many of us have a fully functioning fundraising quadrangle at work that includes some special events yet also ensures that we are systematically asking for annual, major, and planned gifts? As presidents, we must be prepared to offer our time for fundraising, allocate resources to staff, and tool and train our development teams. It's impossible to develop full-fledged annual giving, major gifts, planned giving, and capital campaigns without an adequately staffed development operation that also includes support for less touted but essential infrastructure functions such as prospect research and alumni relations programming.

We must also be patient. The amount initially invested may take years to pay dividends. Some years, the amount invested may not directly result in a profitable yield. We must be focused on the long-term legacy benefits, not the shorter term quick wins that can often result when we first start out. We must convince our boards of trustees of the growing importance of and need for private fundraising. We must be bold in articulating to our college constituents and others the rationale for hiring an annual giving officer, for example, rather than filling another much-needed faculty, support, or administrative position. We must be willing and able to ask for gifts. And, to set an example in building a new campus culture of philanthropy, we must step up and give generously of our own resources.

My own journey in developing a culture of philanthropy on my campus is just over seven years long and requires constant tending. A fundraising program is not a once-and-done presidential priority. Leading, with philanthropy as a core component of our work and thinking, requires a new mindset that is essential to future success. Every job description for a new community college president that I've seen recently includes private fundraising experience as a core, desired presidential skill.

Getting the Green offers a comprehensive and detailed look at private fundraising in community colleges. It's a must-read for aspiring and new community college presidents, academic leaders searching for ways to bring in new dollars to support new programs, and advancement professionals. It's a resource for foundation board leaders and members. It's also a potential read for new board of trustee members, especially those serving as liaison members to foundation boards. It's a book that can inform in-house leadership development programs—both on our campuses and through key organizations. Most importantly, my hope is that the book draws attention to the serious, emerging, and exciting work of community college philanthropy to enable us to attract the talented development professionals of the future to our campuses.

I can't emphasize enough the importance for all of us to start or expand serious and comprehensive private fundraising efforts in our community colleges and to take a long view of the potential impact these efforts will have on our colleges long after we leave them. We have a unique responsibility to be what Galford and Maruca (2006) call "legacy thinkers." A few weeks ago, on a walk through Harvard Yard, I came across a building named Holworthy Hall. A modest plaque read: "Named in Honor of an English Merchant, Sir Matthew Holworthy, who in 1681 gave 1,000 pounds, the largest gift received by Harvard College during the 17th century." I stopped in my steps, struck by the tradition of philanthropy that this once large, but now small gift, set for

Harvard. I was also struck by the sophisticated and subtle stewardship that this plaque symbolized. In community colleges, we have many gifts that have catalyzed our campuses and other gifts yet to be discovered and recorded. It may be more than 400 years later, but as community college leaders we can and must create a culture of philanthropy that will ensure our viability and vitality in increasingly uncertain times by cultivating, asking for, and stewarding our own "Holworthy" gifts.

Getting the Green offers the cultivation, campaigning, and stewardship advice necessary to create the culture and legacy of philanthropy that will be essential to the overall success of community colleges into the future. It's a book that many of us—presidents, development professionals, and novices—will turn to again and again to set and chart or re-chart our private fundraising compasses. It's a book that can help us all become legacy-oriented rather than transaction-oriented leaders of our community colleges.

Karen A. Stout
President, Montgomery County Community College

PREFACE

Your college is stronger than it has ever been. It has earned the trust and admiration of the community. Your classrooms are bursting with students of all ages. Your faculty members are providing informed, up-to-date information to thousands of learners. Representatives from local businesses populate your advisory committees because you provide them with the skilled, trained graduates they need and offer an economical alternative to the first 2 years of a bachelor's degree.

You have reached a point, however, where the demands on your institution have outstripped the resources available to meet them. Government funding and tuition barely meet your basic needs; vital programs and projects depend on raising additional funds. For example,

- You have money for a new building but not enough to equip it.
- You have funds to hire faculty for a new program but not enough to hire the faculty needed to be competitive in the marketplace.
- Newly arrived immigrant populations and other deserving students are clamoring for education, but your scholarship funds can meet only a fraction of the demand.
- Your flagship program is housed in an outmoded building, and there is no money in your budget for renovating or reequipping it.
- Budgets for professional development have shrunk to the point where your faculty and staff members are unable to get the training they need to serve your students.

Imagine that a group of college leaders has gathered to discuss whether they should embark on a fundraising campaign to meet some of their needs. The following are the kinds of questions they may have on their minds.

The president: “I already work 60 hours a week running the college. How can I find time for a campaign? And I’ve never really raised money before. Four years ago I was in charge of academic programs. How will I learn what I need to know?”

The vice president for advancement: “We’ve been raising $400,000 a year for scholarships and some faculty development funds. We do an auction, a golf tournament, and a request to our faculty and staff, and several small local businesses and foundations give us $5,000 to $10,000 every year. How will we raise big money? And who will do it? I’m busy with events and with coordinating public awareness and government relations.”

The foundation board chair: “Our local economy isn’t doing so well. My own business has seen its profits fall, and many of my friends are concerned about whether they’ll ever be able to retire. I joined the foundation because I believe in the college and its mission, but putting together an auction table and procuring some good items is about the extent of my comfort level. Will I have to ask my friends for money?”

A member of the board of trustees: “I’m only on the foundation as a liaison between the two boards. I didn’t get involved in the college to raise money, and if I do, I’ll probably lose friends, not to mention all the time I’ll have to spend. And is there a conflict when raising private funds for a public institution?”

Executive committee members of the foundation: “How will we decide what to raise money for? Raising money has to be expensive—where will we get the money? I already give $1,000 a year. Will I have to give more? The state university just started a $300 million campaign. How can we compete?”

Every year, hundreds of community and technical colleges find themselves in similar positions. They have discovered what other nonprofit organizations in the United States have found over the past 100 years: To take advantage of new opportunities, they must increase their capacity to attract private funding. As government funding at all levels has declined, and most community and technical colleges have changed from government funded to government supported, raising funds from the private sector has increased in importance.

Accepting this challenge will help ensure the vitality of the nation’s community and technical colleges. Hundreds of institutions have already accepted it; a few have undertaken multiple campaigns. They have discovered that the outcome is not only new money for important initiatives; the act of embracing private fundraising on a large scale also raises the college’s profile in the community; builds morale among faculty, staff, and students; and attracts important new adherents to the institution’s mission.

However, the activities involved in bringing about a major fundraising campaign are daunting to those who will hold the power to give it the green light. You, as foundation board members, executive officers, and staff may approach fundraising with a mixture of excitement and fear. You understand the possible benefits to the institution, but you realize the potential pitfalls. What if you fail? What if the community has no interest in supporting you? What if the demands on your administration and staff are too great and the entire institution suffers?

You also have personal concerns, ranging from the financial (How much do I give?), social (If I ask people for money, it'll hurt my relationships), and professional (Do I have the time? Will I risk business relationships if I ask people for money?). You also realize that part of you is truly unsettled by the task of engaging in large-scale fundraising. How will you learn enough about the school to avoid embarrassing yourself? How will you learn the necessary fundraising skills?

Over the past 25 years, I have consulted with more than 300 organizations and thousands of people who have embarked on their first campaign. I have heard almost every conceivable question and helped quell most of the concerns people like you have had. This book combines my experience with knowledge from top consultants, community college presidents, foundation directors, and fundraising staff who've faced the same issues to offer answers to the many questions you may have about fundraising for community colleges.

Acknowledgments

As with any book that reflects more than a quarter century's experience in a field, *Getting the Green* owes its existence to far more people than can be readily acknowledged. College presidents, foundation directors and board members, consulting colleagues, and many others have influenced my work and shaped this book.

No work on community college fundraising can fail to acknowledge its debt to Ray Clements and his late wife Lana, who pioneered in this field and whose company has served more than half of the nation's community colleges, always with ethical and effective counsel. The Clements Group, LC, has been instrumental in introducing community colleges to philanthropy and highly successful in engaging communities with their colleges.

My colleagues at The Collins Group, through their focus on best practices, have also helped shape this work. The firm's founder, Dick Collins, managed one of the first community college campaigns in the region, successfully linking an important project both to its natural allies in business and to the leading philanthropists of the area.

Polly Binns, executive director of the Council for Resource Development (CRD), has been very helpful in providing me with relevant materials and directing me to accomplished professionals in the field. Staff members at the Center on the Advancement and Support of Education (CASE) have also been helpful in providing guidance on technical aspects of fundraising for higher education.

In more than 25 years of consulting with community and technical colleges, I have had the privilege of working with many talented and dedicated presidents and foundation directors. Don Bressler, former president of Renton Technical College, stands out for his ability to encourage his staff and volunteers to take risks and reach ambitious goals. Scott Reardan, vice president for advancement at South Seattle Community College, set high standards with his ability to relate to his board members and inspire them to achieve excellent results. Roberta Greer, also at South Seattle Community College, stands out as a foundation board member who helped move her entire institution to a higher level.

To help provide a national perspective to this work, I had the good fortune of receiving the benefit of the experience of many foundation directors. I want to especially thank three outstanding leaders for their insights. Perry Hammock, executive director of resource development at the Ivy Tech Community College in Indiana provided examples of experience from a statewide multicampus system that has run several successful campaigns. Drew Matonal, president of Hudson Valley Community College in New York, shared his experiences as a chief executive during a campaign. Eileen Piwetz, the vice president for institutional advancement at Midland College in Texas, offered her thoughts on raising money with a strong board and a limited donor base. These and other veterans of the campaign helped confirm my beliefs that while fundraising for community colleges cannot be a one size fits all proposition, the role of volunteers and the college president are key elements of any successful campaign.

Several skilled readers offered useful advice while this work progressed. Pamela Transue, president of Tacoma Community College, provided insights from the standpoint of a president who had recently completed a successful campaign. Kara Hefley, former vice president of institutional advancement at Highline Community College, offered a detailed critique of my approach. Tory Groshong provided skilled editing that helped make the manuscript more readable. Finally, Deanna D'Errico, editor of the Community College Press, offered gentle professional guidance throughout the entire process of preparing this work for publication.

The acknowledgments listed here reflect only a small portion of my debt to others and cannot be exhaustive. I apologize to all those people who have helped shape this work whose names are not listed here. Needless to say, any errors or shortcomings are mine alone.

INTRODUCTION

Many books have been published for professional fundraisers on how to plan and implement a fundraising campaign. In fact, a number of them are cited as resources for this book. But this is the first book, to my knowledge, written specifically with the community college audience in mind. This book is primarily for community college presidents, administrators, foundation board members, and trustees—people who, because they are being called on increasingly to become involved in fundraising, need a basic primer.

Each year, scores of community and technical colleges decide that they have to take a leap forward in their fundraising efforts. They decide that the time is right to expand scholarship programs, strengthen academic offerings, expand or improve facilities, or add amenities to the campus. These decisions result in fundraising campaigns called *capital campaigns* if they involve a building, *endowment campaigns* if they are raising a permanent fund to create income that supports an organization's purpose, or *major gift campaigns* if they seek to support new programs, activities, or provide furnishings and equipment. Campaigns that combine more than one need are labeled *comprehensive*, a common approach for community and technical colleges. Over the past decade, funds raised by community colleges have ranged from a few hundred thousand dollars to more than $100 million in campaigns running from 1 to 7 years.

> In 2008, Americans gave away more than $300 billion, almost $2,000 for every household in the country and about 2.2% of all money earned in this country, a percentage that has remained relatively stable over the past century.
>
> *Source: Giving USA Foundation (2009)*

What sets these campaigns apart from other kinds of fundraising is that community colleges are increasing their capacity, just as a for-profit entity does when it issues stock or sells bonds. They are turning to the community for the additional funds to expand the colleges' ability to fulfill their mission. Just as investors make decisions based on their financial return, donors to community college campaigns will judge colleges based on the social benefit that results from the community's investment in the project.

This book focuses on campaigns with goals ranging from about $500,000 to $25 million. Smaller goals often can be reached without full-fledged campaigns, and relatively few community colleges have goals exceeding $25 million. Nevertheless, because the approaches outlined in this book apply to all fundraising, you will benefit from its advice no matter what you're raising money for or how much money you are attempting to raise.

The chapters are divided into three parts that address what needs to be done before, during, and after a campaign. The fact that the chapters in Part 1, "Before the Campaign," constitute more than half of the total number of chapters is testament to the amount of thought and planning needed even before a campaign is officially launched. In the first three chapters, I address some general issues, including understanding what's specific to community college fundraising (chapter 1), the attitudes key for successful fundraisers (chapter 2), and fundraising ethics. In chapters 4–13, I turn to all the tasks that need to be performed prior to formal launch, including gearing up your campus and getting agreement to move forward (chapters 4 and 6); completing administrative tasks such as commissioning a feasibility study (chapter 5) and developing a master plan, marketing materials, and a system for managing gifts (chapters 8, 9, and 13); and building a prospect list (chapter 11).

> Charitable behavior in the United States is unequaled anywhere else. In any given year, almost 70% of all Americans make a cash gift to at least one charity. Among wealthy Americans with a net worth of $5 million or more, more than 97% make charitable gifts each year.
>
> *Source: Center on Philanthropy at Indiana University and American Express (2007); Center on Philanthropy at Indiana University (2009)*

Chapters 14–23 pertain to the campaign itself, separately addressing different stages (i.e., the board, family, and community campaigns) and types of gifts (i.e., lead and institutional gifts, and public funding), as well as pertinent communications issues (i.e., leveraging the media and jumpstarting stalled campaigns). Chapter 15, "Preparing for the Ask," provides detailed guidance on cultivating donors, and Chapter 20, "Forming Additional Solicitation Committees," stresses the importance of having a sufficient number of volunteers to approach donors. The two chapters in Part 3 touch on celebrations and continuing stewardship when the campaign concludes.

Throughout the book, I have tried to avoid describing in detail things like how to write a brochure, how to organize an annual campaign, or how to track prospects and donors. These are all matters for which foundation staff members are responsible; my goal was to help my audience understand the basics of organizing and managing a campaign. What I have done, however, is to supply some useful materials in the appendixes and, through sidebar material and a comprehensive resource list, direct readers to as many outside resources as possible so that they can explore issues of particular interest to them, or beyond the purview of this book, in greater depth.

To undertake major fundraising initiatives, you need both staff and volunteer leaders. Although the fundraising profession has expanded exponentially, nothing replaces the power of volunteers in attracting financial support to worthy projects. This book collects in one place the lessons learned from thousands of volunteers who have shared their wealth, enthusiasm, and talent with organizations.

Some Useful Facts About Fundraising Campaigns

- According to the Giving USA Foundation (2009), about 75% of charitable gifts made in 2008 came from living individuals; another 7% came from bequests and 6% from family foundations, resulting in 88% of all gifts having their origins with individuals rather than institutions such as corporations or public foundations.
- Although community colleges receive a higher percentage from corporations and businesses than do other charities, they still need gifts from individuals. A small percentage of gifts come from bequests and trusts.
- Campaigns are governed by the rule of 12. One of the few constants in any campaign is that about half the money comes from a dozen (or fewer) gifts. You won't raise a million dollars by having 1,000 people each give $1,000. By the time you finish this book, you'll see why.
- The single most effective and efficient way to raise money is for volunteers to ask people they know for gifts, face to face.
- It takes money to raise money. Generally, you should expect to spend from 5% to 15% of the campaign goal on fundraising. Large campaigns might cost less as a percentage but will still cost a lot on an absolute basis. The percentage is usually higher for first campaigns, small campaigns, or campaigns that feature expensive parties.
- Money comes from people you already know and who know you; the majority of funds will come from donors within 50 miles of the college. Don't expect gifts from new or prominent donors across the country. Oprah Winfrey is probably not going to make a large gift.
- Publicity alone does not raise money. Good publicity creates an environment conducive to raising money, but donors rarely write big checks simply because they see a story in the newspaper.

Part 1: Before the Campaign

CHAPTER 1

Understanding What's Different About Fundraising for Community Colleges

We take comfort in believing that our challenges are unique, that no one has ever had to climb so steep a mountain or face such daunting obstacles. This is especially true for organizations raising large amounts of money for the first time. They focus on all the things that can go wrong and all of the real or imagined disadvantages they face. Leaders of community and technical colleges often respond in the same way. And, in fact, they are different from other nonprofits in many ways.

In many respects, community and technical colleges are the new kids on the block. Whereas Harvard University traces its roots back to the 17th century and the major land grant universities were created in the mid-19th century, the first community college opened its doors in Joliet, Illinois, in 1901; even by 1950, only slightly more than 200,000 students nationwide attended a few hundred 2-year colleges. The number of colleges grew slowly, until a rapid increase in the 1960s, when 457 new colleges opened. By 1996–1997, nearly 6 million students were enrolled. (AACC, 2009a). In 2008, that figure reached 11.7 million studying at 1,177 community and technical colleges (AACC, 2009b).

This enormous growth gradually has been matched by access to philanthropy. Initially, community and technical colleges were largely outgrowths of government-funded vocational-technical schools, fully supported by local or regional jurisdictions. Some legislators even questioned whether these colleges could legally seek private support because they were government entities. Although this objection gradually faded, only incrementally did they achieve an independent identity, still funded primarily by government. In the 1970s and 1980s, this began to change, as an increasing number of colleges recognized that their revenue sources were insufficient to meet the demands placed on the institutions.

The emergence of the Council for Resource Development (CRD) in 1973 accelerated this trend, as CRD began providing technical support and continuing education to fundraising professionals. Likewise, the Council for Advancement and Support of Education (CASE) began serving community colleges with its founding in 1974. More community and technical colleges established independent foundations, charged with raising money on behalf of their parent institutions. Adventuresome colleges launched ambitious campaigns to support major initiatives, to the point where campaigns are now common in many community and technical college districts. Increased scholarship availability, enhanced facilities, and innovative programs have enriched the communities they serve.

Seven Types of Philanthropists

1. **Communitarians (26%)**
2. **The Devout (21%)**
3. **Investors 15%)**
4. **Socialites (11%)**
5. **Repayers (10%)**
6. **Altruists (9%)**
7. **Dynasts (8%)**

Source: Prince & File (2001)

Nonetheless, public perception has not kept pace with reality. Individuals, corporations, and foundations have, in large part, maintained the outmoded notion that our colleges receive all required funding from public sources. They regard us differently than private colleges and universities or large state-supported institutions. In many cases, they exclude our colleges from receiving their support, while others assign a low priority to funding our needs.

Just as state-supported colleges and universities have engaged in vigorous education around this issue, we will have to continue our efforts to inform funders that increasing portions of our budgets are paid for by student tuition and fees and that if we are to maintain true accessibility, we will need the aid of private philanthropy. Despite increases in philanthropy, community colleges receive less than 2% of their income from charitable giving, compared with figures that range from 15% for social service and health organizations to 60% for arts and cultural institutions. According to CRD, in 2005 the total philanthropy received by the nearly 1,200 community and technical colleges reached $1.2 billion, barely more than an average of $1.4 million per college. Fewer than 2% of all gifts to higher education go to community colleges, although the amount is steadily increasing (Lanning, 2008a).

This book's focus on campaigns points out a unique aspect of community and technical colleges. For most nonprofits, campaigns emerge from long-standing and successful fundraising programs. They have engaged in annual fundraising, direct mail, special events, and other types of activities that have yielded a large and committed group of donors. At that point, they decide that they have sufficient strength to embark on a campaign.

Community and technical colleges often use a campaign to jumpstart their fundraising efforts. A campaign provides leaders with a reason to talk with their communities, to invite people to be part of their efforts, and to establish a well-staffed fundraising program. For some colleges, it's a way to develop a true spirit of mission for the foundation; occasionally it's the reason why the foundation is formed and supported internally.

Many colleges plan and successfully implement campaigns for $1 million or more even if they have never raised more than $100,000 in a year prior to the campaign. Although they need preparation for the campaign and must spend time and effort to introduce themselves to community leaders and donors, they discover that the campaign focuses their efforts and attracts the resources they need for success. When done correctly, such a campaign serves as a springboard for future fundraising success.

"Don't buy into the myth that alumni won't give. It has always been assumed that those who attend community colleges will only be loyal to the four-year institutions they later attend. . . Babitz's experience shows that alumni from community colleges will give if they have positive experiences at two-year institutions. . . .It pays to build an alumni database. Granted, it will cost money to track down alumni and to buy the proper software to maintain the data, but the community college will be better off in the long run. The key to smart marketing is a good list."

—Angelo (2005)

Our Supporters Are Different From Those of Nonprofits

In their groundbreaking work, *The Seven Faces of Philanthropy*, Prince and File (2001) discussed the various motivations for giving. Using extensive research, they determined that a major source of giving to educational institutions and hospitals was a type of donor they labeled a *repayer.* Such donors gave generously to express their gratitude for what they had received from an institution—a great education, a second chance, the opportunity to play on the varsity soccer team—or, in the case of hospitals, skilled and compassionate care for themselves or loved ones.

Community and technical colleges have two challenges related to encouraging repayers to make the types of transformational gifts they have made at other institutions. The first is that we only have gradually begun to keep track of our alumni. In the era before computers, enrollment records were seldom maintained in an easily retrievable format, making it difficult or impossible to contact alumni in their prime giving years (55+ years old). In a society where almost one fifth of all families move each year and in which others change names, jobs, and spouses, tracking down names from 50 or even 20 years ago is a frustrating and time-consuming process. Although we have done a better job of tracking alumni from more recent years, most community college alumni are under the age of 55, the age at which philanthropy generally rises to its higher levels.

"Repayers have had some experience that changed their life, an experience which created in them a feeling of obligation or gratitude. These experiences constellate around educational institutions and medical events, and Repayers focus their giving on these two nonprofit types. Repayers do not seek recognition for themselves; as a general rule, they prefer that nonprofits focus on constituents. They are appreciative when the officers of the nonprofit are sensitive to their reasons for being philanthropic as well as their own personal situation."

—Prince & File (2001)

A challenge that many colleges have begun to face is our lack of a hold on our alumni as their philanthropy of choice. Even though a small percentage of our graduates regard us as their alma mater, we do not hold that position for most alumni. Simultaneously, we serve as a feeder system for 4-year institutions and as the nation's largest source of postgraduate education. In both cases, our alumni (whether or not they received degrees from us) frequently look to other colleges or universities as their true alma maters. As we talk more to our alumni, this sentiment is changing, but there is a long way to go before we approach the degree of alumni participation at 4-year colleges and universities.

Furthermore, while many prominent people hold degrees from community or technical colleges, most of them are more strongly connected to 4-year colleges or universities. Many of them list their bachelor's degree and advanced or professional degrees on their resumes; fewer include their attendance or degree at a community or technical college. This lack of publicly identified graduates of our colleges helps make our position less visible in the community as a whole. Identifying leaders with community and technical college backgrounds and encouraging them to become more vocal in expressing their gratitude for their foundational education will help our philanthropic efforts.

Community and technical colleges penetrate into every corner of the United States, from Key West, Florida, to Barrow, Alaska. Although we share some aspects of mission, each college differs from the others, and all rely primarily on local economies to support them. Raising money in rural, sometimes impoverished communities presents significant challenges that set us apart from a major symphony orchestra or a metropolitan YMCA.

Despite these challenges, we are not different from any other nonprofit organization located in rural or poor communities. A food bank in rural Louisiana, a mental health clinic in central Alaska, or a historical museum in rural New England all face the challenges of a small population, limited corporate and foundation support, and reliance on the generosity of individuals. All have succeeded in attracting financial support and surviving in the bleakest of economic times. They, like us, must rely on making their missions relevant to their communities and building relationships that ensure ongoing philanthropic support.

We Have Closer Relationships With Local and Regional Businesses

We have fundraising advantages that set us apart from other nonprofit organizations. We already have close relationships with local and regional businesses that recognize the role we play in workforce training. In many cases, our nimbleness and ability to undertake programs rapidly to meet their needs gives us a significant call on their charitable resources. Part of our quick response reflects our ability to request and use equipment and other in-kind gifts to fulfill our missions.

When we create or expand a culinary arts facility, restaurant supply firms have an interest in our students training on their equipment and often provide it as a gift or at greatly reduced cost. Allied health professionals are in great demand; hospitals and equipment manufacturers realize that their training requires access to up-to-date equipment, which is often extremely expensive. As programs at our colleges expand in these and many other fields, suppliers often provide free or reduced-cost equipment, sometimes through computer programs that create virtual facilities, at other times offering the actual equipment. In some parts of the nation, we also have relationships with many trade unions through our apprenticeship programs. These unions provide financial support and reduced-cost services in many cases, allowing our building funds to stretch further.

Many corporations and foundations also understand the need for expanded scholarship aid to ensure a broader pool of potential workers in selected fields. As they seek to improve the ethnic and economic diversity of the workforce, they understand that community and technical colleges offer the most direct path to success for members of minorities and economically challenged families. In 2008, of all undergraduates in higher educational institutions, 55% of Native Americans, 45% of Asian/Pacific Islanders, 55% of Hispanics, and 46% of Blacks attended community colleges (AACC, 2009b). This has encouraged many companies and foundations, large and small, to provide either ongoing or endowed scholarship funds for their specific vocational concern.

Our Internal Challenges Are Different

We differ from other nonprofit sectors because of the extent to which there is, at times, a misunderstanding and distrust of the fundraising function within the college. Community and technical colleges serve placebound students, who often come from modest backgrounds. These colleges believe that they have fewer alumni with great wealth and less access to major donors than do 4-year or graduate institutions. There may be a sense that the very wealthy cannot ever fully identify with the community and technical college mission.

"It is easy to see that community colleges are deserving of public and private support. Indeed, community colleges have the 'best case' for presentation to prospective donors. It is a fact that many people want to be a part of something so exciting. This desire is greatly enhanced because they can make a difference where they live, in the same town where they made their money and where the college is located. We, in community colleges, should never sell short the magnitude of potential support that is awaiting our proposals. The gold is not at the end of the rainbow. The gold is in our backyard. We are living in a time when there will occur the greatest transfer of wealth in the history of civilization.... In a very real sense the door is wide open for us to state our case to them, either personally or through their agents. Remember, the case is strong; internalize it, organize it, commit to it, memorize it, present it."

—Daniel (2002)

From an internal point of view, instructors and staff often have minimal direct contact with the foundation. Instructors, even those with tenure, may only make $41,000 to $56,000 annually (American Association of University Professors, 2009). They may not understand why the head of the foundation or vice president for advancement should make anywhere from $64,000 to as much as $150,000 (see CASE Compensation Survey 2008 at www.case.org; López-Rivera, 2009). At times, they also resent the virtually unlimited access top fundraising staff have to the president and the various perceived perks that come with the job (often including extensive travel and expense accounts).

If your college leaders do not help explain the value that these investments in time and resources bring back to the institution, your fundraising potential can be limited. Simply stated, instructors and staff are among your most effective contacts with potential donors and the best spokespeople for the college. If you allow them to feel alienated from the fundraising process and the campaign, it will result in lost opportunities.

Consulting instructors and staff, including them in planning for the campaign, using them to review campaign priorities, and involving them in committees and task forces related to fundraising will help demystify the process. Although the integration of the entire institution may take awhile, it will be well repaid over time. The extent to which support for fundraising efforts pervades your entire institution is a major predictor of campaign success.

Everyone Is a Potential Donor

A final, more general way in which our institutions differ from other nonprofits is that we boast an almost completely undefined donor base. What does this mean? Some nonprofit organizations have a tightly defined donor base, related to the people they touch directly. It is difficult for a church to go beyond its congregation when it seeks to raise money for expansion. Private K–12 schools define their potential donors as parents, grandparents, and alumni. Local and regional theaters have a slightly larger donor universe, but most gifts from individuals originate with subscribers.

For community and technical colleges, however, the donor universe is much broader. We often touch more than 10% of the families (assuming approximately 2.5 members per family) in our communities each year, an enormous pool of potential donors. Maricopa Community Colleges (AZ) have an enrollment of 267,000 (Bloom, 2009), in a county where about 4 million people live; Miami Dade College (FL) (2009a) has an enrollment of 167,000 in a county with a population of 2.4 million. Obviously, corporations that benefit directly from our programs are potential donors. Alumni may feel the desire to express their gratitude. We also strengthen communities, so almost any individual, business, or foundation that cares about our towns, cities, and counties has a potential interest in supporting us. We have policies of open enrollment and almost unlimited accessibility, so altruistic people who wish to see a more level playing field are attracted to our mission, and government entities feel justified in providing additional (non–operating budget) support. Finally, we provide specialized technical training so that corporations and individuals with a belief in that particular field may be inclined to provide financial support.

We are, of course, not the only institutions with an undefined donor base. Large science museums, state universities, and the humane society are all examples of nonprofits that appeal to a broad spectrum of donors. But we can feel secure that almost any philanthropically inclined person in our community is a possible donor to our cause.

Despite our differences, community and technical colleges do also resemble other nonprofits and have the same challenges and opportunities for fundraising as the local hospital, YMCA or YWCA, theater group, and even the state university. For example,

- We are not as well known in our communities as we would hope and must work hard to gain renown and respect.
- Our initial gifts for any campaign must come from those who know us best—our boards, staff, and clients (in our case, often our corporate and business partners rather than our alumni).
- We must demonstrate community benefit if we are to convince people that they should support us.
- Every major gift we receive results from personal attention and individual strategies, primarily through contacts between individuals.
- We must demonstrate wise stewardship of all gifts we receive.

In other words, despite the many ways in which we differ from other types of nonprofits, the rules for successful fundraising remain the same for community and technical colleges. We are obliged to engage in ethical behavior and subscribe to best fundraising practices as developed over the past century. The following chapters will focus on those techniques and provide you with guidelines for your activities.

CHAPTER 2

Six Key Attitudes for the Successful Fundraiser

To succeed within a campaign, whether as a staff member or a volunteer, you must maintain a relentlessly upbeat attitude. Once you start thinking a campaign might fail, it will. At the same time, campaigns don't get done by themselves, and their success is not preordained. They require true sacrifice and dedication. Attitude isn't enough without hard work.

Most board or committee members think a campaign will be either very easy or very hard. The ones who see it as easy offer many paths to success. Here are some comments you might hear from those who think such a campaign is easy.

- "Let's get an article in the paper. Someone's sure to see it and write a big check."
- "We have 50,000 families in our area. If each of them gives $100, we can raise $5,000,000 in no time."
- "Bill Gates has a huge foundation and loves education. Why wouldn't he give us the money?"
- "A bank will lend us the money, and we can pay it off in 5 or 10 years."

Others see roadblocks at every turn:

- "The economy's in the toilet."
- "The local university's big campaign has all the money."
- "Not enough people really know about us."
- "Our group doesn't have the big money that's on the board at the art museum."

Neither the optimists nor the pessimists have it right. The campaign will succeed because of well-organized hard work. There will always be competition, economic challenges, and setbacks. You won't attract money through public relations or by dividing the goal into equal slices. The vast majority of campaigns reach goals without much help from billionaires. Everyone has fears and concerns about fundraising, no matter what their position in the community, their experience, or the merits of the project.

Fundraising probably fosters even more fears than public speaking. It connects to our unease in discussing money, our fears of rejection, and our concern about forcing our ideas on others. However, it's easy to counteract these fears by assuming attitudes that will ensure success. I describe six of them here.

Six Key Attitudes for the Successful Fundraiser

1. **Giving Begets Joy**
2. **Fundraising Is Not Unethical**
3. **Fundraisers Are Respected Leaders**
4. **Fundraising Benefits Others**
5. **People Will Give Freely if They Can**
6. **The Campaign Will Succeed**

1. Giving Begets Joy

It's easy to fall into the idea that giving is an imposition—something people do against their will and resent. Think about the times you've given money to something you really cared about—a scholarship fund, the local food bank, or other worthy cause close to your heart. You felt good about doing something for the cause. You expressed your love of humankind and helped redress the balance between justice and injustice. Every year, community colleges give scholarships to students who are the first in their family to attend college. Often, they organize an event that introduces the scholarship donors to the recipients. To see how a gift can change a young person's life gives joy and deep satisfaction.

People give because it expresses their deepest values and desires. The result of a gift is joy to the person who gives. In modern society, relatively few people have time to volunteer. We lack the skills to educate the young or heal the sick. Our gifts, however, can accomplish those goals, and when our money translates into a better world, we feel good. Community and technical colleges occupy an especially strong position in this regard. According to a 2007 survey sponsored by the *Wall Street Journal,* more than 76% of all donors say that their prime motivation for giving is attraction to an organization's mission (cited in Donor Advising, 2009). We offer a compelling and easily articulated mission that most people identify with.

2. Fundraising Is Not Unethical

Somehow, although we gladly give money, we fear that asking for money is unethical. We think of the boiler room operations and the dinnertime phone calls. We forget that we've happily given to the Red Cross or the Girl Scouts. When disasters strike, people's first impulse is to give, whether after the 9/11 attacks, the tsunamis in Asia, or Hurricane Katrina. Giving offers a sense that we are all part of a larger effort. In chapter 3, I examine the issue of ethics in fundraising, but for now it is essential that you accept the fact that fundraising, done properly, is not unethical. Ask the right way, and you will never have to compromise your personal ethics.

3. Fundraisers Are Respected Leaders

Many people think that asking for contributions will lose them friends or alienate them from their community. They fear that people will start crossing the street when they see them coming, seeking to avoid unpleasant encounters. Fortunately, reality doesn't bear out these fears. Men and women who raise money for community priorities become role models who do something wonderful—create better communities.

Think of the people in your community whom others admire. In many cases, they have served as chairs of fundraising campaigns. They are the ones who get things done. They are leaders. They have earned respect because they have been brave enough to stand up for what they believe in. Many communities have First Citizen awards. The recipients of that honor have almost universally provided leadership in local or regional fundraising campaigns, demonstrating their willingness to accept responsibility for accomplishing important community goals.

Campaign leadership is both a mark of respect and a testing ground. People ask you to participate in a campaign because they see in you the skills and traits that others admire. They want to follow your direction. Others see you as embodying credibility and integrity, because those are the characteristics that inspire others.

4. Fundraising Benefits Others

When you're part of a campaign, it is too easy to equate what you're doing with begging. You're going to your friends to ask for money, and you may feel that their gift is to you personally. In fact, you are serving only as a conduit for the organization, not acting out of self-interest. This lack of self-interest dictates the need for volunteers to lead a campaign. In their groundbreaking work, *The Trusted Advisor*, Maister, Green, and Galford (2001) wrote about the trust equation. They indicated that you achieve trust by dividing the sum of expertise, reliability, and intimacy by the degree of self-interest. In raising funds, you, as volunteers, bring the ability to talk about your college and its projects in detail. You are discussing something you believe in with people you know, and you will keep your promises. You provide all of the positive attributes of trust with a minimum of self-interest. Not only are you not making money from being part of the campaign, but you are also making a substantial gift and providing large amounts of your time without compensation.

Your friends understand that you are asking them to support a cause you believe in. They listen to you because they respect you, but they'll give because they believe in the mission you're there to talk about. If they say no, it is not because of any lack of respect for you. Your request for money derives from a desire to do good, not to advance your career or your finances. Before you've asked anyone else for a gift, you've spent dozens of hours learning about and shaping the project. You've also made your own gift to demonstrate your belief. Your request for your friend to join you simply gives him or her the chance to achieve joy through supporting a good cause.

5. People Will Give Freely if They Can

We all know the feeling. You are about to ask a friend for a gift, and you fear that he or she will feel pressured to give. You're afraid that it will seem that you are using your friendship and the goodwill between you and your friend to manipulate your friend. You think of a used car salesman and the martial arts metaphors of strong-arming, hot-boxing, or arm-twisting.

Except that isn't what happens. People in today's world are sophisticated about charitable giving and their own personal priorities. They won't give to something they don't believe in, and they will never give more than they can afford. You are serving as a matchmaker, establishing a connection between friends and a cause they might find joy in supporting. Just as a real-life matchmaker doesn't always succeed in creating a marriage, you won't always find the perfect match. Your friends have free will, and you will not lead them astray. On the other hand, they can't give if they're not asked.

6. The Campaign Will Succeed

If you've ever played golf, you know that a belief in your ability to hit a shot properly is central to your success. If you think you're going to hit the ball into the rough, you probably will. If you are convinced that you'll land it in the middle of the fairway, your chances for a straight drive are better.

Fundraising is no different. If you can focus on your feeling of accomplishment at the campaign's completion and imagine the satisfaction you'll feel at having played a role in the project's success, you will do better than if you contemplate the humiliation you'd feel if you failed. While it's human to retain a little nervousness and fear, your primary focus should be on the inevitable success of your efforts.

Your belief has a basis in fact. Whatever the economic climate, whatever the cause, whatever the region, more than 9 out of 10 campaigns succeed. The ones that fail usually reflect extraordinary, but avoidable, circumstances. Communities band together to follow the initiative of those brave enough to lead. Hidden wealth appears, known wealth extends itself to new levels, or new wealth emerges in response to worthy causes. You provide the magic ingredient of leadership that creates a catalytic effect on others.

With few exceptions, everyone (volunteer or staff) involved in a major campaign starts with some fear and concern. However much staff members and consultants try to ease these concerns, fundraisers on the verge of a campaign still have them. What most participants in campaigns find, however, is that by the end of a concerted fundraising effort, they have evinced the six key attitudes. They discover that their efforts are appreciated by others, succeed in the great majority of cases, and achieve goals that the community values. They find themselves cast into the role of leader by their friends. They discover that they were giving others the chance for joy. They discover that asking for support is fun and strengthens existing relationships. They make new friends. Perhaps most important, they find a level of satisfaction in their project's success that they had not expected could exist. Talk to people you know who have been part of successful campaigns. In all probability, they hold these attitudes. After you provide leadership, you will, too.

But success also depends on empirically proven fundraising methods. Just as other professions have standards and rules, so does fundraising. It has ethical standards (see the next chapter) and methodologies that have been shown to work in peer-reviewed, replicable research. The approaches suggested in this book reflect both the ethical and empirical bases of fundraising:

- Campaigns must be something other than business as usual. Both volunteers and donors receive motivation from a well-organized, focused campaign with a designated start and finish and a clearly stated goal.
- Campaigns request large sums of community funds. In return for these funds, you must demonstrate the social benefit of the investment you are requesting. The more concrete you can make the outcomes of the campaign, the more likely you are to succeed.

"Upon my wife's death, I was motivated to set up a scholarship in her name to honor her and to leave something in this community that has been our adopted home for 25 years… I can attest that there is no greater feeling of satisfaction than sharing funds we have been fortunate enough to accumulate over our life time."

—Patrick H. Norton, benefactor to Monroe County Community College (in Budd, 2006)

- Donors and volunteers respond to bold and innovative visions. The larger the vision, the more likely your community is to provide an enthusiastic response.

CHAPTER 3

Fundraising Ethics

We all get fundraising calls from people asking for money for obscure organizations with names that sound vaguely familiar or that invoke respected institutions. Those calls from the State Patrol Widows' Fund or the Firefighters Garden Club interrupt our dinners and irritate us. We sometimes find out later that they're scams, with no relationship to the organization whose name they invoke, and that the vast majority of funds go into the pockets of a fundraising firm.

If we've fallen for these pleas, we get mad. If we haven't given money, we probably also get mad, and we allow this anger to reflect on our attitudes toward fundraising in general. We also read about the questionable behavior and improper use of money by a small number of charitable organizations. The head of a national nonprofit used his expense account to finance his relationship with a teenager. Money given to an organization for a specific disaster was put aside to use for future disasters. Can we trust that the money we give or that we ask for will go to the purpose for which it's meant?

Fundraising often seems to rely on techniques that make us feel uncomfortable. We equate fundraising requests with high-pressure sales calls. Even the casual or informal terminology of fundraising reflects this attitude. How many times do we hear about the need to "put the arm on" a friend, or refer to a charitable request as "hitting someone up" for a gift? These phrases and tactics sound and feel unsavory.

The Association of Fundraising Professionals (AFP) has more than 24,000 members worldwide. Its code of ethics and the accompanying donor bill of rights can be found on its Web site at www.afpnet.org. The Giving Institute (formerly the American Association of Fund-Raising Counsel [AAFRC]) also has a code of standards of practice for its members, who represent the largest and best-known consulting firms in the United States (Giving Institute, 2007).

Certified Fund Raising Executive (CFRE) International certifies fundraising professionals who demonstrate the knowledge, skills, and commitment to the highest standards of ethical and professional practice in serving the philanthropic sector. CFRE International fulfills this mission by establishing and administering a voluntary certification process based on current and valid standards that measure competency in the practice of philanthropic fundraising. CFRE certificants must agree to uphold the Donor Bill of Rights and abide by CFRE International Accountability Standards.

CASE has several clear and compelling ethics statements (all available at www.case.org), including the CASE Statement of Ethics, the CASE Principles of Practice for Fundraising Professionals at Educational Institutions, and the Donor Bill of Rights (AAFRC, Association of Healthcare Philanthropy, CASE, & AFP, 1993). Network for Good (2008) has also developed an e-philanthropy code of ethics. These codes of ethics provide universally accepted approaches to fundraising that rule out the noxious practices of boiler-room efforts and high-pressure sales. The rules that follow are consistent with the professional standards of fundraising but are expressed in nontechnical terms.

Three Principles of Ethical Fundraising

We want to do things that establish us as leaders and demonstrate that we are ethical and honest people. How do we engage in fundraising in a way consistent with those desires? The answer is simple. We should make sure that our organizations and we, as their representatives, behave in ways that are totally and unarguably ethical. Our actions should reflect three main ethical principles, as follows.

Respect for the Donor

Donors should give only because they want to give, not because they feel obliged to do so. They should give because it gives them joy and reflects their personal values and desires. Your task is to make certain that the people you ask to support your cause feel good after they give and continue to feel good about their gift. These simple concepts should dictate your approach:

- What they care about.
- What appeals to them and what doesn't.
- If they don't care about your project, they shouldn't give.

Your request must focus on the impact the donated funds will have rather than what they will build. Donors won't want to build a new allied health professions building; they'll want to improve your community's health-care system. They don't want to endow a new professorship in welding; they want to ensure that your local construction companies have the skilled workers they need to thrive. They don't want to double your first-generation scholarship fund; they want to guarantee the possibility of a good education for hard-working, bright young people.

Honesty and Transparency

Those dinnertime phone calls bother you because they're so vague and evasive. The callers expect you to give without knowing about the organization they represent. When you ask them financial questions, they may not be able to tell you exactly how the money will be used. You, on the other hand, are not paid to ask for the gift and have no financial interest in whether or not your friend gives. Your involvement reflects your own passion for the college's mission. You're proud of the college and everything it does.

To an almost total extent, everything about your college is part of public record, including budgets, salaries, and even evaluations of specific programs. As a result, there is no reason not to tell your friends virtually anything they want to know about the organization, since it's all available anyway. You should display a policy of complete transparency about

- the college's financial situation
- how money is used
- the percentage of the gift that goes toward the project
- why the project is important
- whom the project will serve
- how the project will make a difference

The Donor Bill of Rights

Philanthropy is based on voluntary action for the common good. It is a tradition of giving and sharing that is primary to the quality of life. To ensure that philanthropy merits the respect and trust of the general public, and that donors and prospective donors can have full confidence in the nonprofit organizations and causes they are asked to support, we declare that all donors have these rights:

I. To be informed of the organization's mission, of the way the organization intends to use donated resources, and of its capacity to use donations effectively for their intended purposes.

II. To be informed of the identity of those serving on the organization's governing board, and to expect the board to exercise prudent judgment in its stewardship responsibilities.

III. To have access to the organization's most recent financial statements.

IV. To be assured their gifts will be used for the purposes for which they were given.

V. To receive appropriate acknowledgement and recognition.

VI. To be assured that information about their donation is handled with respect and with confidentiality to the extent provided by law.

VII. To expect that all relationships with individuals representing organizations of interest to the donor will be professional in nature.

VIII. To be informed whether those seeking donations are volunteers, employees of the organization or hired solicitors.

IX. To have the opportunity for their names to be deleted from mailing lists that an organization may intend to share.

X. To feel free to ask questions when making a donation and to receive prompt, truthful and forthright answers.

Source: AAFRC et al. (1993)

You'll answer the questions you can and offer to help them find answers to those questions you can't answer. They will make their decision based on complete information.

Accountability

After your college receives a gift, it must communicate with the donor. This begins with a timely acknowledgment of the gift, tax receipts, and other legally required documentation. It continues with ongoing communication about how the money is being used on the project. For very large gifts, it might mean a personal tour of the construction site, semi-monthly updates on campaign progress, and other factual and complete information. When the project is over, the accountability continues, with a focus on outcomes rather than facilities or endowment.

Donors who have given gifts that include permanent recognition should be invited to see the space or plaque containing their names. If you have a grand opening, they should receive an invitation and tour. As operations start in a new facility, they should receive reports on how the facility allows you to do a better job of fulfilling your mission. Donors to an endowed faculty position or program should meet the staff and students involved. Supporters of scholarships should receive a report summarizing the progress you've made in expanding scholarship support and have the opportunity to meet individual scholarship recipients.

The wonderful part of total accountability is that it offers a reason for you to remain in contact with your donors. They will become part of the organization and feel a sense of ownership for its people and programs. When it comes time to launch your next campaign, they will be prepared to help you.

If you follow the three principles of ethical fundraising, several of your fears will disappear. Your friends and acquaintances will do something that gives them pleasure, based on complete and honest information. They will receive acknowledgment and recognition for their gifts and take pride in the achievements they have made possible. You will feel certain that your fundraising involved neither coercion nor manipulation. The donors will have engaged in an even-handed relationship in which you have given them the opportunity to fulfill their most deeply held values. Through transparency and accountability, your organization will also ensure the proper use of donated funds. You will obey all accounting rules, establish the correct controls over handling of contributions, and be able to show where every dollar went.

CHAPTER 4

Gearing Up for a Campaign

This chapter is addressed to the college as a whole. The processes described here will be led by your president and carried out by the staff, overseen closely by the trustees of the college. It is vital, however, that these processes occur and that foundation board members and staff internalize and understand the results. Although college presidents will find this chapter the most useful, all campaign participants should read it to understand that a campaign flows organically from their institution's mission, vision, and strategic plan.

When you embark on a campaign, by definition you are claiming that the campaign will help your college achieve high-priority objectives. You are not simply chasing money or responding to opportunism. It follows that campaigns must emanate logically and organically from your institution's mission, vision, and strategic plan. In addition, you should test your priorities against those perceived by the community to ensure that you can attract financial support for your efforts. You should also be certain that the projects encompassed within your campaign are sustainable once the campaign reaches a successful conclusion.

Getting Technical Elements in Order

Mission and Vision Statements

Often, organizations issue a collective groan when asked to consider (or reconsider) their mission and vision. Yet, properly done, such an effort is richly rewarded. An organization's mission defines its reason for existing. What do you do that sets you apart and guarantees that you serve your community? Whom do you serve and how? What are the most important values you represent (such elements as excellence, ensured access, diversity, and innovation). A mission statement offers a promise to the community; your success as an institution is determined by the extent to which you measure up to the standards you establish in your mission statement. In overwhelming measure, we, as a sector, have clear and compelling missions that state our goals and make manifest our reasons for existence.

Visions are another story. Few institutions are willing to set lofty visions for themselves or to phrase their visions in a manner that is oriented toward community benefit. They do not fully answer the question, "If we do a really good job at attaining our mission, what difference will it make to our stakeholders?" A successful vision statement inspires those who read it—both your internal community as it seeks support and the external community as it considers whether to provide support. Big gifts require big visions; small changes and improvements attract less dramatic giving.

A vision statement should be ambitious but realistic, soaring in its audacity but down to earth in its outcomes. Vision statements focus on the outcomes of your activities and the way in which you will alter your institution and service area through your activities. Many community colleges share elements of their vision statements. If you maintain open access, your community will prosper economically because of a well-educated and trained workforce. If you reach out to those who are disadvantaged, you will create a more integrated, harmonious community. If you uphold the promise of diversity, your institution will reflect your commitment.

Having the right policies in place before beginning a campaign will help your board members reach comfort levels in working with donors and ensure uniform communication. Foundation policies should include the following:

- College–foundation operating agreement
- Investment, asset management, and payout policies
- Naming policy
- Confidentiality policy
- Revocable or irrevocable pledge policy
- Gift acceptance policy
- 990 Form–related policies:
  - Conflict of interest policy
  - Whistleblower policy
  - Document destruction policy

Many vision statements are inwardly focused, expressing how great the college itself can be. One of the nation's largest colleges, Miami Dade College (2009b) in Florida, starts its vision statement with the following: "Miami Dade College is committed to being a college of excellence" before providing details of the impact that excellence will have on its students, employees, and programs. Another large system, Maricopa Community Colleges (2009) in Arizona, takes a more outward view, claiming as its vision "A community of colleges—colleges for the community, working collectively and responsibly to meet the lifelong needs of our diverse students and communities."

Others combine outward and inward aspirations. Ilisagvik College (2006) in Barrow, Alaska, describes itself as "a two-year tribal college offering quality post-secondary academic, vocational and technical education aimed at matching workforce needs. We are dedicated to perpetuating and strengthening Inupiat (Eskimo) culture, language, values and traditions." Community College of Vermont (2009) states, "We strive to acknowledge and respond to change and apply our resources to identified needs. We seek to be a respectful, welcoming community that challenges economic and social barriers and excludes no one who has an ability to benefit."

Vision statements are vital to successful fundraising because they offer the inspiration that leaders need, along with the outcomes that faculty, staff, and donors hope to achieve through their participation in the campaign. As opposed to a mission statement, which describes what you must do now to fulfill your role, a vision statement opens up future possibilities.

Some vision statements evoke visceral responses. When a major research institute states as its vision "to eradicate cancer as a cause of human suffering and death," almost everyone can respond with a heartfelt, "amen." When an organization seeks money to build a shelter to fulfill its vision that "Every woman in our county should have a safe place to sleep every night," community members can nod their heads in agreement. And if your community college announces a scholarship initiative whose ultimate result will be that "Every person should have affordable access to quality education and training," your community will embrace the vision wholeheartedly.

In examining your vision statement, you should test it to ensure that it is

- Specific to your college: No one else could lay claim to the same vision.
- Compelling: If achieved, your vision would make a real difference that your community would applaud.
- Wide reaching: If achieved, it would touch many people, including those beyond your staff and student body and corporate partners.
- Believable: As much as we all want world peace, your college can't guarantee it. The scope of your vision must be commensurate to your ability to deliver on it.

"The tendency of institutions to focus their attention on the size of the goal of their proposed campaign rather than what they should and can realistically achieve is probably the greatest cause of dissatisfaction with campaign results. The primary purposes of the campaign should be to enable the institution to fulfill its mission, accomplish its strategic goals, and enhance its educational quality and access. The primary purposes should not be to meet a particular financial target, raise more money than another institution, or set a new fundraising record."

—CASE (2009)

Why do you need a vision statement? As you look to the future, you need a clear focus on where you are going and what you will achieve. A better future for your constituents serves as the rationale for asking for support. A fundraising campaign is a request for recapitalization of your college. In effect, you are looking to investors to provide you with the funds needed for you to do more, and do things better, than you do now. Unless you have a clear vision for where their investment will lead, it is hard for them to justify their investment. Doing the same thing over and over doesn't require or merit expanded funding. Increasing your capacity to achieve your vision does.

Vision statements also provide broad guidelines for strategic plans. They offer the result you hope to achieve by completing your plan and provide a benchmark for determining whether your strategic plan is focused properly. If you, like Tacoma Community College (2009) in Washington, have as part of your vision "a commitment to innovation and excellence," your strategic plan should address those issues in its goals, objectives, and strategies.

The Strategic Plan

The college needs to know where it wants to go and what it wants to do. It has to have clearly defined concrete goals and objectives and possess the strategies needed to achieve them. All other elements of a campaign must emanate from this strategic plan.

Many colleges have adopted a strategy called appreciative inquiry in creating or revising strategic plans. This approach invites all of your stakeholders to participate in the planning process and promises that their concerns and desires will be heard. Constituencies both from within the college and from the broader community are represented. The process commits to ensuring that all points of view are represented and listened to respectfully. Appreciative inquiry focuses on what works within your institution and how to build on positive elements, rather than concentrating on fixing elements that are broken. Generally, the plan that emerges from this approach reflects the best elements within the institution and provides a solid foundation for future growth.

Campaign-Related Policy Models

Sample policies can be found on the CRD members-only Web pages under *Resources/Foundation Resources* at www.crdnet.org.

Whatever approach your college uses, your strategic plan must offer a coherent, clearly focused path to future success. It must offer a relatively small number of goals, measurable objectives that will allow you to know when you've achieved those goals, and specific strategies and tactics that will offer a path to attainment of your objectives. The best strategic plans can fit on a few sheets of paper and offer an exciting and easily understandable list of your institution's priorities. It should also be a living document that you revisit regularly to update and use to benchmark your progress. If your strategic plan is not on the desks of your leaders, providing them with ongoing guidance, it's probably dead and will soon be buried. Strategic plans are vital to fundraising campaigns because they engage your entire institution and its constituents in priority setting. They establish the areas you need to work on if you are to move toward reaching your vision and allow you to compile a list of those areas where you require recapitalization.

Needs Assessment

Once your organization has either developed a new vision statement or confirmed the old one, it's time to relate this vision to your future. The first step is to test your vision against the reality of the marketplace for your services. If you want to build and equip an allied health professions facility, you need to know that area health-care providers will hire your graduates. If you think you need a day-care center for your students' children, you need to survey your students to determine how great the need for such day care will be. You also have to develop an operating plan that ensures that the facility will be able to continue operations once it opens.

Performing needs assessments often results in pleasant surprises: South Seattle Community College, which prided itself on its culinary arts program, realized that it needed to update its equipment and facilities. It talked with representatives of the local hospitality industry and discovered that there was a need for more trained chefs and restaurant professionals, who indicated that the campaign would gain much more support if the college promised to expand the number of graduates, rather than only improving the training of the current number. The campaign doubled in size and was more successful than the institution hoped—all because it had done its homework before starting.

> *"A capital campaign should not be thought of as an isolated activity to raise funds. Rather, it should be seen as a significant step in a long-term journey to enhance private-sector awareness, partnering, and resource development."*
>
> —Culp et al. (2008)

Some needs are easy to demonstrate. If you receive three times more scholarship applications from qualified students than you can fund, you can easily explain the need for a scholarship campaign. If local hospitals come to you pleading for more nurses, then funds for expansion of your nursing program are easy to justify. Sometimes, however, you discover your potential supporters do not appreciate your plans: When North Seattle Community College approached potential donors about a proposed center for high technology training, it discovered that local corporations did not see the institution as the appropriate one to train students for high-tech occupations. The negative results of the needs assessment prevented the college from embarking on a frustrating, unsuccessful campaign and allowed it to maintain its focus on its traditional offerings.

Project Sustainability Statement

Community and technical colleges are essential institutions that the community regards as ongoing resources that will always be there. No matter the economic climate or the state's budget crisis, the colleges will continue to fulfill their mission. Unlike a museum or a theater company, your college does not have to demonstrate that it is sustainable on a long-term basis. That's a given.

However, if you're launching a new program or initiative with private funds, donors will want to know how the program will survive in the future. Will it generate earned income through tuition and fees? Will it be incorporated into an existing department's budget? Do you expect an additional state budget appropriation once the program proves itself? Your donors will want to know that you will sustain what they start.

Sample Project Definitions

- The addition to the automotive service training center will provide 30 new service managers to our local repair shops.
- A $3 million scholarship endowment will let 30 students annually be the first in their family to attend college.
- Approximately $2 million will allow us to equip our new allied health professions building with the modern equipment that will ensure that local hospitals can hire graduates ready to go to work the first day.

Project Definition

Defining a project precisely will help you raise money and strengthen your organization. Never forget that the building, endowment, program initiative, or other goal is only a vehicle for helping you achieve your mission and vision. People won't give money for a new science building or an endowment. They'll give money to guarantee that regional businesses will have the skilled workforce they need or that they are helping to level the playing field through scholarships.

Communicating With External and Internal Constituents

Introducing the Community to Your College

As was mentioned in the first chapter, often your campaign will be the first major foray you have made into fundraising. As a result, your fears that the community doesn't fully understand what you do, and why they might not consider donating to your projects, are probably well founded. It's up to you to do something about that.

What should you do before you consider launching a campaign, perhaps before you even know what you hope to raise money to support? Your most important task is to talk with the people who need to know about you. Who are your area's major leaders, donors, businesspeople, and civic and political leaders? Who are the people you want as allies as you seek support? Who doesn't know as much about you as they should? Depending on the size and scope of your institution, this list might constitute 40 names or several hundred.

What are you telling these people? At this point, you're telling community leaders about the college. If you're the president, you can talk about the programs, the students, the instructors, and the outcomes. Most people won't know that community colleges are the largest source of postgraduate education in the United States or that students who have completed their first 2 years at community colleges do as well at 4-year institutions as students who started there. They probably don't know that community and technical college students excel in competitive testing in almost all fields, including nursing and accounting. And they certainly don't know the specific strengths of your college. You are not asking anyone for a gift at this point or even discussing the campaign. Instead, you are increasing the community's familiarity with your college in general and explaining how you are financed. These conversations will ease their inevitable transition from interested citizens to partisans of community and technical colleges.

Who should make contact with your potential leaders and donors? The college president is the appropriate contact for some potential donors. Some people only want to meet with the person in charge and desire the respect that such an invitation implies. Certainly, having a member of a foundation or advisory board who is acquainted with the person is also appropriate and helpful.

Before You Launch a Feasibility Study . . .

- Revisit your mission statement.
- Review your vision statement and perhaps expand it.
- Renew your strategic plan.
- Perform a needs assessment to confirm the demand for your project.
- Do the financial due diligence to ensure that your project is sustainable.

For other people, the most natural way of arranging a meeting is for the foundation staff or board members to host them at the college. You don't need to invent a reason for them to visit your college. Every week you have an athletic event, a lecture, a concert or recital, a special class, or an exciting student presentation or exhibit that would give a visitor a clearer sense of who you are and what you do. Bellingham Technical College in rural Washington hosts a welding rodeo each year, "Junkyards War," in which students compete to create sculptures out of spare parts. Their work is amusing and clever and displays enormous skill. What better way to focus attention on their program than to invite the president of a local construction company to help judge the event? Bowling Green Technical College in Kentucky runs a chef's camp for kids each summer. This brings in dozens of kids who learn useful skills, while publicizing the college's culinary arts program.

Needless to say, it also brings in parents and grandparents who learn about the college in a personal fashion (see Kentucky Community & Technical Community College System, 2009). At Ivy Tech Community College (2009) in Indiana, the Hospitality Administration Program stages a seven-course French dinner annually at an "April in Paris" event that draws a large audience to appreciate the college.

You can also ask instructors and staff to help reach out to the community. Often, instructors whose programs will benefit from the campaign will know local leaders personally, through church membership, civic organizations, or other activities. They can invite their acquaintances to campus to meet the president and foundation board members and to hear more about what you do. For example, at Tacoma Community College (WA), art instructor Marit Berg, with the help of her students, decorated a new restaurant. She introduced the restaurant owners to the college's president, and what followed was a long-lasting and significant relationship between the restaurant and the college, culminating in the creation of a scholarship fund for art students. It began, however, with the art instructor recognizing an opportunity beyond simply painting a mural (see Tacoma Community College, 2006).

Fostering a Fundraising Mentality at Your College

For your college to be successful in fundraising, the entire campus has to participate. All instructors and staff members should understand that they have a role and be willing to talk about their area of responsibility if called upon to do so. They should be enthusiastic about the college and articulate in their support of your mission. Obviously, the president sets the tone, but it's the whole college that raises funds. The foundation leads the way, with the college president providing a constant, public face. However, they won't get very far if your community does not perceive the entire institution as deeply invested in the fundraising process. This doesn't mean that your college's departmental staff members will ask millionaires for gifts. It means that they will be part of a larger process, rather than on the front lines of fundraising.

Remember, the fundraising process focuses on creating a lasting, meaningful relationship with a potential donor that might take months or years to ripen into substantial financial support. It may include meetings with the president, but it may also include discussions with faculty, staff, and students; visits to campus; and receipt of information about the college and its programs. Over time, your college will become part of the potential donor's life, culminating in a gift. This process will be discussed later in the book, but it is vital that you begin this series of actions even before you start a campaign.

CHAPTER 5

Commissioning a Feasibility Study

"Everyone I've talked to thinks this is a great idea. Why waste money having a consultant talk to the same people?" "Consultants always say you should go ahead with a campaign. Why waste the money when the result is preordained?" "It's a lot of money to spend to talk to 40 people. We could just have our foundation director do it."

Those are some of the things you're probably thinking when someone on your board suggests doing a feasibility study. You've been out in the community talking up the technology center or performing arts building, and you haven't heard one word against it. Everyone you talk to agrees you need a new building, or that you should raise money for more scholarships or to start an emergency medical technician (EMT) program. You just know that fundraising the $2 million or $5 million or $20 million you need will be easy. Or do you?

Have you heard definitively from anyone that they'll make the $250,000 (or $1 million) gift necessary to get the project off the ground? Has anyone talked to the local corporations to see if they think that community and technical colleges are really worthy targets of philanthropy, because government supports them? Do local businesspeople fully understand what you provide for the benefit of the community? Are your foundation board members excited about the project, and are they willing to represent it to the community and to potential donors? These are just a few of the things that a professionally run study can tell you. A good study can help you avoid embarrassment and make sure you organize your efforts most effectively.

In CRD's Resource Paper 16, *The Feasibility Study: A Road Map to Success*, Culp, LeRoy, and Armistead (2008) outlined the process and outcomes of a feasibility study. Although its intended audience is foundation staff members, the document may be helpful to readers of this book. The paper reinforces a strong recommendation to execute a feasibility study before embarking on a campaign.

Hiring a Consultant

No matter where you live, you can probably find people who say they can do a study cheaply and accurately. Maybe they can. But before you proceed, here are some things to think about.

- Do you feel comfortable trusting your project to them? Are they the type of people you want representing your project to the broader community? Do you believe they'll tell you the truth, even if it means telling you things you don't want to hear?
- Have they completed at least 10 studies, including several on projects somewhat similar to yours in terms of size or focus?
- Do they belong to regional and national organizations and possess appropriate credentials? The Giving Institute is the gold standard of the profession, but membership in the Association of Fundraising Professionals and the certified fundraising executive credential are good signs as well. On its Web site, CASE lists consultants who work specifically with educational institutions, including community colleges, as educational partners (go to www.case.org). Do a Web search and see whether they've made speeches, written articles, and won acclaim in the field. Check with the American Association of Community Colleges and its affiliate, CRD, to see whether they have developed a good reputation among community and technical colleges.
- Do they have strong references? Call four or five of their past clients—not just the ones they suggest.
- Are they trying to sell you a package deal, asking you to agree to both the study and the following campaign management? Such a package means they have a stake in showing that a campaign is feasible, lessening your chances of an objective study.
- Are those selling the contract the same ones who will be carrying it out?
- Are you impressed by their preparation for the interview? If they do their homework before they meet with you, there is a good chance they will be prepared for a future engagement.
- Most importantly, do they seem to actually know and care about your project?

When beginning your search, don't start by putting out a general request for proposals (RFP). Instead, establish a small search committee to carry out the first steps, listed in Table 5.1.

You'll notice that there has been no mention of cost. Fit is a much more important criterion. That said, the least expensive consultant is often not the best choice, nor is the most expensive. If you absolutely can't spend more than a specific amount, it's not fair to hide that from your prospective consultants and then disqualify or penalize their proposals for more than that amount. You should also provide a timeframe. If you need the study within a set time, let the consultant know. Studies take from 2 to 6 months to complete, depending on the size and complexity of the project; most take at least 3 to 4 months. Don't shortchange yourself by thinking you need an answer tomorrow. Assign one person to answer the prospective consultants' questions. Nothing's worse for a consultant than to guess at your intent or interest.

Give the consultants at least 2 weeks to respond. Then, review the proposals and get back to them within a week or 10 days. If all the proposals are responsive and specific to your college's needs, interview all the candidates. If two stand out, then only interview those.

Table 5.1: Preliminary Steps of the Search Committee

- Call six to eight colleges (and possibly other large nonprofits) in the region that have recently done capital campaigns, and get recommendations.
- Search the Internet for a Giving Institute consultant in the area, or visit the CASE Web site to locate local or national consultants affiliated with CASE.
- Look in the Yellow Pages to see if there are any specialized consultants in the area.
- Contact half a dozen or so consultants or firms, and request that they send their qualifications (not a formal RFP, since that is asking them for a significant investment with little chance for return).
- Develop a short list of two to four firms that seem to be a good fit for the college.
- Once a short list of candidates is identified, prepare a formal but brief RFP to explain the project, the organization, and the goals of the study.

The committee should spend at least an hour with each finalist. All committee members should be present at all interviews. You may be able to get it done in a day, or you may have to spread the interviews over a week.

Make clear that you want the candidates to present for no more than half the time, and leave the rest for give-and-take. Prepare questions beforehand, and ask the same core questions of each group. If you have questions about a specific proposal, ask. If one of the finalists quotes a very high or very low price, request an explanation. Remember that $10,000 represents a very small part of your entire project.

Make your choice, and ask for a contract. Make certain that there are no hidden costs or surprises, that the specific people who will perform the work are identified, and that they can get the study done within the period you need.

Estimating and Covering Costs

How much should a study cost? Not surprisingly, costs vary widely. Firms that work nationally charge anywhere from $15,000 to $100,000 for studies, depending on the size of the project and the number of people they will contact. For most projects that require raising between $1 million and $20 million, you should be able to get a good study for $50,000 or less (Culp et al., 2008). Your decision should focus on the product you want and the feel you get for the consultant. The following questions will help you determine the variables that will affect the cost of the study:

- Does it include an evaluation (sometimes called an audit) of your current fundraising? If you have a large department (or even two or three people), such an audit might add $10,000 or more to the cost.
- Who is preparing the materials that describe the project? If the consultant is responsible for writing, designing, and printing the case statement (described later), it could cost $5,000 or more. If consultants are skilled at such activities, it's well worth it.
- How many interviews are they doing? Make sure they're doing enough to get a good cross-section of information. You can often save money by offering to schedule the interviews at a central location to save travel time. On the other hand, remember that a feasibility study is different from a public opinion poll. You're not trying to interview everyone in town—just those who can make a difference.
- Are they charging you to travel to your site? Out-of-town firms will generally charge you for plane fare and hotels. If they have to make half a dozen trips, this can add up, especially if you're not near an airline hub. Encourage them to consolidate travel to lower costs.
- Are they doing focus groups or mail or e-mail surveys? These also will add costs but provide valuable information.
- How many people are they assigning to the study? More people cost more but often provide a more balanced view.
- How detailed a report will they present to you? A brief report takes less time to write and may contain the basic information you think you need. A more detailed report may be read by only a few people but contains the nuances that will help shape a successful campaign.

In any event, the cost of the study is less important than the trust you feel for its conclusions. A cheap study is wasted money if you don't have the information you need or can't trust the information it presents. A more expensive study that provides trustworthy and detailed information can shorten the campaign, make it more successful, and save you hundreds of thousands of dollars in fundraising and financing costs.

How will you pay for the feasibility study? Colleges ordinarily pay for studies in one of three ways:

- They use cash reserves they have amassed for precisely the purpose of launching a campaign. These funds will help pay for all of the work entailed in a campaign, including a needs assessment, architectural work that defines what will occur in the building when it is finished and what spaces will be required (a functional program), and the feasibility study.
- A generous patron or patrons might provide the funds either as a gift or as a forgivable loan that doesn't have to be repaid if the campaign doesn't move forward. Some local foundations are willing to provide this type of grant, and some organizations have angels who will invest in the organization's future.
- The organization's board members may put up the initial funds to get the project off the ground. If the campaign moves forward, it is accepted practice to use funds raised to repay the cost of the study if they were taken from institutional coffers.

Assembling Study Components

The consultants you hire will ask to review information about your organization and the project. Usually, they'll want to work with a small oversight committee that will provide guidance and make certain they're answering the questions you need them to address. They'll need your help with three aspects of the study: the case statement, defining critical issues, and determining who to interview.

Crafting a Case Statement

Whether you or the consultant writes the case statement, the document has to be carefully prepared. It should be brief enough to be read within 5 minutes and establish how the community will benefit from the funds you raise. It must inform its intended audience (the people you will interview during the course of the study) about your college, the proposed project, and the community benefits resulting from the campaign.

A good case statement will provide a strong sense of what will happen to those the project touches. It will explain how a new performance center will not only give your students a place to present live performances but also provide cultural and educational opportunities to the entire community. It will explain how equipping your new technology center with computers will benefit low-income students who don't have Internet access and how this will create better- prepared employees for all businesses in the region. It will explain how improving faculty skills will create better students and better future employees.

Many colleges have found it useful for the president to compose a white paper that outlines a vision for the institution. Your chief executive often has a clear sense of where he or she wants the institution to go and why. That vision statement can serve as an excellent jumping-off place for the case statement. It will be a logical outgrowth of the processes described in the preceding chapter, reflecting your strategic plan and vision.

Depending on the project and your community, the case statement can be simple or ornate, a few pages of word-processed text or a full-color brochure. It can be on your organization's letterhead or in a well-designed four-color brochure. Generally, you want to avoid looking as if you are being wasteful, but also transmit a sense of competence and significance for the institution. If you get the printing donated, feature that fact prominently, both to recognize the donor and to let the community know how carefully you steward your financial resources.

The study oversight committee reviews the case statement and suggests changes. Key staff and administrators also provide input to ensure accuracy and adherence to college standards. If the consultant writes the first draft, your public relations officer will also review the document to check that the messages offered in the case statement are consistent with those the college has been using.

Defining Critical Issues

One overarching concern defines all feasibility studies: Do enough people care about your project to provide the money needed to get it done? That is always the bottom line in every study, but many separate issues make up that ultimate determination. These issues can be grouped into six categories.

Organizational Issues

- Is your college the right one to take on this challenge, or should it be cooperating with others?
- Do people have confidence in your college? Do they regard it as competent and creative?
- Is your college strong enough to take on new challenges? Does the community see you as having the firepower to achieve your goals?

Leadership

- Are good volunteer leaders available (often members of your foundation board or other prominent community members associated with your college)?
- Do people regard you (the foundation board) as up to the task? Do your group members have the reputations that speak positively for the worthiness of the college?
- Is your president seen as an effective leader?
- Will respected community leaders not currently closely allied with your college step up to provide leadership for the campaign?
- Is there an obvious candidate for campaign chair?

Perceived Value

- What does the community see as the most important benefit of your project?

- Is the community convinced that your project will make a significant difference to its well-being?
- Do your projected outcomes (e.g., people served, changes made) strike people as worth the amount of money you're raising? If you're raising $5 million to equip an allied health professions building in which only 20 people will be trained annually, potential donors might question whether the investment is commensurate to the benefit.

> *"In short, the feasibility study is the first step in positioning a college as a solution provider to community needs while also addressing whether the college meets the six essential campaign criteria necessary to move forward with a successful campaign: an essential need, a compelling case for support, inspired and influential leadership, sufficient prospects, a plan of action, and sound management."*
>
> —Clements Group (2009)

Giving Potential

- Will the sources you count on the most give the size of gifts you hope for?
- How far away from your core group can you go and still hope to get large gifts?
- Will local and regional foundations and corporations make gifts?

Readiness

- To raise money, you need staff, software, hardware, and systems. Where does your organization stand in regard to these needs?
- Is the foundation board prepared to be part of a campaign or not?

Timing

- Are people optimistic enough about the economy and the direction of their lives that they'll make big charitable gifts to you? As this book is being written, we have entered into a major recession. Does your local community believe that gifts to you will help cushion the effects of the recession in your community?
- Are there no competing campaigns preventing you from starting your campaign?

If the answers to these questions are mostly positive, you can launch a campaign; if they're mostly negative, you should reconsider. Feasibility studies provide accurate information if competent, experienced consultants do them. Either they find potential gifts, or they don't. The community tells them you're a strong, deserving organization, or they mutter a collective "Huh?" Either the study identifies strong leadership or it doesn't.

As a foundation board member or a college administrator, you have to remember that consultants return with community perceptions—not their personal opinions. Resist the temptation to kill the messenger if you're unhappy with the message. If you have done all you can to make the study a success by making sure the consultant asks the right questions and talks to the right people, then you can rely on its conclusions.

Determining Whom to Interview

You can't talk to everyone; you're not conducting a marketing survey. You want a consultant to talk to people who can make big gifts—identifying those dozen or so gifts that will guarantee the success of the campaign. You want to identify your leaders, and you want to learn what pitfalls might await you. Generally, between 35 and 60 people will provide you with all the information you need. These will include potential leaders, donors, opinion makers, and spoilers.

If you're located in a small community and trying to raise $1.5 million to equip a new life sciences building, 35 people will give the information you need. If you're a multicampus urban community college with 50,000 students and a service area of 10 million people, testing multiple initiatives within a $25 million campaign, you'll probably need 50 to 100 interviews, with perhaps several focus groups to reach specific constituencies.

Sample RFPs for feasibility studies are available from Council for Resource Development (CRD) on the members-only Web pages. Go to www.crdnet.org and click on Resources/Foundation Resources.

Why so few interviews? Because you are consciously seeking an elite group of people—the few people who can determine success or failure. No matter how large the campaign or how big your organization, 12 or fewer gifts will make up 50% of your goal. Similarly, you need four or five dynamic, committed campaign leaders to provide you with instant credibility and clout. If you can't identify the 30 to 50 people amongst whom you're likely to find those 12 large gifts and the 8 or 10 who will yield the 4 or 5 to provide the necessary leadership, you're not ready to do a study.

You should also recognize that it's primarily up to the foundation and others associated with the college to come up with the list of potential interviewees—not the consultant. Your foundation staff and board know the community and your current donors and have the ability to ensure that your potential leaders and donors will talk with your consultant. They also know who the potential donors are (individuals, corporations, and foundations) that have not contributed to you, but might if properly motivated.

Your consultant may have some ideas about potential interviewees and can certainly provide you with the criteria to determine how to use consulting time most effectively. However, you can't expect *them* to arrive with a ready-made list of prospects if *you* don't already have contacts. Your consultants will also provide a process to expand and vet your list, using the small oversight committee.

An additional source of potential interviewees, although one frequently costing $5,000 or more, is obtained by submitting a list of possible donors to an asset screen. This process can crunch many thousands of donor names and indicate their past giving to other nonprofits, potential giving levels, and other useful data. These screens are done both by consultants and software companies that market them under the rubric of "analytics" using publicly available information. Often, the results are more useful after you've completed your study and have assembled your campaign team to review and interpret the data. The raw data itself is seldom helpful during the study process, in part because you lack relationships with potential donors and don't have time to develop them within the period of the study.

> *"It is critical to recognize that the feasibility study is neither a poll nor a survey. It is designed to answer questions related to program appeal, availability of financial support, and availability of leadership. It also provides the information necessary to prepare a plan for a campaign that will organize the people and the programs to maximize an institution's success."*
>
> —Culp et al. (2008)

Leaders

I began this book by telling you that leadership is the most important element in the success of fundraising campaigns. So, it's no surprise that the first priority of a study is to find leaders for your campaign. Review your donor list, event attendee lists, alumni list, and advisory committee member lists. Are there any people whose participation would ensure your success?

Look for logical connections and reasonable expectations. Even if a tycoon gives you $10,000 annually, it doesn't mean that he or she has the time to be part of your campaign—or even that your cause is a major priority. Leaders don't have to be rich or famous; they do have to care about your college, be willing to approach others on behalf of the campaign, and have sufficient local renown to confer credibility on the campaign. For example, Renton Technical College, located in a rapidly growing Washington suburb, called upon King Parker, the owner of a local appliance store and city council member, to help lead its campaign. He agreed and provided (in part because of his TV ads and years of local service in community endeavors) immediate recognizability and credibility. He made a generous gift and met with people who made the lead gifts to the campaign, which raised more than $800,000 for a technology resource center (Renton Technical College, 2005).

Donors

Talk to the people who are already your major donors. Anyone who provides 1% or more of your annual fund should be interviewed. You should look carefully at those donors who've given money for many consecutive years or who are among your top 10 cumulative donors.

Talk to corporations and foundations that already know about you and that have provided occasional support, especially if their executives sit on your advisory committees or if you have training programs tied to them and their industry. There might be regional or national foundations that you should talk to, but make sure they have a logical reason for supporting you. Talk to a few current non-donors who give to similar organizations. Remember that you serve the entire community, and they might not support you because they don't know much about you. A feasibility study interview is a great way to begin developing a relationship with new donors.

Community and technical colleges receive substantial support from all levels of government. Your consultant should meet with appropriate representatives to determine whether there are public sources to augment the private funds they identify. If you have an institutional lobbyist, they can be helpful in directing the consultant to the proper contacts. If not, members of your board probably have contacts with your representatives in the Congress, the state legislature, county council, and city government.

Opinion Leaders

Think about who sets the tone in your community. Whose participation or support seems to be part of everything important that happens? You'll want to know whether they're on your side or not, and why. Although interviews are normally strictly confidential, opinion leaders frequently preface their comments with "I want your board to know that." The interviewer, after clarifying that the opinion leader is serious, is entitled to carry these thoughts back to you. Opinion leaders can include the local newspaper editor or publisher, the head of the local chamber of commerce, the mayor or council members, and even a popular blogger. Certainly, you should talk with your internal opinion leaders and the heads of your faculty and staff unions and faculty senate to make certain they feel fully invested in the campaign.

Spoilers

Some people love to spoil other people's plans. They glory in being power brokers with the capacity to make or break a project. It's important to let them talk to you first, both to give you a clearer view of where they stand and to ensure that they feel part of the process. Ask around town to find out who's gossiping about the project and leading backroom bickering about it. That's the person you have to talk to before he or she poisons the community. It's actually not a bad idea to talk with the president of a competing college or with someone who has criticized your college for not meeting local needs.

From your point of view, not much will happen during the study. The consultant team contacts people and arranges interviews. Usually, this will instigate some talk throughout the community's inner circles because it's the first public word about your plans. Sometimes your friends will stop you on the street and ask you, "Why am I not being interviewed?" If you realize that they should be part of the study, inform the consultant. If not, just say, "Well, we had a limited budget and we can't talk to everyone, unfortunately." Ask them whether they'd like to be informed about the study results, and make sure you follow up.

Otherwise, for a 4- to 12-week period, you'll only receive occasional reports on how the study process is going—if there are any difficulties in getting interviews or whether people are anxious to talk. The consultant may ask for your help in acquiring interviews with key people and for additional background information on interviewees.

What a Feasibility Study Will Tell You

- Who will step forward as a leader and what leadership structure will work best.
- How much money you can raise and who your big donors may be.
- What the most and least attractive aspects of your project are.
- How people regard your college.
- What competition or roadblocks you face.
- What internal preparation you need before you can launch a campaign and what staff and resources you need to add before starting.
- How soon, if at all, you can start your campaign.

The consultant will meet with the committee overseeing the study and then with the entire foundation board and key staff. A representative of the trustees should also be present. It's imperative that all board members read the completed study carefully and that the meeting with the consultant team allows enough time to get all questions addressed. Make certain you understand how the consultants reached the study's conclusions, and be certain they can defend them. Now is the time to get your questions answered—if you wait until after the campaign has started to second-guess the study conclusions, it's too late. Once you've reviewed and discussed the study, you're ready for the next step—confirming your support for an actual campaign.

CHAPTER 6

Deciding to Move Forward

The feasibility study is complete. You and your fellow board members have heard the results, discussed them, and reached a crossroads. Should you proceed? In almost 200 studies that I have been involved with, the consultant recommended moving forward about 75% of the time, a figure almost identical to one reported by CRD (Culp et al., 2008). In fewer than 25% of the cases, findings came back that were so negative that moving forward with a campaign was inadvisable. Your consultants will lay out their results clearly and with a thorough explanation for why they are making specific recommendations.

Let's assume that you've received positive news, and the consultant has recommended that you move forward. You have some potential leaders and donors. The community likes the project and ranks it as a high priority. All agree that your college has the ability to achieve your goals. No major roadblocks to a successful campaign have emerged. In most cases (almost two thirds, according to Culp et al., 2008), however, you will have to adjust your financial goal and your hoped-for outcomes, as illustrated in the following example.

You tested raising $10 million: $3 million to equip a building, $2 million for a scholarship endowment, $3 million to expand your workforce training program, $1 million for professional development for the instructors over a 5-year period, $500,000 to plan a branch campus in a neighboring suburb, and $500,000 to support fundraising expenses for the campaign. The consultant thinks you can raise about $6 million altogether, with the strongest support coming for scholarships and little enthusiasm for expansion planning or workforce training, which the community believes to be a government responsibility to fund.

The consultant also has discovered that your top choices for leadership are unwilling to chair the campaign, although they're willing to participate at some level. Your fundraising department is not ready for a campaign without additional staff. And the local Boys and Girls Club, with strong ties to local businesses, plans to announce a $5 million campaign within the next month. What should you do?

Establish a date by which the board will make a decision, assuming that you are not ready to make one now. Give yourself a few weeks to answer the basic questions that will allow you to decide whether to move forward:

- What can you achieve with a total of $6 million?
- What constituencies do you have to meet with before you can cut down your campaign to reflect the results of the study?
- Are there any alternative sources of funding for all or a portion of the projects that the community expressed a negative response to?
- Will your ideal leaders help assure success, making a few key calls and serving as spokespeople, even if they won't serve as chairs?
- Is the board willing to support expansion of the development staff?
- Will the other campaign provide competition for major donors? Will anything be gained by waiting?

The Reconciliation Process

As discussed in chapter 1, community and technical colleges face an unusual challenge in that our instructors and staff (not to mention students) often know little about fundraising; in fact, some of them both dislike and distrust the process. If you have involved them in campaign planning, you may have allayed some of their concerns. If, however, you ignore their interests in responding to the feasibility study, you risk forfeiting the trust you've gained. Treat them as potential donors and leaders, and they will develop a sense of empowerment and become an integral part of your campaign team.

Before you started planning the campaign, you received the help of several departments to create a project description tied to the building and project you hoped to support. You discussed scholarship needs and professional development concerns with the appropriate departments. You enlisted your workforce training staff to help describe how and why the program should be expanded. You laid out your plans for a branch campus to your entire internal community, fueling considerable excitement and high expectations. Now you have heard that the external community failed to share your excitement and that some expectations will not be met. How should you proceed?

A highly participatory and inclusive reconciliation process frequently can provide the answer. You can offer presentations at regularly scheduled meetings of the instructors and staff as well as at an executive staff meeting. The better members of your internal community understand the situation, the more likely they are to support your eventual decisions. They should be invited to make suggestions. Can some initiatives be postponed for a future campaign? Can important objectives be reached if you raise only a portion of the desired goal. For instance, will $250,000 allow meaningful progress in professional staff development? Will $1.5 million buy enough equipment to make your new building usable?

After the president has heard responses to the study, he or she should formulate an action plan in concert with the chief fundraising officer and the foundation board. This plan should be shared with everyone on campus to ensure that they understand the extent to which their suggestions have been heard and incorporated into the campaign. The plan and the financial goal are what the foundation board will consider in determining whether to move forward.

The Board's Decision

The foundation board should schedule a meeting to discuss the feasibility study findings, the reconciliation process (if one occurred), and the president's recommendations. Foundation board members must accept the decision-making meeting as a major priority and should schedule it to maximize attendance, with enough time to permit full discussion.

The president, board chair, foundation executive director, and consultant should present a united front, offering their opinions and recommendations for future action. They should fully explain their conclusions and then open the floor for discussion. If they have recommended moving forward, they should bring with them a formal resolution of support, distributed after their presentation. That resolution should become the basis for discussion once a motion is introduced to pass it. A sample resolution appears in Table 6.1.

After you discuss the resolution, take a vote to ensure that everyone agrees. If the resolution doesn't pass unanimously, continue discussions with the possibility of making emendations. Once a satisfactory resolution is passed and signed, it's final, and its provisions bind all board members. Board members are bound to make a gift that is significant to them. The resolution is a public affirmation of the board's commitment and will be shared with potential donors.

It is possible that you can gain the support of 18 out of 20 board members, but are unable to achieve unanimity. It is far better to have one or two board members leave if they cannot support the campaign than to have them fighting a rear-guard action for the next several years.

In almost all cases, however, the board will reach agreement and all members will sign the resolution with enthusiasm and excitement. It represents a major commitment that should be taken with immense seriousness, but is also a cause for celebration.

A capital campaign strains every sinew of an organization. If the basic fabric of your foundation, held together by the board, is not strong, the entire enterprise can dissolve quickly. Engaging in debate and discussion before you start, no matter how painful, will help create the strongest possible fabric that can withstand any possible tension during the campaign.

Table 6.1: Sample Resolution to Launch a Fundraising Campaign

Whereas, the Perch Falls Community College has provided high-quality, low-cost education to Perch Falls and the surrounding area for the past 32 years, and

Whereas, the College has grown to the point where we have a large waiting list for many courses, unsatisfied demand for our offerings in nearby Salmon Springs, a desperate need for scholarships for deserving but economically challenged students, and a highly motivated group of staff and faculty hungering for additional professional development activities that will strengthen their ability to serve the community, and

Whereas, our administration, faculty, and staff support moving forward with a campaign to address these needs on behalf of a supportive community,

Whereas, the community has indicated a willingness to provide financial and leadership support for our efforts, and

Whereas, we are confident that achieving the goals outlined in our campaign case will allow us to serve our community better and achieve our mission of "providing access to those who need us and opportunity to all for a better life,"

Therefore, we, the Board of Directors of the Perch Falls Community College Foundation, do solemnly resolve to:

- Raise a minimum of $6 million, of which $2.2 million will be used to equip our planned science building, $2.5 million will create an endowed "first-generation" scholarship fund, $750,000 will support professional development for staff and faculty, $250,000 will support planning for our Salmon Springs branch campus, and $300,000 remain available for campaign expenses;
- Seek support for our workforce training programs, with the understanding that they may have to await government funding;
- Support the fundraising effort enthusiastically and without reserve, including making our own significant gifts;
- Represent the College and the campaign to our friends and neighbors in the most positive possible fashion; and
- Not be satisfied until we have successfully completed these efforts. Unanimously agreed to, on the ___th day of ____________, 2____ (signed)

CHAPTER 7

Establishing Campaign Central

It is always tempting to think you can raise money without spending very much. After all, presidents and board members don't need to be paid for asking for gifts. The foundation's executive director or the vice president for advancement gets the same salary as always, although he or she will do a lot of work on the campaign. You probably already have a chief fundraising officer and support staff. You can get a couple of extra computers from the local bank and jury-rig something to handle the campaign database. Right?

Wrong.

Campaigns require skilled, specialized staff members and consultants in addition to your current staff. You need top-of-the-line computer equipment and specialized software. Saving money in the end will cost you money now. Using fewer staff will mean a longer, less successful campaign and reducing your ability to develop and sustain donor relationships that guarantee your long-term viability. It'll take several months after the campaign begins before money starts coming in. You need a war chest to pay salaries, buy equipment, and create campaign materials. As with the feasibility study, it is considered ethical and responsible to use campaign proceeds to pay campaign expenses.

Financing the Campaign

Estimating Campaign Costs

In Appendix A, you will find a grid you can use to estimate the costs of running a campaign. Generally speaking, it is difficult if not impossible to run a campaign for less than 10% of the goal, no matter how much you are raising. This percentage rises for smaller campaigns, although the absolute numbers will be much smaller.

First-time campaigns are generally the most expensive because you are starting from scratch in building both systems and relationships. You will have to provide enough staff to do research, arrange meetings, enter data, and perform all the other campaign functions. These start-up costs are proportionally less when you've done a campaign within the last 5 years.

Campaigns in small towns tend to be less expensive than those in large cities. There are fewer prospects and fewer media outlets to try to influence. You have access to leaders and donors without convoluted strategies. Staff costs are often lower as well because the cost of living is lower.

Consulting Fees

It is unethical and against the canons of professional fundraising for a consultant to be paid on a percentage or contingent basis. There are many reasons for this, but the primary one is that campaigns must reflect shared risk—the organization and the consultant must have skin in the game for a campaign to have the best chance to work. This issue is addressed in both the CASE Principles of Practice for Fundraising Professionals at Educational Institutions and the CASE Statement on Commission-based Compensation (both at www.case.org). If the onus is on consultants, and they won't be paid unless funds are raised, the college's volunteers are likely to sit back rather than participate wholeheartedly in the campaign.

Percentage-based fundraising is also unethical because it appears to create a situation where a portion of the gift goes directly into the consultant's pocket. Although sophisticated donors understand that there is a real cost to raising money, they bridle at the thought that consultants may be seeking a gift largely to line their own pockets. Finally, percentage-based fundraising has been abused in the past by consultants who began a campaign by pursuing easy, large gifts to collect their fees and then walked away during the vital, but more difficult, portions of the campaign.

Ethical fundraisers usually set their professional fees based on the number of days per month they plan to spend working on the project. Fees vary based on experience and success rates. You should choose a model that fits your campaign's needs rather than conform to a preconceived budget. If your campaign is complex and will require many committees and extensive work with funders over a large region, you should retain a consultant with experience in such campaigns. In all cases, you want to retain a consultant or firm with whom you feel comfortable and whom you believe will make a good impression on your board members, volunteers, and the community as a whole.

The amount you pay your consultant will depend on how you've structured the campaign. If you are a large, multicampus college with a well-developed fundraising operation and have many staff members working on the campaign, your consultant will focus on providing strategic counsel. If you're a small college with a single capital campaign staff member, the consultant will spend much more time on the campaign, performing a variety of campaign-related tasks.

Consultants' daily fees cover a wide range. A consultant who is a sole practitioner and works locally may charge $800 a day. A nationally renowned consultant who has performed hundreds of campaigns may charge $4,000 a day, including travel and expenses. Cost should not be the determining factor. A more expensive consultant may get the campaign done more quickly and raise more money. A bargain consultant may be less experienced and cost you money in the end.

Staffing

Raising money is about relationships between people. It requires people who are part of your organization to communicate with potential leaders, donors, vendors, and other prospective participants. You must keep close track of all of these relationships, record past meetings' outcomes, schedule current meetings, and plan future meetings. A campaign operates as a continuum, not an isolated series of events. You must keep accurate, detailed records of all campaign activities.

Managing these relationships and records is the responsibility of "campaign central," the nerve center of the campaign, composed of paid campaign staff and consultants whose sole job is to ensure the campaign's success. To raise $1 million or more requires at least one full-time staff person dedicated to the campaign. You will also probably require some level of fundraising consulting and perhaps additional clerical help.

Larger campaigns require more staff. If your campaign is to raise $5 million or more, you will probably need an additional staff person whose primary job is to establish and develop relationships with foundations and corporations, including writing grant proposals. You will also probably require an additional full-time clerical person to handle the increased volume of activity and ensure that no potential donor slips through the cracks. As the size of the goal increases, so does the complexity of the campaign. You may need a part- or full-time public relations officer to coordinate publicity efforts or an additional person to work with committees that focus on smaller gifts. You will probably also need the capacity to do research on potential donors.

"Community colleges must recognize the need for development staff. The Valencia Community College Foundation in Orlando, Florida, has a staff of 9 and a 60-member board dedicated to development efforts. As of March 31, 2007, the foundation had an endowment totaling $52 million—almost a quarter of the endowment of the entire 2.6 million-student-system in California."

—Lanning (2008b)

Campaign Manager

At the heart of every successful campaign stands a competent, committed, and energetic campaign manager who keeps the campaign moving forward, ensures that volunteers perform properly, and always has his or her finger on the pulse of the campaign. Ideally, managers have at least 3 years' experience as professional fundraisers, have participated in a campaign, and have top-rate skills and a professional demeanor. They may or may not be current employees of a foundation or college.

Estimating staff costs for your campaign is difficult because the costs vary widely depending on the size and location of your college and the magnitude of the campaign. If several organizations in a large city are undertaking major campaigns, they can get into a bidding war that raises salaries beyond normal levels. A small campaign in a rural area might pay a campaign manager $40,000 a year, while a large system in a major metropolis may find that it will pay $100,000 or more for a qualified professional. Salaries and benefits are all legitimately included in the overall campaign goal. The term of employment is ordinarily for the duration of the campaign plus at least another 6 months to launch an effective stewardship plan.

Campaign Assistant

For almost any campaign, the quantity of data that you will enter will exceed the ability of current staff to oversee it. Lists of prospective donors and leaders, donor lists, gift acknowledgments, donor records, and all other detail work must be handled with absolute accuracy and great tact. A good campaign assistant will make the work of your committees much more efficient and successful. Depending on the skill and experience level of the campaign assistant and the location of your college, salaries can vary greatly but are generally in line with the market for high-level clerical help.

Qualifications start with two vital characteristics: excellent computer skills and attention to detail. Campaign assistants handle specialized software; they must keep perfect track of myriad details and be able to provide required information instantaneously. Campaigns flounder if they rely on inaccurate or insufficient information.

Consultants

Most campaigns for raising more than $1 million will benefit from hiring professional campaign counsel. If the head of your foundation has run campaigns previously, if your college president is an experienced campaigner, and if your foundation board already has demonstrated the ability to cultivate and solicit large gifts, you may not require a consultant. As Perry Hammock, a long-time foundation executive from Ivy Tech Community College of Indiana remarked, "We've done 11 campaigns over the past decade and used consultants for 10 of them. They helped our regional chancellors, helped train our high-level volunteers, and made certain we got our campaigns off to a good start. If you asked our volunteers, 90% of them would say that consultant fees are money well spent" (personal communication, February 3, 2009).

Consultants are most important for organizing the campaign, providing strategic guidance as the campaign progresses, and evaluating the campaign at each step along the way. They help train your volunteers, provide a constantly reviewed campaign plan, and offer ongoing reassurance that you're making satisfactory progress toward success. They generally do not perform staff functions, although occasionally, especially for small campaigns at rural institutions, they might write grants, coordinate meetings, and engage in other activities that are normally carried out by staff members.

Working with a seasoned consultant lets you profit from past experience and ensures that you follow the most appropriate and effective path to success. Consultants offer a dispassionate outside voice to remind you of best practices and assure you that you're making correct decisions. They provide ongoing oversight of the campaign and prevent you from embarking on wasteful detours. A competent consultant can explain to the overenthusiastic volunteer why things are done in a specific way. A good consultant discourages fruitless efforts—for example, chasing after gifts from donors far removed from the college rather than focusing on donors connected to the project—and ensures that you ask for gifts only after appropriate preparation.

If you've been happy with the consultant who did your feasibility study, your discussions should start with him or her, although you will want to consult with your finance office to ensure that any proposed expenditures meet institutional purchasing guidelines. Get a bid on how much the campaign will cost, including both fees and expenses. Gain an understanding of precisely what the consultant proposes to do in exchange for the fee. How often will you meet? Will grant writing be included, or will you have to hire an additional person? Will the consultant help you hire your campaign manager and assistant? Does the consultant's company have the capacity to help create campaign materials, do you have the capacity to develop materials in house, or will you have to retain another company for that purpose?

Acquiring Hardware and Software

Ten years ago, hardware was a major issue for colleges considering campaigns because computers were relatively expensive and the expertise to operate and support them was at a premium. Today, that is no longer a problem. Your college probably has an information technology (IT) office that will help you choose the needed computers and peripherals and decide whether you need desktops, laptops, or other types of

"If your institution has not invested in training staff appropriately to use the current software, then it is likely that brand new software will not change a thing. In fact, if training is not seen as a high priority, then five years from now your Foundation staff will be in the same situation as they are now with their current software—believing it doesn't work."

—Grant (2008)

devices. The IT office will also work with you to integrate your campaign software with the programs the college already uses.

Avoid any temptation to accept gifts of used computers from local businesses. If the computers are not good enough for them, they're not good enough for you. Get new, state-of-the-art computers. It's good for morale and good for efficiency. A high-speed color printer/copier is a good investment that can save trips to the copy center.

Many medium and large colleges already possess contact management software that is sufficiently sophisticated to manage a capital campaign. Often it is part of a large, integrated software system that handles admissions, alumni records, and many other college administrative tasks. But many smaller colleges lack both an integrated system and a sophisticated contact management system, relying on either paper records or some form of generic database such as Microsoft Excel. Although this may be sufficient for annual fundraising, it will not work for a capital campaign involving more than several dozen potential donors.

You will need some form of easily manipulated contact management software. Such software allows you to keep track of your prospects and volunteers, usually along with donors, advisory committee members, and any other supporters. More sophisticated programs will permit you to generate correspondence, check changes of address over the Internet, and even do prospect research.

You will also probably want to have access to your software from multiple computers or work stations, which usually means purchasing licenses for each computer. Whatever system you use, it must allow you to track all communications between the organization and its prospective donors. You will have to generate lists of donors sorted by category and according to the volunteer who has been assigned to work with them. You will need a field in which you can record notes on each transaction and another to provide ticklers for future actions.

Good software programs are easy to use, produce reports that are highly legible and easy to understand, and can be updated as new features are added. They also should come with appropriate technical support. Talk with similar-sized colleges, get recommendations through CRD, or visit the CASE Web site (www.case.org) to explore vendors. You'll quickly determine what program is right for you.

CHAPTER 8

DRAFTING A MASTER PLAN

You know you're going someplace, but you're not sure how to get there. You've signed a resolution, you know you're going to pursue gifts, and you hope that somehow everything will come together. But how will that happen? That's why you have consultants and campaign managers. Their job is to create, with your participation, a clear and detailed master plan that gives you the confidence to know where you're going and what you're doing and provides a clear schedule marked with tasks and accomplishments and the sequence of events. This plan may be rendered in a variety of ways:

- A narrative that enumerates the steps.
- A detailed calendar of events showing what, when, and who will be responsible for what.
- A timeline that breaks the campaign down into phases.
- Regardless of the method used to draft the plan, every master plan should include the components described in this chapter.

POTENTIAL SOURCES

Every campaign should know from the start where the money is coming from. You need goals for giving by boards, staff and faculty, foundations, corporations, government, and others. (But see CASE's position on government funds, p. 163.) Staff and faculty giving is important because it demonstrates that those closest to you support the campaign, but the rate of participation is generally more important than the amount. For some colleges, local corporate and business support will provide the largest portion of the campaign. For others, individuals will offer the majority of support. The feasibility study should inform the plan in this regard, indicating what portion of the campaign will come from each sector. Whatever combination you hit upon, you must set goals by sector and have a clear idea of who your prospects are and how you will reach them.

Size of Gifts Sought

Long division is the biggest enemy of successful campaigns. Let's say that in addition to funds the state is providing, you need $2 million to renovate and modernize your main classroom building. You're located in a county with 200,000 families. All you need is to find 400 businesses and individuals to give you $5,000 each, and you'll reach your goal. Simple, isn't it?

But that approach will invariably fail. Why? Because fundraising is not democratic. People can't, don't, and won't give the same amount. For some people, $5,000 is too much. For others, it's not enough. What works for almost any campaign is proportionality. The institutions or people with the most capacity and connections give the largest gifts. People with less wealth and fewer connections give smaller gifts. There are always variations, but the shape of a campaign resembles a pyramid: a few big gifts will be on top (remember the rule of 12—in every campaign, approximately 12 gifts make up at least 50% of the campaign goal), with most gifts at the bottom. More specifically, according to the 2008 CASE Campaign Report, of community college campaigns that were active in 2008, 58% of funds raised came from the top 1% of donors, and 77% came from the top 10% of donors (see www.case.org).

As part of your planning process, your consultants and staff should prepare a gift chart (see Appendix B) that shows how many gifts at each level you need to reach your goal. This chart will provide you with simple, easy-to-track goals. At any point in the campaign, you'll be able to compare the gifts you've raised to those you've projected. This offers an easy way to judge your progress and chances for success.

What to Consider When Drafting a Campaign Master Plan

- Potential sources of funds (e.g., individuals, foundations, corporations, government, etc.). (But see CASE's position on government funds, p. 163.)
- Size of gifts needed.
- The order in which you'll pursue different sizes and sources of gifts, and the strategies you will use to pursue gifts from various constituencies.
- What collateral materials you'll need and when.
- How to use marketing and public relations effectively and in concert with the college's overall communications plan.
- What the construction schedule will be and how it will mesh with fundraising.
- What benchmarks you're going to meet.
- How you'll continue to make your donors feel good about their gifts (your stewardship plan).

Then the plan has to indicate whom you go to first. Most campaigns go to the board first, then to the biggest individual donors, then to foundations and corporations. But there are exceptions to most rules—other than going to the board first. In general, you start with the constituencies closest to you, including the board, faculty, and staff. With those gifts secured and demonstrating your college's support of the campaign, you can go to your largest potential donors, whatever constituency they represent. Then you approach donors who will make smaller but still substantial gifts representing 1% or more of the campaign goal. Only after you secure those gifts do you appeal to the broader community.

Public Relations and Marketing Plan

It is vital to determine where you need efforts to increase public awareness. More important, however, is determining who your audience is. From whom will the majority of your support come, and what's the best way to reach those people? Increased public awareness seldom generates immediate support from the public, but as you see the community better informed about the college, it makes you feel confident enough to ask others for support. Your campaign plan should delineate the purpose of public relations, its timing, and the audience at which it is aimed. You should develop strategies to reach all major donor constituencies, not forgetting your internal supporters—your board, faculty and staff, advisory committee members, and others who may not be big donors but will influence others. Your messages must be consistent and tailored to your constituency. They should also be consistent with the larger messages the college uses in its comprehensive communications plan.

As is discussed in the next chapter, you'll need marketing materials, and you have to expect to pay for those materials. You don't necessarily need them at the very start of the campaign. For your initial gifts, you may not need anything fancier than a two-page letter on your organization's stationery. Your fundraising plan should lay out what materials you will need and the point at which you'll need them. Working back from the due date, you can then construct a schedule indicating when you must make decisions and when you will have to reserve time at the printer.

"Campaign marketing should be proportional and appropriate to the institution's goals, requirements, and values. Although campaign case statements and other literature or presentations should inspire and motivate donors, such materials should not distort institutional accomplishments, characteristics, or capabilities. Institutions should consider the perception of extravagant spending and availability of actual funds as important marketing considerations. Campaign managers should also be careful to balance the marketing of outright, irrevocable deferred and revocable support in their presentations, ensuring that the separate goals for these forms of gifts are well articulated."

—CASE (2009)

Construction Plan

If your campaign focuses on a building project, it should use the concrete timeline of the building project to motivate volunteers to get the fundraising to a predetermined point. In general, the single most important benchmark is groundbreaking. Organizations should have at least 80% of the funds they need pledged before they break ground. If your total project cost is $5 million, your supporters should have pledged or given at least $4 million before you stick a shovel in the ground.

Once ground is broken, fundraising urgency abates for many people because they assume you wouldn't have started the project without having the money to finish it. Volunteers begin to focus on the physical project rather than completing the fundraising for it. Having 80% committed is safe because you will have other gifts in process, and a few people will prefer to wait until they know the project is a "winner." That said, 80% is a minimum—less than that and you risk running out of momentum before the campaign is complete.

Your contractor or project manager will create a project plan for construction. Your campaign manager or consultant should suggest other benchmarks for you to use in your campaign. These may be internal, such as moving forward to design documents (a very expensive step), or external, such as groundbreaking, topping off, or the grand opening. In all cases, they will help gauge whether your fundraising is ahead of or behind schedule.

CASE on Campaign Planning

"Campaign planning should begin with a careful review of the institution's strategic priorities and long-range aspirations. Planners should then identify ways in which the campaign can directly contribute to the fulfillment of those priorities and aspirations. A written campaign plan should be prepared for review by all appropriate bodies of the institution. This document should describe, at a minimum,

- the institution's financial needs that will be addressed
- the campaign reporting policies to which the institution will adhere, including the treatment of outright gifts and pledges, irrevocable deferred gifts, revocable gifts, and gifts-in-kind
- the manner of considering and acting upon exceptions to those policies
- the tentative goal for both featured objectives (usually endowment and construction) and other objectives (usually expendable programmatic support and annual fund revenues)
- an objective analysis of the fundraising potential of the institution
- the purpose and duration of the quiet or nucleus phase of the campaign
- the duration of the public phase of the campaign"

—CASE (2009)

Stewardship Plan

One of the most important truths to remember while you're in the midst of the campaign is that your fundraising is only starting. The money raised to create a building or an endowment is only a down payment on your future needs. If you look at capital campaign gifts as the ultimate gift your donors will ever make, your future is likely to be bleak. Your goal is to ensure that every campaign donor becomes an annual donor and a prospect for future capital campaigns and will want to cement their relationship by making a planned gift—leaving you a bequest or other gift from their estate.

Your plans for the future begin with the capital campaign plan. You should determine how to connect your donors to your mission and to demonstrate to them on an ongoing basis that their gift is allowing you to do a better job of carrying out your mission. Your success will gratify them and make them feel great about their gift, eager to do more. Your plan should outline a communications plan and an event plan that serves to tie your donors to you. They should share in your good and bad news and be asked to participate in all events marking your progress.

CHAPTER 9

Designing Effective Marketing Materials

Most community and technical colleges have collegewide communications plans. The plan represents your college's efforts to attract potential students, expand community awareness, and ensure that the college is perceived in the most favorable light possible Most colleges develop a limited number of messages that dominate their communications, often focusing on accessibility, responsiveness, and other positive attributes of community and technical colleges. The plan seeks to make the college an attractive organization within the community, positioned as an appropriate target for community support and an excellent place to gain an education.

As you enter a campaign, you will want to ensure that the messages you broadcast to the community through your public relations and marketing plan are congruent with those that are at the center of your current communications plan. If you are launching a scholarship campaign, you must focus on the ways that this will expand accessibility rather than implying that you are not currently accessible to low-income students. If you are enhancing your nursing program, you must be clear that the current program represents the highest degree of excellence; the campaign will only move the program to the next level and allow you to serve more students. In a similar vein, it is essential that your materials reflect the style and approach existing materials have adopted. Although your campaign brochure, logo, and other materials will clearly identify with this special effort, they should never clash with the materials and look you have undoubtedly worked hard to achieve.

Staffing the Communications Function

Many colleges already have a communications specialist on staff. Some do not, and for a large campaign, the workload will expand beyond the point where a single person can perform all the necessary work. Campaigns can attract additional attention from the community and offer the opportunity to broaden your renown among all of your constituencies. You should not waste this chance to heighten public awareness.

Your communications committee can do much of the work involved in planning and implementing a detailed communications plan for the campaign. However, it is unrealistic to expect volunteers to undertake the day-to-day tasks of communications, such as contacting media members, writing press releases, overseeing production of campaign materials, and managing interviews and other contacts with the public. For such activities, you need a staff member who is trained and experienced in communications and who can step into this role with minimal training. Ideally, this person will develop an effective partnership with your campaign manager and your volunteer leadership. He or she will provide scripts for public events and ensure that your messaging is powerful and consistent.

In most campaigns, the needs for a communications specialist specific to the campaign do not exceed a half-time position and might be handled either internally or by a consultant who will work on an hourly or daily basis. The position will have more work to do at the start of the campaign and during the community phase, a financial consideration that should be reflected in your budgeting. If your college determines that current staff members can absorb the additional load, it is important that it budgets the necessary time to ensure that the campaign receives the attention it requires for success.

Targeting the Right Market

Car manufacturers create beautifully illustrated glossy brochures filled with photos of their cars from every angle, often decorated with attractive models and placed in dramatic settings. They also have DVDs and other audiovisual aids to help you imagine how wonderful you'll feel in their cars. On the Internet, you can see photos of the car and even get a price quote with the precise options you want. Yet few people buy a car based solely on these materials and without visiting a dealership or otherwise experiencing the auto firsthand. Automakers are good at selling cars. Why do they spend millions of dollars on these tools when people are going to make up their minds based on personally experiencing the product? They create the materials, of course, to establish the correct preconditions and atmosphere for a sale.

By sampling a car through the printed and video word, you get a feel for whether it's the right car for you. The impression being made on you is created partly by the look and feel of the brochure—a Kia brochure looks and feels a lot different from one for a BMW or a Lexus. Part of the message appeals to your style. For example, hip-hop music is more likely to be used on a DVD targeted to young people. Trendy colors dominate ads for Gen Xers, as opposed to the primary colors aimed at older generations. Perceived expense of the marketing piece also makes an impression. A brochure for a Suzuki is not going to be effective if it appears to be incredibly expensive, with embossed covers and die cut inserts. A Mercedes probably won't show up effectively in a brochure with thin paper.

Your project is no different. You need materials. Your potential donors need to be able to look at something that summarizes what you hope to do and how you plan to do it. They need to know your budget, both for the project and for its operations once it's open. You need an identity, so that anyone receiving information about your project knows it's from you. You want to make certain that your newsletter isn't mistaken for a direct mail appeal.

However, you don't need a Cadillac brochure to sell a Saturn. In fact, expensive, glossy materials will probably turn off potential donors to a rural technical college. Your materials have to be appropriate to the project. For appearances in front of the Rotary or Kiwanis, you might need a brief video or a professionally prepared PowerPoint presentation or slide show, especially for those who have difficulty in translating words into images without visual aids.

Stating Your Case Compellingly

To establish the merits of your project, you need to make a clear case. This goes back to your feasibility study, when you created a case statement. Your potential donors and leaders reviewed your case and suggested ways to strengthen and improve it. Now's the time to take their advice and create the most compelling, clearest, simplest case statement possible. Start by reducing what you want to do to its most important outcomes. For example, "We're going to increase our scholarship program by 50%" or "We will install state-of-the-art equipment for our EMT training program." Then, translate those outcomes into benefits for the community and add that to your case statement. For example, "Our high school kids will stay in school and graduate at a higher rate because they'll be able to look forward to a college education." Or "The community will get needed emergency services from the best-trained EMTs in the state."

These outcomes and benefits will form the core of your case statement, driving everything else you write. From them, you can derive the project description. You'll be able to relate what you're doing to specific community needs and explain why your solution is best. You'll show how much the project will cost and how you will sustain it. You'll feature stories that bring the project alive and that lend themselves to illustrations through photos, video, or drawings. Choose representative students who personify the diversity of your student body by ethnicity, age, gender, and other demographic factors. When possible, use interviews with actual students to demonstrate the benefits of your project in a compelling and convincing manner.

Utilizing a Communications Committee

In planning your communications strategy, the presence of a communications committee that will help form and guide your efforts often provides broad (and at times unexpected) benefits. The committee should be organized on the premise that it will meet frequently at the very beginning of the campaign, with meetings at a diminishing frequency thereafter. The committee should include a combination of your college's communications staff (if any), your foundation director, one or two members of your board and campaign cabinet with declared interest in public awareness and communications issues, and representatives from the community who bring defined skills and connections to your efforts. The creative director at an advertising agency, a local television or radio personality, or a video production professional are examples of the members you might seek. They bring both knowledge of the community and useful skills to your efforts.

An early task for the committee is to undertake a review of existing materials, both to determine what other elements will be required and to ensure that campaign messages are consistent with existing ones. Often, the committee will find innovative and cost-saving ways to reuse existing materials. For example, if you have a promotional video that includes interviews with successful students, these can be repackaged as part of a campaign-focused video. Similarly, if you have done a series of newspaper ads featuring your college's diversity, these can be incorporated into your brochures. In the initial meetings, the committee should review and revise a communications plan developed by your staff members or consultant. The committee should also be used as an ongoing test site for your campaign messages, materials, and overall campaign communications strategy.

Often, the committee plays an additional, cost-saving role. It frequently can help you connect with vendors to produce your campaign materials and provide creative services at reduced rates or even as the vendor's campaign contribution. Often, they can themselves provide such services if they are excited and motivated by your campaign goals. A well-known radio personality serving on your committee might agree to do the voice-over for your video or your public service spots. A local television anchor might agree to serve as the emcee for your kick-off event.

The committee will meet more sporadically as the campaign progresses. It is often helpful in troubleshooting problems that arise. For example, it will help develop messages to respond to the departure of your president or foundation executive. On a more positive note, if you are about to exceed your campaign goal and decide that you want to continue raising money for new initiatives, it will help you find the best way to introduce this concept to the community.

Creating a Distinctive Brand

A campaign brand (logo or tagline) can take a long time to create. It's worth the effort to create something that is effective and inspires volunteers and donors Your communications committee will provide an initial useful response to your ideas; it may be possible to convene focus groups of your potential donor constituencies to provide additional feedback. You should certainly include your college family members in testing your brand and logo, since they are the ones who live your messages every day. Your plan tells you whether you need a logo now, later, or never.

In general, the broader the audiences you are trying to reach, the more likely it is that you should invest in a logo. Your need to establish an easily recognized image that your campaign volunteers, college family, and potential donors recognize increase as the breadth of the campaign expands. If you expect to get the great majority of your gifts from a very small group of people, the need for elaborate branding is minimal. If you are attempting to reach a broad metropolitan area with many competing efforts, establishing your individuality through a distinctive brand can be a valuable effort.

For comprehensive campaigns, the campaign brand and slogan can often be generic, such as "Building for Our Future." For more targeted campaigns, the brand and slogan can be more focused. For example, "Stirring the Pot" might work for a culinary arts center campaign. "New workers, new hope," would be a possibility for a new workforce training center. For a campaign for a multicampus college, you might have one overarching theme, with subthemes for the individual projects. Slogans and logos should be rendered in a variety of sizes, colors, and file formats so that they can be readily incorporated into campaign materials (e.g., on campaign stationery, newsletters, brochures, etc.).

Matching the Medium to the Message

Print Media

You will need letterhead, envelopes, a template for a campaign newsletter, note cards and matching envelopes, a pledge form, return envelopes, and other materials with the campaign logo and slogan on them. Your volunteers will recognize immediately which mail is from the campaign and which relates to normal college business. Separate letterhead will give the campaign a sense of identity and begin the process of branding the campaign in the community.

Once you have your logo and a basic case statement, you can start to decide how you will display your project and which mediums will work best. If many of your meetings are going to be one-on-one briefings, you might put your case statement and supporting materials into a view book, an easily altered notebook that provides talking points. The book is useful for people who don't need to be impressed—just informed. Depending on how elaborate the book is, it can cost $10 to $50 each. Since it's meant only for a limited number of donors, it allows you to approach your initial donors at minimal cost.

You'll probably need a brochure specifically for major donors (e.g., prospects for gifts of $5,000 or more). Such a brochure has about an 18-month shelf life and will be expensive to produce. It tells your story in an attractive way. More importantly, it gives you consistent talking points when you meet with donors. The brochure acts as a prompter, ensuring that you stick to the script. Even more important, a well-done brochure lets you speak to prospects knowing that you've defined your project and that you have something that makes it concrete. In a sense, the brochure isn't selling the prospect on your campaign; it's selling you on your ability to present your case effectively.

The major donor brochure should be appropriate to the project. If you're creating a child-care center, you can create a beguiling and attractive brochure in the form of a kid's storybook. If you're raising money to equip a culinary arts building, you could create a brochure that contains testimonials from successful graduates, perhaps with a few of their favorite recipes. If you're creating a first-generation scholarship fund, profiles of previous scholarship recipients and donors would help illustrate why such a campaign is vital to the community. What does not work is a brochure that is filled with detailed text and abstract explanations of the project's importance. Tell your story clearly, simply, and in a way that allows readers to understand why they will benefit from your success.

To Video or Not to Video?

Mary Kaufman-Cranney, long one of the YMCA's leading fundraisers and a frequent speaker at the North American Association of YMCA Development Officers summed up the case against videos in a discussion with me in late 2007. She asked, "Why would I want a prospective donor staring at a computer screen for five minutes when I could have my campaign chair talking to him in person about her excitement concerning the campaign? Nothing beats a peer-to-peer meeting, no matter how excellent the video."

Unfortunately, however, you can't always have a campaign leader available to make a presentation. In addition, some volunteer fundraisers are more likely to meet with a prospect if they can introduce the campaign with a professionally produced video. In addition, you will have some alumni, corporate officers, and other potential donors that are located out of town, and a video offers a convenient way to tell them about the campaign. If you have an attractive and frequently visited Web site, you can post the video on it to capture viewers who are interested in your college and its campaign. Finally, if you are addressing large groups, a video can be effective in conveying great deal of information effectively and in a short time. You can allow your local Rotary to meet students, faculty, and alumni, while also enjoying visuals of campus activities. For many of them, it will be an effective introduction to your college, especially if they haven't visited your campus in the past.

Videos can now be transferred onto DVDs, are cheap to reproduce, and, done well, can convey the excitement of your project in a personal way. Videos are also portable: You can show them on your laptop at the drop of a hat when you meet somebody who's interested in your project. Videos aren't for everyone, though, so before deciding to use this medium, you should investigate potential costs and venues for using them.

A top-level video company will charge at least $15,000 for a 4-minute video and as much as $50,000 for something longer and more elaborate. You don't want to try to do it yourself, because it will probably scream "amateur!" If a video is primarily a "talking head," it won't hold up well for large audiences, and no one will be interested if the video is too long or too dull. So, before proceeding, ask yourself what a video could do that you couldn't do better by talking about the project animatedly or doing a high-quality brochure.

If you are going to do a video, one approach that works well is to splice together a number of news clips from coverage your college has received on local television stations. A well-known news anchor talking about your college is much more effective than a talking head bragging about the institution. The station will generally give permission for such use, providing you give the appropriate credit.

A video works best if it tells a compelling story and focuses on people talking about how your organization affects them personally. You also need clear plans as to how you will use the video and how you can update it as needed. Can you put the video on your college's Web site, allowing the public to view it on demand? Can you entice people to your Web site to ensure that they view the video, or will it receive so few hits that your effort goes unrewarded?

College and Foundation Web Sites

Most potential donors expect your college to have an attractive, informative, easy-to-navigate Web site. They click on your site to learn about your course offerings, your instructors, your specialties, and other information. They will often gain their initial opinion of your worthiness from a quick perusal of your site. If the site is welcoming and easy to navigate, they'll get a positive impression. If they can't find what they want intuitively, they'll be suspicious about your claims to be fully accessible.

Your site is an excellent place to feature your campaign. Since by definition your campaign is one of your top priorities, that significance must be reflected in your public portrayal. Your Web site can be an invaluable resource to your campaign. At the very least, it offers a way to describe what you're doing in words and images. You can include access to your brochure, video, architectural plans, and other materials. You can also offer links to most media coverage and provide updates through a Web-based newsletter. Equally important, you can use the Web to collect names and contact information, expanding your prospect base. It's easy to honor volunteers and donors on your Web site as well as keep your constituents informed of your progress.

Ideally, whether your campaign Web site is housed on your college's server or a host server, it should be prominently displayed on your college Web site, because that's where most potential donors or campaign volunteers will initially expect to find information. The site can be used to host an Intranet campaign site that allows password-protected access to information volunteers need. It is an ideal way to store assignments for volunteers and to disseminate an internal newsletter and other information that is for insiders only.

A staff member should be responsible for keeping the Web site updated. The time and money to create an attractive Web site will be wasted if you do not keep it fresh. Ideally, large gifts, news stories, campaign milestones, and other notable occurrences should be posted as soon as they happen. This gives your constituents a reason to return to the site repeatedly rather than discover that what they're looking at hasn't changed in the past month. Such upkeep should be budgeted for and time should be set aside to ensure that it occurs.

The campaign should establish its Web strategy as early as possible, involving your communications committee in consulting with the college's information technology department or consultant. You should understand the costs of creating the various Web-based components and receive expert advice on what results you can realistically expect from your efforts. It is important to understand that nationally, only a very small percentage of all gifts are generated through Web-based philanthropy and that for large gifts, nothing replaces face-to-face cultivation and solicitation.

Electronic Fundraising

Internet fundraising should be a component of your overall fundraising strategy. It is not, however, an appropriate means of soliciting donations for a capital campaign until the very end of the campaign when you are willing to accept any size gift. Your focus has to be on face-to-face requests for lead and major gifts until you enter the community phase of the campaign. Providing potential major donors with the opportunity to give small gifts, without personal contact, is usually a mistake. Even if you use your Web site to solicit and receive annual funding, you should not offer the option of making capital gifts through electronic means until the last stages of the campaign.

Most colleges are accustomed to communicating with their supporters by e-mail. There are many campaign-related strategies that allow you to continue and expand this approach. You can send frequent updates on the campaign to those closest to the college. These updates should be brief and punchy and make the recipients feel like insiders. Notification about large gifts, significant campaign milestones, and other breaking news are all likely topics for such communications.

"Conversations around all community colleges are already occurring on the likes of Facebook, Twitter, and other social networking sites. It is imperative that we add our college's voice to that already on-going conversation; we fail to do so at our own peril. The next arena for student recruitment and alumni engagement is social networking sites, and if you are not involved, then you will be left out of the game entirely."

—Erik Williams, alumni relations and annual giving coordinator, Virginia Western Community College

Social Networking

As each week passes, it seems, new technology emerges that uses electronic means to reach organizational constituents. Among such technologies that have emerged over the past few years, photo and video sharing, podcasting, microblogging (Twitter), and social networking have attracted hundreds of millions of adherents. These newer approaches joined blogs, message boards, and chat rooms as means of connecting people through virtual networks. The last presidential campaign brought attention to the potential power of such technologies, both as a means of viral messaging and as a platform for significant fundraising. The question that community and technical colleges face, of course, is whether they can use these technologies in connection with their fundraising efforts.

Facebook, MySpace, Twitter, and other social networking Web sites offer a powerful and popular tool for connecting to your constituencies, especially with alumni. It is relatively inexpensive to develop a home page for Facebook or take out an ad requesting people to become friends or fans. You can then e-mail your alumni to invite them to view your page and to link up with you.

Many sites provide suggestions for social networking strategies. All are updated frequently to ensure that you will receive contemporary information rather than advice that is "so last month." Three sites with useful information on social networking and fundraising are Meyer Memorial Trust (www.mmt.org), NPTech (http://nptech.info), and Doshdosh (www.doshdosh.com).

Your hope is that people who sign up will then contact other alumni whose e-mail addresses you don't currently have. Eventually, you will have a large number of alumni as "fans" or "friends," who will follow your efforts and perhaps join them. What you must remember, however, is that all of these technologies are essentially about creating and cultivating relationships, and relationships cost money to maintain. When people become your friends or fans, they are expressing an interest in the college, rather than agreeing to either actively support you or make a donation. It may take months or years for them to determine that they truly wish to be part of your effort.

Successful viral marketing through social networking sites depends on your ability to drive people to your Web site, Facebook site, or other vehicle. During the past presidential campaign, constant media attention, the excitement of a new face, and widespread interest in change resulted in two candidates using these methodologies with great success (Ron Paul and Barack Obama). In all probability, your campaign will not receive comparable coverage or generate as much excitement. You will have to determine whether the considerable effort social networking requires will create acceptable results. "Frogloop" is the name of a nonprofit online marketing blog (www.frogloop.com). One useful post is a tool for determining the return on investment for social networking efforts (see Perkins, 2007). The "ROI calculator" allows you to factor in all of the elements involved in establishing, maintaining, and exploiting an online network and to determine whether the results are worth it.

Another type of networking available to your college is provided by Web portals that share their income with you. Each time one of your alumni registers with such a Web site, all of their activities that generate income for the Web host are shared with you. For example, if one of your alumni signs up and then purchases travel through the portal, the travel site pays a commission to the portal. The socially conscious Web site will share that revenue with you, at times up to 50%. One such company that will be available to nonprofits is Globalmojo, which is in its final testing phase as this book is being written. Other such sites exist, each with its own rules and approaches. Such sites encourage your alumni to identify themselves and also provide ongoing unrestricted income for your college.

In general, modern technology offers many opportunities for you to reestablish contact with your alumni and perhaps generate support. Follow-up, however, is essential. City University in Seattle did an online survey of its alumni in 2007 and received a response rate of almost 20%, demonstrating a high level of interest in the college. Almost 40% of respondents indicated that they would at least consider making a gift. Even with that information, however, the college was unable to launch a fundraising campaign immediately because it lacked staff resources (E. Ryan-Rojas, personal communication, June, 2007).

Budgeting for Marketing Materials

Expenses for marketing materials are as legitimate as those for staff, consultants, and new telephone lines. You should be sure to budget fully for all the materials identified in your public relations and marketing plan. Realize, however, that it is often possible to find local businesses willing to donate services such as design, printing, or photography, or sponsors who will pay for such services in exchange for recognition. You should plan to spend a minimum of $25,000 on materials for campaigns of $1 million; costs increase from there depending on the size of the campaign, although not proportionally. It will cost little more to publicize a $25 million campaign than it would a $5 million one, since the major cost of preparing materials is considerably greater than that of duplicating them. Brochure design will be the same for either campaign; an additional 500 copies will add perhaps $1,000 to the cost.

If you are part of a multicampus system with different projects at each campus and separate committees working on the campaigns, you should consider creating one comprehensive brochure covering all of the projects, with less elaborate, less expensive materials dedicated to the individual projects. Thus, you might have a single "Going From Good to Great" campaign logo and brochure, but individual campuses might have specific materials relating to their initiatives. In all cases, the cost for campaign materials should fit within the overall campaign budget. Use the template in Appendix C to estimate costs.

Things To Do Before Developing Marketing Materials

- Determine that the top priority is to ensure you have what you need to make your initial calls. You will soon realize that marketing materials are part of the supporting cast, not the star.
- Appoint a small editorial advisory board to which you entrust all decisions about campaign marketing materials. Accept that you're not going to love everything the advisory board does, but trust the advisors to get close enough to perfection to satisfy your needs.
- Be sure that you have a clear vision statement and focus before you start developing your materials. Make sure you are at a point where you will discuss how to best convey your vision, not where you are still trying to define your vision.

In difficult economic times, it is frequently tempting for colleges to cut budgets for public awareness and communications initiatives. Severe cuts can cripple campaigns, because campaign volunteers are less likely to make their calls if they lack effective materials. Possessing an informative and attractive major gift brochure, a professionally produced PowerPoint or video, and a well-maintained Web site gives volunteers the confidence they need to make calls.

If your college's budget is limited, it is better to find ways of doing things less expensively rather than eliminating them. Seeking donations of creative and production services will often garner generous contributions from the community. It is less expensive to recycle existing materials than to start from scratch. If a local television station has done several features on your students and faculty, it will often be willing to edit them into an effective video.

As a last resort, you may be able to use an intern or volunteer in place of paid staff. A recent graduate of a top-rate communications program may not yet have a job and could benefit by using your campaign to assemble a portfolio. The danger in this approach, of course, is that the intern may leave mid-campaign, leaving projects unfinished.

It is important to get the campaign under way quickly and to maintain momentum once it's started. Nothing brings a campaign to a grinding halt quicker than arguments over campaign materials. One major community college spent more than a year creating its case statement, holding back the fundraisers who were anxious for materials that would allow them to start raising money.

The worst materials are the ones that are picked over until they lose all life. The best materials are the ones that get you out the door and in front of potential donors. Remember why you have these materials—to ensure that everyone is singing from the same music and that all volunteers and staff members have confidence in their shared story. The materials will never convince your donors to give if your passion doesn't show.

CHAPTER 10

Understanding the Roles Played by Campaign Team Members

Campaigns are a team effort. Participation, whether as a donor or a campaign participant, reverberates throughout the campaign, and the failure of one team member to participate has a negative effect on the entire campaign. For example, if the president is resentful of time spent on the campaign, the foundation board and others will speculate on whether the outcomes of the campaign are truly important. If the foundation board members don't give generously, others in the community will ponder the implications. If instructors ignore the campaign, they will send a strong and negative message to the community in general and their students in particular. If, on the other hand, all participants play their roles and fulfill their responsibilities well, your campaign will succeed.

The College Trustees

College trustees are appointed or elected to represent the community's interests. They hire and oversee the president, set goals and the policies to achieve them, and represent the college to the community. Although fundraising is not considered one of the primary responsibilities of trustees, the Association of Community College Trustees (2009) lists their roles and responsibilities as including "support the foundation and fundraising efforts," and "promote the college in the community." These roles have been widely interpreted as suggesting that trustees have an important role in college fundraising campaigns.

Trustees carry the greatest moral authority concerning the college's worthiness of community support. They know the institution intimately and have the responsibility to ensure that it obeys its mandate to serve the community. Having trustee support for a campaign carries great weight and should involve at least three commitments from each trustee:

- To familiarize themselves with the goals of the campaign and express their support for them.
- To make a gift to the campaign commensurate with their own financial standing, sufficient to attest to their sincere belief in the campaign's aspirations.
- To serve as spokespeople for the campaign in appropriate venues, offering public witness to their support of the college and its campaign.

In many cases, individual trustees will be even more closely involved in the campaign, serving on committees, making one of the largest gifts, or soliciting gifts from friends and colleagues. Although these are not expectations of each trustee, trustee support engenders community support.

The College President

Until the early 1990s, most community and technical college presidents did not view themselves as occupying a central role in fundraising for their institutions. As colleges began to require greater nongovernmental support, however, this view changed. It is now broadly accepted that a community college campaign demands the avid participation of the president. Eileen Piwetz, long-time foundation director at Midland (TX) College stated, "If your president doesn't accept his role as the fundraiser-in-chief, you're in big trouble" (personal communication, January 21, 2009). There are numerous reasons why the president's participation is critical, including the following:

- The prominent position that the president holds in the community makes him or her the most visible representative of the college.
- The president is expected to hold the major stewardship role for raising and spending funds wisely for the college.
- The president is the college's chief visionary, holding the clearest picture of where the college is going and what it can achieve.

Internally, the president's participation is even more important. As the leader of the college, the president acts as cheerleader, inspirer, example, and pacesetter during the campaign. Reflecting these roles, the president must do following:

- Make a significant gift, often as much as 3% to 5% of the total salary over a 5-year period (a $200,000 annual salary would

generate $6,000 to $10,000 annually, for a total gift of $30,000 to $50,000). This gift will serve as a testimony to the president's passionate belief in the campaign and as an example to other top administrators and staff.
- Serve as a consistent and enthusiastic advocate for the campaign internally, making clear that it is an institutional priority.
- Join the campaign leadership and give ongoing support to the efforts of the foundation board and staff.
- Devote a significant amount of time to the campaign, including meeting with potential leaders and donors, attending meetings, and speaking to community organizations. Presidents report spending between 25% and 50% of their time on the campaign, especially in the early months. Of course, many of them might claim that they spend 50% of their time on the campaign, 50% on supervising direct reports, and 50% working with the state and other external entities.

Campaign Team Members

- College Trustees
- College President
- Foundation Board Members
- Advisory Committee Members
- Consultants
- Foundation Staff
- College Instructors and Staff
- Campaign Committees and Task Forces

Foundation Board Members

Foundations exist to support the college's mission. Engaging in a campaign often represents the highest form of such support. The board members have a special responsibility in this regard because they are ultimately responsible for the success or failure of the campaign. Their roles, which will be discussed more fully in subsequent chapters, include the following:

- Making a significant gift to the campaign, often the largest single charitable contribution they have ever made.
- Serving as a consistent advocate for the college and the campaign.
- Overseeing campaign progress and holding the foundation staff and president responsible for meeting goals and staying within budget.
- Soliciting friends and colleagues for campaign gifts and accompanying the president on cultivation and solicitation calls to potential donors.
- Maintaining a relentlessly upbeat attitude toward the campaign and the college and fulfilling their responsibility of institutional loyalty.

Advisory Committee Members

Most community and technical colleges have advisory committees that help ensure that specialized programs remain up-to-date and meet community needs. Whether it's advocating for a program in welding, an allied health profession, dentistry, or cosmetology, such committees connect your college to the real world. They are also invaluable in connecting you to potential sources for cash and in-kind gifts.

Advisory committee members spend valuable time providing your college with advice, usually on a quarterly basis. They have close connections with your instructors and staff and carry your message into the community. You should provide them with the opportunity to make a gift to the campaign, join a campaign committee, and serve as advocates for the campaign within their sphere of influence.

Consultants

Larger campaigns will often use professional consultants who have worked with many other colleges and other nonprofit organizations. These consultants bring valuable experience and knowledge to the campaign and can offer essential guidance as you move forward. Their role is to shape your campaign plan, provide training and preparation for staff and volunteers, and offer ongoing counsel as you move forward. Effective ones are often there to congratulate you on successes and commiserate with you after defeats. They also serve as scorekeepers and referees, letting you know whether you are making appropriate progress.

It is not proper for consultants to make major solicitations, because they are not part of your college. In a sense, they are mercenaries, guns for hire, providing expertise to institutions that pay them for it. They will be with you for the duration of the campaign and perhaps a few months more, but then they'll move on to other projects. Your goal is not simply to raise money but to establish lasting relationships between your college and your donors. Consultants cannot substitute for the foundation board members or the president in establishing such relationships.

Foundation Staff

Most community and technical college foundations have three or fewer staff members. A campaign will result in adding at least one person and sometimes more. They are the glue that holds everyone's efforts together because they provide you with your prospect lists, organize meetings, prepare the proposals that go to all donors, and process gifts as they arrive. At the same time, they have to continue your ongoing foundation efforts, whether these include special events, direct mail, telephone solicitation, or other approaches. It is essential that they have enough time to do their work and that you don't lose any donors because of inadequate stewardship.

Your foundation staff may not be most effectively used as campaign fundraisers. First, their primary task is to facilitate activities undertaken by the president and foundation board members and other volunteers. Additionally, many community and institutional leaders might not regard staff members as peers, which is an important aspect of soliciting major gifts.

For higher education institutions, especially for 4-year and research universities, senior fundraising professionals often develop strong relationships with some donors, eventually reaching the level of a trusted advisor. This involves long periods of time and interactions that demonstrate both their reliability and their interest in serving the college and not themselves. Few community colleges have sufficient staff members to use this model.

Foundation staff members are expected to be leaders in the campaign to gain financial support from other college staff members. They have to demonstrate their personal belief in the campaign through their own gifts and be enthusiastic advocates for the campaign in all their campus discussions. They will not actually solicit these internal gifts, however, as will be shown in chapter 16.

College Instructors and Staff

A fundraising frame of mind should permeate your college during a campaign. Every member of the college family should be aware of the campaign and support it financially and emotionally. They should also consider whether they know others who might be willing to contribute—former students, neighbors, and businesses they patronize. Any donor visiting your campus should receive a warm welcome and get the sense that your instructors and staff believe deeply in your institutional mission. This helps them believe that the college is moving in the right direction and has the full support of its internal constituencies.

Faculty and staff giving is sometimes a contentious issue, since often both groups feel underpaid and may even be mistrustful of the fundraising process. Running a special campaign to secure their support offers an excellent educational device to familiarize them with your broader goals and excite them about the role their personal gifts might play. It is vital that there is never any sense of coercion or compulsion surrounding their gifts and that their participation is perceived as more important than the size of their contribution.

The family campaign, focused on faculty and staff, may take as long as six months. Representatives from the campus make the best leaders, rather than foundation staff. Often, they organize the campaign by department (e.g., humanities, business, or health professions) or function (e.g., maintenance, security, or administration). The foundation can help prepare materials to explain the campaign and provide support in organizing campaign-related events. The emphasis of these campaigns is on participation rate rather than the amount of funds raised. Drew Matonak, president of Hudson Valley Community College in Troy, New York, praised the internal campaign at his college as follows: "By emphasizing participation, we were able to raise our internal support from 6-7% to more than 50% over a six-month period" (personal communication, December, 2008).

Campaign Committees and Task Forces

Steering Committee

Fundraising campaigns rely on committees and task forces to complete discrete elements of work. The first committee to be formed is the campaign steering committee (sometimes called the cabinet or executive committee). It usually consists of the college president, foundation director, relevant administrators and faculty, and an all-star group of community leaders with responsibility for making major campaign decisions and overseeing the execution of the campaign. It includes chairs of the various campaign subcommittees. The steering committee is the only committee that operates for the entire duration of the campaign and meets regularly for the entire period, often once or twice a month.

Ongoing Committees

Once the steering committee is in place, the communications committee should be formed, to help guide the public phase of the campaign. Its members include foundation board members, college staff, and community volunteers with useful expertise and connections. Its work is heavily front-loaded, and it will often meet frequently at the start of the campaign but only sporadically thereafter. In rare cases, if the campaign is for a building project and the college desires additional help, it may choose to create a building advisory committee.

Task Forces

The first solicitation group to be formed is the board gifts task force, which is made up of leading foundation board members and college trustees, the college president, and the foundation director. Generally, the committee consists of one fourth or one fifth of the total number of board members, requiring each volunteer member to make only three or four calls to fellow foundation board members or trustees. This task force ceases to exist once it has completed the board campaign (see chapter 14).

The faculty and staff gifts task force is made up of non-foundation employees of the college responsible for organizing and implementing the faculty and staff campaign. It works closely with the foundation staff, receiving all needed strategic and logistical support. It exists only as long as necessary to fulfill its task, seldom more than three or four months.

Most campaigns use a donor evaluation task force to ensure that volunteers feel confident in asking potential donors for specific amounts of money. Task force members use foundation records, the results of donor screenings (see chapter 11), and public records of previous gifts to set appropriate request amounts. Using materials prepared by foundation staff, the task force has a single charge: reviewing the top campaign prospects and assigning potential solicitation amounts for each individual, corporation, or foundation. Ideally, the donor evaluation task force will meet no more than once or twice.

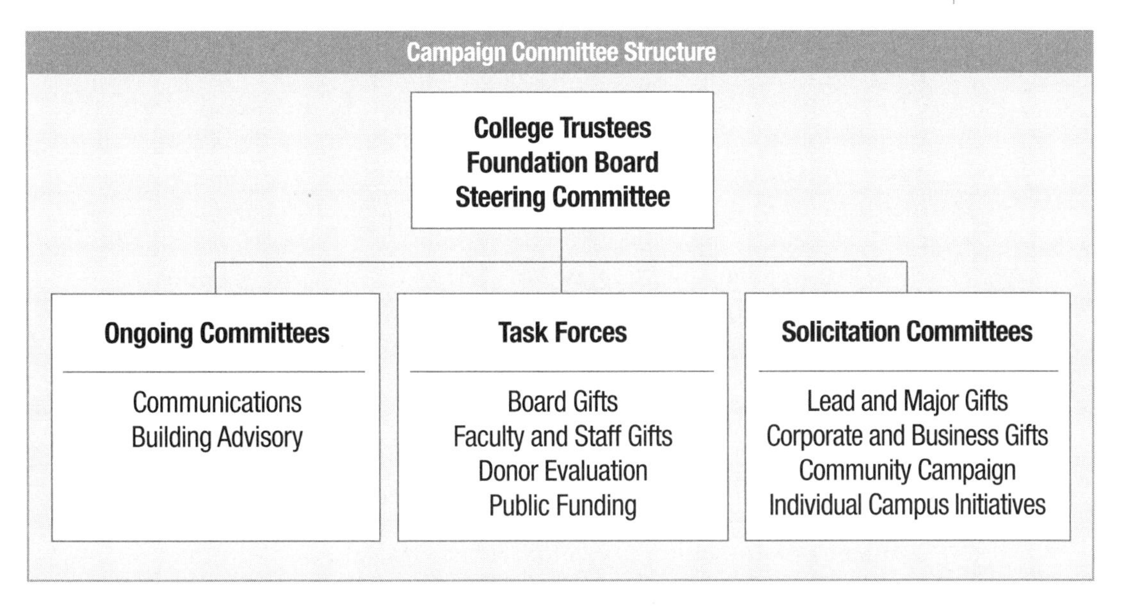

Because of the variety of potential donors, task force members must represent knowledge of all potential donor constituencies. It is helpful, therefore, to have people such as well-connected bankers, accountants, attorneys, real estate agents, chamber of commerce presidents, major philanthropists, and members from each of the most prominent golf or country clubs (if they are important to your community) join foundation staff in making these assessments. All task force discussions should remain strictly confidential; colleges also often ask that task force members remain anonymous as well. The reason for confidentiality will become apparent as conversations about request amounts unfold: Task force members will be providing information about personal wealth, changes in financial situations, or private information such as pending divorces.

Once these deliberations are completed, staff can assemble a qualified prospect list in descending order of potential gift size. This will allow the various solicitation committees to determine who will be paired with whom to pursue potential gifts. It will also provide the final test to ensure that the campaign has sufficient prospects at high enough target amounts to make fulfillment of the rule of 12 possible.

Finally, as discussed in chapter 21, a public funding task force that includes board members, community leaders, civic and political leaders, and others is helpful if you expect to receive a substantial amount of funding from the public sector. Such a committee should have connections to all levels of public funding and the ability to influence decisions at the local, regional, and federal levels.

Solicitation Committees

Lead and major gifts committees are the most important of all the possible solicitation committees you may set up. Ideally, they are made up of significant donors who are strong partisans of the college. Their responsibility, working with the support of the president and the foundation staff, is to identify potential donors and solicit gifts after appropriate cultivation. Generally, a lead and major gifts committee is formed within a few months after the campaign starts and continues until its work is done.

Campaigns in large metropolitan areas may have enough potential donors to warrant creation of a special committee composed of business leaders to cultivate and solicit gifts from corporations and businesses; smaller colleges in regional areas may form committees for obtaining gifts from local small businesses. The community campaign committee is formed in time to plan and implement the community phase of the campaign, which is discussed in detail in chapter 23. Depending on the size and complexity of the campaign, the committee might consist of a handful of community volunteers or it could be a group of 30 people divided into subcommittees that focus on special events, a "brick campaign," or other elements of a community campaign. Either this committee or a separate one also plans the celebrations that mark the completion and success of the campaign. More complex or multicampus campaigns have additional solicitation committees that focus on specific projects and initiatives. They are composed of interested board members, community volunteers, and others, all supported by foundation and college staff.

CHAPTER 11

Building a Prospect List

In the first chapter, you read that one of the characteristics that makes community and technical colleges different is that they possess undefined donor bases. On one hand, most colleges have a relatively small number of donors. On the other hand, their potential donor base includes more possible donors than they can ever reach. How do you identify your real potential donors and ensure that you concentrate on your very best prospects?

One important way is to avoid chasing phantom donors. Too often, people look for gifts in OPM—Other People's Money! They assume that Willie Sutton was right when asked why he robbed banks: "Because that's where the money is." And so, they look to famous rich people, whether in their community or halfway around the world, to fund their project. They make that intuitive jump—that because a rich and famous person cares about ethnic minorities and your college focuses on increasing access and opportunity for minority populations, the rich and famous will jump at the opportunity to fund your project. But, whoever your biggest donors and best prospects may be, they're probably not Denzel Washington, Madonna, Warren Buffett, the Rockefeller Foundation, Wal-Mart, or Tiger Woods.

We've all heard about the check from an angel that arrives unexpectedly, the free cars that Oprah Winfrey gave away, or the huge gifts that Bill Cosby made to his alma mater. And we ask ourselves, "Why shouldn't we get those same gifts?" Because there are more than 1 million nonprofit organizations in the United States and tens of thousands more around the world, and donors—even Bill and Melinda Gates—have to set priorities and limit themselves to a small percentage of possible recipients.

Equally important, the rich and famous tend to give to causes close to them, with which they or their trusted advisors are familiar.

Like anyone else, they give to express their personal values and their individual experience. If a famous actress or basketball player got started at your college and has acknowledged their gratitude in the past, they might be excellent prospects. If you are approaching a rich and famous person for no reason other than their wealth and fame, you will probably be expending effort unwisely.

Outside funds, if they materialize, will come only if your college has a proven community benefit, regional importance, and a strong track record of local funding. The Bill and Melinda Gates Foundation, for example, has announced that it will support community colleges. Their support, however, will most likely go to colleges able to demonstrate strong local and regional support and the ability to sustain programs started with Gates Foundation money. Otherwise, your most likely donors are people you know and who know you, who see the benefits of what you do either directly or indirectly, and who want to see you move to your next stage. You're probably starting with too many prospects rather than too few, and your primary task will be to whittle down your list to those on whom you should focus.

Identifying Potential Donors

Giving starts with the people this book is written for: foundation board members, trustees, college presidents, top college administrators, and members of the campaign leadership. If you are reading this book, you are part of the college's core supporters and will give generously to the campaign. Your gifts will be among the first to be registered by the campaign.

The next group of most obvious potential donors will be those individuals, corporations, and foundations that have given in the past. People talk about donor fatigue, suggesting that individuals and organizations get tired of giving to the same organization. The truth is precisely the opposite. Once someone commits to your college, they are not simply a donor. They also have become an investor, with a strong interest in all of your activities and a passionate desire to see you succeed. If you have kept them informed about your plans, such as through including them in your feasibility study, they will be enthusiastic participants in the campaign.

The third group of early donors includes your administration, instructors, and staff. They will be the direct beneficiaries of your campaign, whether in a specific or general way. A scholarship campaign will strengthen the entire institution. A campaign to equip the library or technology center will improve student performance. New programs will add students and jobs and increase your college's service to the community. Funds for professional development will offer them opportunities to attend conferences and symposia, hone their skills, and feel better about the jobs they do. Although many of the gifts these groups make will be modest, each is vitally important to demonstrate to others that there is internal support for the campaign.

The fourth group of prospects includes your retirees. Many of them spent decades at the college, overseeing the growth of the institution and participating in the improvement of the lives of generations of students. Many of them would enjoy making a gift that cements their relationship in perpetuity, whether by endowing a scholarship, contributing to a new facility, or leaving a bequest to the college to be used where most needed. Many colleges stay in contact with their retirees, hosting annual receptions for them, keeping them informed about new initiatives, and calling upon their expertise. These wise institutions will find the process of discussing gifts with their retirees easy and rewarding.

The fifth group of early donors will be the members of your advisory committees, especially if the campaign benefits their area of interest and expertise. If you are seeking to equip an allied health professions building, your advisory committees for those fields should be approached early in the campaign to demonstrate their support. Of course, you will have discussed the project with them and sought their advice throughout your planning stage. When the campaign begins, they will be pleased to offer personal and corporate support to your efforts.

The sixth group of obvious prospects is composed of the local and regional corporations whose employees you train and educate. These gifts will often take longer to develop because you have often been a below-the-radar partner in their efforts. One local technical college was the largest single supplier of training for employees at a nearby multinational corporation. College staff worked with mid-level managers to provide up-to-date training for many trades employed by the company. The company's top executives, however, all came from major state and national universities. The prestige of those research institutions outweighed the practical value of the technical college's contributions in decisions concerning charitable support. Only after a lengthy educational process involving the college president and responsible managers within the company did a significant gift emerge.

Finally on your most likely potential donors list are public-sector donors (but see CASE's position on government funds, p. 163), starting with your city or municipality and extending to county, state, and federal sources. If you have staff or consultants who focus on public-sector funding, they will provide guidance in this regard, but direct contact between volunteers (foundation board members and college trustees) and representatives of government decision makers is vital for success in this regard. While there are specific funds available for community and technical colleges, personal contact is indispensable in gaining access to them. In the case of local governments, you often have to convince elected officials that your college is a good investment for public funds and will benefit the entire city or county.

NARROWING THE LIST

Using an Asset-Screening Service

After assembling lists of the potential donors representing these groups, you can probably identify at least half the gifts you need to achieve your goals. To reach your financial goal and increase the number of college supporters, you must use new and different approaches to identify potential donors. One tool available to you is an asset screen. This service, provided by many firms throughout the country, consists of submitting a list of potential donors to a computer program that matches names to publicly available data that indicate wealth. Some categories include stock ownership, possession of boats, houses, or airplanes over a certain value, and service on corporate boards. The screen will also utilize records of charitable gifts to other nonprofit organizations.

In choosing the names to screen (often 5,000 to 100,000 names, depending on the size of your district) you should make sure they meet several criteria:

- They have previous contacts with you as full-time, part-time, or not-for-credit students.
- They live in your community within neighborhoods that indicate the capacity to make substantial gifts.
- They have attended your auction, played in your golf tournament, or provided financial support in other ways.
- They are known to support other educational, health and human service, and arts causes in your community.

Clearly, these characteristics frequently overlap, but a skillful asset-screening firm will identify duplicate names and offer you a useful product. They will take your names and return to you a list of people within your universe who have the capacity to make a significant gift.

Some services go further and actually predict what the size of such a gift might be. Usually, the asset-screening process yields a return of at least 5% and as many as 15% of your list of people who have the capacity to make a significant gift. This reflects the concept of the "millionaire next door," the hidden wealth of whom we are unaware but who are surprisingly numerous. *Forbes* magazine estimated that, as of 2007, 9.2 million families in the United States had a net worth of $1 million or more, not counting the value of their houses (Farrell, 2008). Although this number may fluctuate with the economy, it remains surprisingly high, and according to more recent estimates, it is still close to 7 million families (Spectrem Group, 2009).

After the screening, you are likely to have hundreds or thousands of potential donors, more than you can possibly approach during your campaign. How do you go from dealing with too few donors to assessing too many donors? When you receive the results of the asset screen, the first step is for a staff member to vet the list of matches to make certain they refer to the right people. There are many William Woods and Diane Youngs in the world, and you want to make certain that the one identified as having the capacity to make a $50,000 gift is the same one that owns the grocery store or restaurant downtown. If you have 1,000 names that match, it will probably take a month or more for your staff to review them.

What's next? Now it's your turn. It's why you're on the foundation board. You represent the community and have ties to many of your area residents. If your board is properly constituted, you have the ability to reach into every sector of the community and provide connections to the great majority of people with wealth and social position. It is your job to go through the list and indicate the best prospects and then determine whether you are the appropriate person to initiate contact with them.

You may think, "Isn't that the job of the staff? Or the consultant? They're the ones who are paid to raise money." Why is it your responsibility to review these names and identify who should be considered a top prospect? If you have 20 people on your board, and each of you knows 10 different people on the list and can vouch for their ability and possible interest in making a $5,000 gift, you have just helped assemble a potential donor list capable of making a total gift of $1 million. If one fourth of them could make a gift of $25,000, you've created a list that adds up to $2 million in potential giving. If a dozen can make gifts of $100,000 or more, you've compiled a $3 million list. Your fundraising staff might come up with a list a fraction this size without the connections to the prospects that you have. They also would probably not have the detailed knowledge of the prospects' interests and values that you, as peers, have.

Identifying Types of Donors Most Likely to Give

The top criterion is whether supporting the campaign and your college in general will constitute an expression of their most deeply held values. Are they passionate about education and outspoken in their support of increased access for economically disadvantaged and minority students? *The Seven Faces of Philanthropy* (Prince & File, 2001) offers guidance on what motivates different types of donors. Are your prospects people who benefited from community or technical colleges in their own lives (repayers), for example? John A. Hall, president of Rainier Pacific Bank in Tacoma, has frequently stated that without the ability to attend a community college, he would never have received an education. He helped direct a significant gift from his bank's foundation to his college's campaign and was an effective ambassador for the college in the broader community.

Does your prospect own a business that employs students trained at your college? The owner of a restaurant chain (who wished to remain anonymous) made a generous gift to the South Seattle Community College culinary arts campaign because so many of his chefs and line cooks had received their training in the community college's culinary arts program. At Shoreline Community College near Seattle, during a campaign for an automotive service-manager training program and facility, several local car dealerships united to make a lead gift, knowing the benefits that the program would bring to them. Such donors represent investor types, who make gifts that they think will benefit themselves and the broader community. They see their philanthropy as leveraging future development and are willing, at times, to make extraordinary gifts even if they are not the direct beneficiaries of the outcomes, because it is good business to do so.

Most Likely Donors

- College leaders (foundation board, trustees, president)
- Past individual donors
- College administrators, instructors, and staff
- College students and alumni
- Retirees of the college
- College advisory board members
- Local and regional corporations
- Local, state, and federal governments (But see CASE's position on government funds, p. 163.)

Communitarian donors are another variety of donor likely to support your campaign. Is someone on your large list a major booster of your city or municipality? Are they trying to bolster economic growth and make your area a better place to live and work? IKEA, a multinational company with a destination store in a small community, wanted to encourage more arts and culture. It made a $100,000 gift that supported an auditorium at Renton Technical College suitable for lectures and readings. Henry Schatz owns a plastic-extrusion company in Tacoma. After meeting with Bates Technical College president David Borofsky, he gave $500,000 to the college for scholarships in ten specific areas. According to Bates College Foundation executive Kimberly Pleger, Schatz is very committed to the mission of the college and very passionate about the need for a skilled workforce. According to Pleger, "He wants to make sure that there aren't financial barriers that are preventing students from learning the skills necessary to pursue their chosen career" (K. Pleger, personal communication, June, 2009; H. Schatz, personal communication, June, 2009).

Some donors can be classified as altruists. Such people believe that they have the obligation to help others help themselves, and they seek opportunities to do so in an effective way. An anonymous local philanthropist made the decision to support Tacoma Community College's early childhood education center with a $1 million gift because of the college's commitment to helping students who might not be able to obtain an education elsewhere (P. Transue, personal communication, June, 2009).

Knowing a potential donor's values and his or her ability to make a significant gift can guide you in narrowing down your prospect list, but there is one other major criterion to consider. Do you have the means to connect with this person or company? If a business owner lives in a gated community, plays no part in community affairs, and has never supported any local cause, and no one on your board could call her up and expect to receive a return phone call, she's probably not a good prospect. Perhaps you can put her on a second-tier list and work to establish a connection, but you should focus on people who have capacity, motivation, and connection.

Honing the List to Prime Prospects

The initial review process by the foundation board is a holistic process—quickly reviewing a large list and choosing the most likely prospects. You will probably produce a list of 200 to 500 names, depending on the size of your original list, the number of board members, and the degree of connectivity your board possesses. The two next steps will winnow your list down to a manageable size and offer a list of 50 or so top prospects.

The first step is to bring together a more formal donor evaluation task force, as described in the previous chapter. The task force will review your prime prospect list on a name-by-name basis and assign ratings to them. Ratings are based partially on capacity to give, partially on the likelihood of giving (motivation), and partially on the ability of the board to connect with the prospect. Obviously, wealthy people who currently support the college and are close to board members or the president would be the very best prospects. Wealthy people who have not supported the college in any significant way but are connected to its representatives might be the next level of prospect. Those with wealth and only vague connections would be lower; people of lesser wealth but with closer connections would be better prospects.

What Motivates Different Types of Donors?

- **Communitarians**—Are interested in bolstering the economic growth and development of the municipality they live in.
- **The Devout**—Believe that doing good is God's will.
- **Investors**—Make gifts because it's good business.
- **Socialites**—Think giving is fun.
- **Repayers**—Have benefited from the college in the past (e.g., former students and local business people who hire workers trained at the college).
- **Altruists**—Believe that they have the obligation to help others help themselves.
- **Dynasts**—Give as a way of carrying on family traditions.

Source: Prince & File (2001)

As mentioned in chapter 10, the task force must keep this process absolutely confidential but also be candid and free-ranging in its discussions. Comments such as "He won't have much money after his divorce" or "She doesn't want anyone to know, but she's planning to marry her high school sweetheart and move to Guam" must be permitted with the assurance that they will not leave the room. That type of openness permits a CPA to say, "I can't say where the money came from, but if she made a $250,000 gift, it would really help her tax situation."

As your plan indicates, you need to assign each of the prospects to the appropriate committee. Then you rank them by priority, starting with the biggest gifts. If you have several gifts that are the same size, a close friend with a long history of support for the college who can give $100,000 is a better prospect than a person who could give $100,000, but who has never been closely allied with you.

The community will want to see support from those closely allied with your organization. Otherwise, big gifts generally influence small gifts and take priority over them. Big gifts from highly respected community members are the most powerful of all. The important rule is to avoid pursuing a small gift from a rich person to start the campaign. It will set a low and harmful giving level. Never forget that each gift is a campaign in itself and occupies a specific position within the entire campaign.

CHAPTER 12

Recruiting Effective Campaign Leaders

Leadership is the key indicator for success. If your college can attract strong campaign leaders, you can make up for any other deficiencies. If you can't, the campaign will struggle. The first step in establishing leadership is to recruit a powerful, highly committed chair (or co-chairs). When asked what their greatest challenge is, most colleges cite the difficulties in finding good board members and other volunteers for high-level policy and fundraising. This difficulty multiplies exponentially when it comes to recruiting campaign chairs. This may be because of what chairs are expected to do:

- Make a big gift (it doesn't have to be the biggest in the campaign, but it has to be significant for them).
- Attend at least two meetings a month to maintain campaign momentum and unity.
- Help recruit other steering committee members.
- Help with major solicitations.
- Attend a limited number of special events, and provide inspiration to the entire organization.
- Speak at local civic events, be available for newspaper interviews, and generally represent the organization.
- Remind other steering committee members about their responsibilities and assignments.

Recruiting Chairpeople

Characteristics of an Effective Chairperson

If the responsibilities just described sound like those for a CEO of a

The Three Most Common Traits of Effective Campaign Chairs

- passion for the college and its mission
- sufficient time to devote to the cause
- an ability to motivate other people

successful corporation, that's no accident. Your college is raising more money than ever before, and you're involving more people than at any time in your history. The project is probably the most complex activity you've ever undertaken. Someone in the private sector would be paid a lot to run it, while your campaign chairs receive nothing other than personal satisfaction and recognition. So, it's no wonder the person in charge has to be energetic and multitalented, possess excellent interpersonal skills, and have the respect of everyone associated with the organization—and be passionate about your mission. Do such people exist? Every community has people that others respect and admire. They're not always the richest or best known, but they share these characteristics:

- They are seen as leaders.
- They hold the best interest of the community at the center of all they do.
- Others look to them for advice and counsel.
- They are considered wise, honest, and fair-minded.

When considering possible chairs, some questions might help in winnowing the field:

- Who would guarantee that the campaign is a success—people so prestigious that their involvement will convey a sense of inevitability about reaching your goals?
- Who can reach out to all portions of the community and communicate effectively with them?
- Who would be extremely hard to say no to and would get their phone calls returned?

You want those people as your chairs. During your feasibility study, the people you have interviewed will suggest possible chairs. A strong consensus among their recommendations provides an excellent starting point in focusing your efforts. You must take care to ensure that you are following good advice, however.

Chairpeople can be community volunteers, business leaders, or respected professionals from law, medicine, accounting, or other fields. Professional athletes, well-known politicians, television or movie stars, or other celebrities tend to be too busy and have too many other pulls on their time to take on volunteer responsibilities. There are exceptions, but few. Honorary chairs, offering their names but not their hearts, don't provide effective leadership. Effective campaign chairs are passionate about the college and its mission, have sufficient time to devote to the cause, and have the ability to motivate other people. Add to those traits unquestioned integrity and a stellar reputation, and you have a great leader.

Tacoma Community College found a great leader in its chair of its board of trustees. Dave Edwards was a retired CFO for Weyerhaeuser, had long been a committed advocate of the college, chaired its governing board, served as chair of a capital campaign for the local children's museum, and also served on the national board of Catholic Health Initiatives. He had a gregarious and pleasant nature and was respected by other community leaders with whom he had worked in business and on community projects. He was also generous, having made lead gifts both for the children's museum project and to the college's campaign. He led a successful campaign that exceeded its goal by almost 40%, and he was involved in many of the largest requests. He spent hundreds of hours on the campaign and was a reliable and effective partner to the president (P. Transue, personal communication, December, 2007).

Thirty years ago, the local bank president would chair the campaign and call up his friends to collect his outstanding chits. Those days are gone forever. Campaign leadership may not be as high profile as it once was, but it is spread out more evenly among men and women, among the very wealthy and the passionately committed, and among people of different races and backgrounds.

Co-chairs may split the work. One chair may be very good at running meetings (an invaluable skill), while the other is good at public speaking. One chair may be well-connected in the business community, while the others are more involved with the town's social elite. Sometimes one chair is a political office holder or even a judge, who cannot actually raise money. He or she brings prestige and integrity that attracts other volunteers who are willing to raise funds. No one model provides certain success; a variety of structures can work. The key is to ensure that you have the ability to reach sources of large gifts, and that the chair engenders respect that will attach to the project.

Leadership Contracts

Sometimes you know that a potential co-chair or other lead volunteer cannot spend much time on your campaign. That person may be out of town much of the time, have pressing personal issues, or feel so frail that he or she doesn't have the energy to perform many of the normal tasks of a lead volunteer. On the other hand, that person would bring you prestige, connections, and other positive attributes. What do you do?

If you're in this situation, avoid using honorary chairs, which exist primarily as an excuse for volunteers to do nothing. Most potential donors see through this ploy. They know that it's easy to get someone's name without getting their actual participation.

Instead, consider using leadership contracts. In these documents, you list the precise tasks you hope someone will undertake on your behalf. For example, you might wish to involve your former Congresspeople in your campaign, but they might be reluctant to commit to the position, because they are too busy campaigning for elective office and are seldom available. You might respond by suggesting that they could provide invaluable help by serving as campaign co-chairs with the following, finite expectations:

- Attend three major events, and give inspirational speeches.
- Help obtain gifts from two businesses to which they are closely attached.
- Make a limited number of calls to public funding sources asking for support.
- Give the featured speech at the end-of-campaign celebration.

These tasks require a time commitment of perhaps 25 hours over a 2-year period. From their standpoint, the exposure would help political aspirations. Your college, in return, would receive high-profile leadership, and the community would see a well-known person setting a good example.

The Steering Committee

Once the campaign chairs are in place, they will help you choose and recruit members of your campaign leadership, starting with the steering committee. This committee, which may be called a campaign cabinet, campaign executive committee, or other similar name, comprises fierce partisans of your college who also are widely respected within the community on which you're relying to support the campaign. The steering committee plays three vital roles:

1. It oversees development of campaign policies and plans, recommending passage to the foundation board and to the college trustees for approval.
2. It provides a public face to the campaign, with its members serving as the major spokespeople for the fundraising effort.
3. It is usually responsible for both making and acquiring a large portion of the largest gifts to the campaign.

In a campaign, the steering committee maintains momentum by holding regular meetings (usually at least once or twice a month) and ensuring that the fundraising efforts remain concentrated and effective. The committee monitors campaign progress and holds itself and staff responsible for achieving goals and benchmarks on schedule. Although most volunteers claim to dislike frequent meetings, they find that well-run, crisp (1-hour) meetings that are results-oriented are both enjoyable and fruitful. Such meetings develop an invaluable *esprit de corps* among the members and create a sense of engaging in an important and enjoyable endeavor.

During the feasibility study, you will discover a number of people who think of themselves as possible campaign leaders and whom the community perceives as ideal leaders. Generally, the steering committee should include

- Several of your lead donors who set the example for the entire community.
- The college president.
- The CEO of the foundation or the vice president for advancement (often the same person).
- The campaign manager and the director of development (if there is one).
- The foundation board president and several enthusiastic and effective foundation board members.
- Community leaders who have not necessarily been previously involved with fundraising for the college.
- The dean or deans of those portions of the college most closely involved in the campaign.
- The chairs of other campaign committees, if not included in the categories listed.

The steering committee should include 15 or more members to ensure that you can reach into the entire community as fully as possible. A larger committee becomes unwieldy and cannot make decisions quickly. A smaller committee often lacks the ability to take on all the necessary tasks. Overall, without a strong steering committee, your campaign will not succeed. If the people you're counting on for big gifts can't see a group of recognized leaders with credible records of accomplishment, you will probably struggle to gain support.

Focus of Primary Volunteer Committees

- prospect evaluation
- public relations
- gift acceptance and recognition
- public funding
- community outreach

Volunteer Committees

Here are a few guidelines to keep in mind when forming committees of volunteers for your campaign:

- Large campaigns have more committees than small campaigns.
- Each specialized constituency needs committees or subcommittees to work within it.
- Most campaigns need committees that focus on businesses that benefit from the college. Committee members who work for

large companies with training programs associated with the college, local chamber of commerce directors, and respected local business owners all offer useful connections to potential donors.
- At the start of a campaign, you will need a prospect evaluation committee that determines who can give how much to the campaign.
- A public relations committee oversees the campaign's public awareness efforts, including its publications.
- A gift acceptance and recognition committee oversees creation of policies concerning what gifts can be accepted and how they are acknowledged and recognized.
- A committee that focuses on public funding creates strategies and coordinates their implementation, as well as makes contacts with government decision makers.
- Large campaigns need separate committees for various levels of giving—one that focuses on the top 30 to 50 gifts, another that focuses on the middle range of gifts, and a third that focuses on the smallest level of gifts you will be soliciting face to face.
- You may also need committees or subcommittees for more narrow constituencies—for example, a local business committee or a health-care professions subcommittee.
- If you are part of a multicampus system, with each campus seeking separate initiatives, you will require individual committees for each campus.
- If you plan to approach the entire community for support, you will need a committee or subcommittees that focus on special events, house parties, the sale of mementos, and other means of attracting support.

How to Recruit Volunteers

It is one thing to ask people for money. All they have to do is decide yes or no and decide on an amount. It's another thing to ask them to make a commitment to help a campaign reach its goal. You're asking them to spend time and risk their reputation. That's commitment. Just as you wouldn't ask someone for $100,000 over the phone, you're not going to request a commitment from volunteers in a note or e-mail. You're going to prepare to meet with them and have materials that explain what is expected. You have to be totally open and honest about their roles and responsibilities.

For filling important positions early in the campaign, the foundation board chair and the college president or the foundation executive should make the call; once you have a campaign chair(s) in place, they should be involved in recruitment. Ideally, one of the reasons you've recruited the chair is for his or her ability to attract other top leaders. When you visit with potential leadership candidates, you'll need to have the following ready:

- A detailed job description that lays out responsibilities and expectations, including time commitment and financial expectations, and a brief, easy-to-understand project description, so that they know what they're supposed to represent (see Appendix D).
- A list of others involved in the project, including your board and any volunteers you've already recruited.
- A goal and supporting budget for the project(s) at the core of your fundraising campaign.
- For outsiders, your college's annual report.
- Any campaign literature you've already developed.
- A campaign organizational chart, so they can see where they fit in.

Just as in requesting funds, there are no magic words. You have to go into the meeting with optimism and be willing to answer all questions. You have to listen carefully and be prepared to alter your plan. If potential leaders share your enthusiasm for the project and express a willingness to take on the challenge, they will make successful volunteers. If they say yes but only to be good sports, you won't really be able to count on them. It's better to seek out your second choice than to accept a halfhearted commitment. Leadership makes or breaks your campaign. Passion is the secret ingredient. The best volunteer wakes up every morning thinking about what the campaign needs for success.

Responsibilities of the Foundation Board

A surprising number of college foundations believe that their boards are too weak to lead fundraising campaigns effectively. The boards use this as an excuse to cede the leadership role to the steering committee and expect a free pass in relation to the maelstrom swirling around them. Other than making a gift, they avoid the campaign and hope that others will make it work.

This is a recipe for failure. You, as a foundation board member and the steward for donated funds, must also take on a strong supervisory role in a campaign. Along with making all policy decisions relating to the campaign, you must continue to serve as organizational safe keeper. At least eight major responsibilities fall to all board members, whether or not they are members of the steering committee or actively involved in soliciting gifts (see Table 12.1).

Volunteer Subcommittees May Be Subdivided by

- gift levels
- specific constituencies
- individual campuses

Campaign organizational charts should reflect the expected sources of campaign contributions and the specific needs of the campaign.

The structure should also represent reality, showing committees that exist for a purpose, meet regularly, and are held accountable for specific outcomes. In a way, the organizational chart should graphically display your entire campaign strategy, with each committee demonstrating how you are going to reach out to a specific constituency or achieve a specific task such as public relations or gift recognition. As is true of all elements of your campaign plan, it should be reviewed on a regular basis to ensure that it continues to reflect the progress of the campaign. You may find it helpful to eliminate a committee, combine two committees, or add a new committee to the campaign.

Table 12.1: Responsibilities of Foundation Board Members

- Making a personal investment, through a significant gift—ordinarily one of the largest a board members has ever made—as a reflection of passion for the project.
- Managing the campaign process, ensuring that the campaign does not begin until the proper preconditions are in place, including leadership and staffing.
- Being an ethical steward, making certain that the campaign lives up to the college's mission statement and is conducted in an ethical fashion at all times.
- Managing resources, by investing in appropriate and high-quality planning and ensuring that campaign funds are spent wisely.
- Maintaining quality control by ensuring that all campaign materials reflect well on the organization.
- Forging connections to potential donors and leaders; leveraging position and commitment to expand the college's circle of influence.
- Advocating for the project throughout the community.
- Getting involved in any of the various campaign activities.

CHAPTER 13

MANAGING AND RECOGNIZING GIFTS

Keeping track of and recognizing gifts will mostly be the responsibility of your staff members. They will develop policies, acknowledge and track gifts as they come in, and file reports to both the public and the government. As board members of the foundation, you will approve these policies and are responsible, ultimately, for ensuring that they are followed and enforced. You will also have many questions concerning these policies, and so will those people with whom you're discussing potential gifts. You will need to know the ramifications of specific types of gifts (or at least be aware that you have to check with staff members to determine the implications). The specific areas of concern for tracking and recognizing gifts include the following:

- Having policies and procedures governing which gifts to accept, what to do when a gift presents problems, and acceptable ways of recognizing different kinds of gifts.
- Establishing how to count gifts—what counts toward the campaign total and for how much.
- Deciding how to credit your donors, especially for in-kind gifts, for gifts of property, and for facilitating matching gifts.
- Determining the parameters for recording the value of gifts in your financial reports.

Your foundation office and consultant will help you craft policies that keep you out of trouble. A gift acceptance policy will mean that when someone wants to give you a Ferrari Testarossa that isn't street legal, you have a reason to either refuse it or assign it a value that reflects the difficulty you'll have in selling it. It will mean that you can turn down timeshares in Zimbabwe or vacant lots in swamps; you can have rules about accepting polluted properties.

The policies should cover all fundraising, not just raising money for the campaign. They should be appropriate to your organizational culture. They should also give your board some flexibility in special circumstances, because the board can't foresee every eventuality. The main thing is to have your policies in place before you ask anyone for money, which will help you prevent many problems.

Counting Gifts and Assigning Credit

A challenge that every campaign for any purpose faces is how to count gifts and how to provide credit for the gifts. The issues that arise in these regards are varied and complex. Consider the following scenarios:

- A donor gives $5,000 that is matched by her company, for a total gift of $10,000. Who gets credit, and for how much?
- A 55-year-old donor informs you that he has left you $50,000 in his will. In all probability, you will not receive this gift for another 30 years. Do you count it, and for how much?
- A board member gives you a fancy sports car that has been appraised at $75,000. When you sell it, the market has weakened, the auctioneer was expensive, and you clear only $45,000. What is the value of the gift?
- A member of your steering committee gives you a gift from an advised fund at the local community foundation. What goes on the plaque?

Fortunately, CASE (2009) provides simple and logical answers to these and most other questions surrounding counting and recognizing gifts in its *CASE Reporting Standards and Management Guidelines for Educational Fundraising*, 4th edition, which establishes guidelines for annual giving and campaigns for educational fundraising. The CASE approach is straightforward and reflects common sense. The guidelines emphasize one basic precept: that campaign totals from one college should be easily comparable with those from another. Your campaign that raised $475,000 should represent similar results to a campaign for $475,000 completed by a college across the country. Your list of gifts should represent the same standards as those from every other college.

CASE's guidelines apply to all institution types, including community and technical colleges. One obvious difference between campaigns for community colleges and those for 4-year and research institutions is the size and duration of the campaign. Many comprehensive campaigns for universities last for 7 years, with goals of hundreds of millions of dollars or even $1 billion or more (CASE recommends that a comprehensive campaign not exceed 8 years). Community and technical colleges seldom launch campaigns for amounts of more than $10 million, with only a few recorded as raising $20 million or more.

CASE guidelines work for smaller campaigns. They call for counting gifts only to the extent that they actually benefit your campaign: They count in-kind gifts only for the actual benefit you receive and gifts of property only in the amount they contribute to the campaign, regardless of appraised value. They now allow counting conditional pledges and revocable gifts, such as bequests, under certain circumstances; however, for the sake of transparency, these gifts must be reported separately from outright and irrevocable deferred gifts. The guidelines describe in-kind gifts as follows:

> Gifts-in-kind are generally defined as non-cash donations of materials or long-lived assets, other than real and personal property. . . . Gifts of materials or long-lived assets that are directly related to the mission of the institution should be reported at the face (or fair market) value. . . . For all gifts-in-kind, especially items such as equipment and software, report the educational value (if an educational discount is offered)—that is, the value the institution would have paid had it purchased the item outright from the vendor. This point is key. Regardless of what estimated value a vendor may place on a gift-in-kind, the recipient should only count as a gift the amount it would have paid for the item or items were they not donated. (CASE, 2009)

Although you maintain strict guidelines in counting, it is always better to be generous (but consistent) in recognition. You can count a matching gift only once, but you should give recognition (soft credit) both to the donor whose gift triggered the match and to the organization that provided the match. Gifts from advised funds should be counted once but credited both to the community foundation that produced the check and to the individual or family who provided the initial funds. Pledges can generally be counted for a maximum of only 5 years, but they can be credited for the entire amount. A donor will receive credit for the full $100,000 of a 10-year pledge, but you will count it initially only as $50,000, with a new entry during the 6th year. You may choose to not count a bequest in your campaign total, but you will enroll the person who has made the bequest in a legacy club that honors the donor and helps ensure that the bequest remains in the will in the future.

Your college's accounting department (or the foundation's, if it maintains separate books) will be responsible for keeping track of gifts and reporting to the Internal Revenue Service (IRS). You should be aware that there are very specific rules (known as GAAP, Generally Accepted Accounting Procedures) that govern how gifts show up on your financial statements. Multiyear pledges are discounted, provisions are made for nonpayment, and standards are provided for counting various types of deferred gifts. These provisions affect neither recognition nor counting but are important for you to be aware of, because otherwise you will be shocked to see your statements displaying less money raised than what you had thought.

The other important element for you to know about IRS rules is that they preclude nonprofit organizations of any type from offering advice with appraisals or tax deductions. If a donor wants to give you a house and requests that you provide a valuation, you are required to have the donor get his or her own appraisal from a qualified source not attached to the college in any way. Donors who want to establish trusts for the college, to be used for scholarships, might ask you what tax deduction they can take. You must direct them to their own accountant or tax advisor.

Recognizing Gifts: Your Real Work as a Board Member

At the minimum, as soon as a donor signs a pledge form and makes a campaign gift official, the thank-yous should start. Your foundation board chair or campaign chair—if not both of them—should jot a quick thank-you note. The president and the chief development staff person should write a thank-you note. Whoever solicited the donor should send a thank-you note. The fundraising department or campaign office should send a thank-you note, along with the official acknowledgment of the gift's value. Although oral thanks are never out of place, written gratitude is much weightier.

The gift should be entered into your gift processing system. Whether the foundation or the college's accounting office is responsible for gift processing, the basic attributes of the system should be the same. Best practices indicate that different people should receive, enter, and deposit gifts. Detailed records should be kept about any conditions attached to the gift (e.g., anonymity, payment over time, restrictions on how the gift is used). Once gifts are received, they should be acknowledged as quickly as possible, ideally within 48 hours. If the gift was pledged, there should be a tickler system that reminds you when to send notification that the payment is due. This is all pro forma and reflects your foundation's legal responsibilities.

Sometimes, thanking people isn't enough. For many donors, especially board members, this may be the biggest gift they have made and the biggest gift they will ever make. It may represent the equivalent of 3 months' salary, the value of a new car, the cost of a dream vacation, or perhaps the equivalent of a new house. Many people want and deserve special recognition for gifts of such magnitude. They may want to have something to point to when they take their children or grandchildren to your campus. They may want a permanent connection to the building, program, or endowment, so that in 50 years, people receiving the benefits of the structure or the fund will associate their gift with this project. A gift to a major fundraising campaign is one path to immortality (or at least a big chunk of time when your name will be in front of the community). How many people would remember Carnegie without his libraries? Getty or Guggenheim without the museums? Stanford without the university?

Those sorts of recognitions exist at tens of thousands of other sites throughout the United States and the world. If you visit Ephesus in Turkey, part of the ancient Greek empire, you'll find the names of patrons on the temples. If you look at many of the great religious paintings of the 15th century, you'll see small portraits of patrons included in masterworks. Think of your town and the people whose names are on buildings, in art galleries, on walls in your church, or at the entrances to your parks. In all likelihood, you respect them as community leaders and are aware of their contributions to your personal enjoyment. You may think that you'd like to someday have your name on a classroom building, in a room within the building, or at least on a plaque recognizing all donors to your campaign, so that your descendants can look with pride at the contribution their family made to your college and community.

Or, you may have no such desire for recognition, but want to honor a parent or a favorite teacher. Haven't you ever thought how wonderful it would be to dedicate something to someone who helped you reach your current position in life? Not everyone wants or needs recognition, but it is sufficiently universal that it serves as both an impetus and a reward for giving. Donors stretch a bit to reach a level high enough to earn permanent recognition. They see their gift as meaning more if it's attached to naming rights, whether for themselves or others. The community sees the entire project as enriched and enhanced by its association with their leading citizens.

"Campaign managers should take special care to devise appropriate ways of recognizing all contributors during a capital campaign (keeping in mind IRS and CRA regulations on premiums and corporate sponsorship), even those whose gifts technically fall outside what is appropriately counted according to the CASE reporting standards."

—CASE (2009)

Managing Named Gifts

Although many donors don't need additional incentives, some will want to know what type of named giving opportunities are available. Take the time before the campaign begins to establish policies for recognizing named gifts, using the following questions as your guide:

- What are you trying to accomplish through named gifts?
- What's the lowest level for permanent recognition?
- What's the lowest level for any type of public recognition?
- How do you value gifts other than cash or pledges? Are there any rules about planned gifts?
- How will you recognize bequests that may be withdrawn?

So, how do you determine named giving opportunities? Let's assume you are launching a comprehensive campaign for your college. You hope to find $2 million to furnish and equip a new criminal justice building, $1 million to create an endowment for scholarships in your health professions departments, $500,000 to launch an EMT program, and $250,000 to support professional development for faculty and staff. You'll also need $400,000 to support your fundraising efforts. You have, of course, created a gift chart—that tool that helps you estimate how many gifts at what size it will take to complete your campaign (see Appendix B for models). You know that to raise a total of $4,150,000, you'll need at least one gift of $500,000, three gifts of $250,000, five gifts of $100,000, and eight gifts of $50,000. So, that means that you should establish the top named giving opportunity (naming a building or program) at $500,000. Wrong.

If you set up your named giving opportunities that way, it means that no one has the incentive to give more than $500,000. The family that just sold its business for $10 million will not have any reason to provide you with a $1 million gift. Not only that, but for whatever reason, most people are shy about contributing the top level of gift, fearing that they're either being made a dupe, or that they'll appear to be showing off.

The Italian Leather Sofa Theory

Go into a furniture store where most of the sofas cost $2,000, and you'll generally notice that there's a really expensive sofa, sometimes soft Italian leather, very impractical, very beautiful, and on sale for $5,000. You sit in it, luxuriate in the soft and supple leather, and appreciate the lustrous shine. Then you feel good about spending $2,000 on a much more practical, almost as handsome, sofa that fits better with your house and your pocketbook. Although you had wanted to spend no more than $1,500, seeing and rejecting the $5,000 Italian leather sofa makes you feel more secure in getting a good deal.

Named giving works the same way. Maybe no one will ever take the top naming opportunity, which in this case might offer naming the criminal justice building for $1 million. Donors might not jump at the chance to have their name on a building for that amount of money. They might, however, find naming the high-tech forensics laboratory to be a bargain at $500,000. Naming the main lecture hall for $250,000 would be an absolute steal, as generations of future law enforcement professionals would receive their educations in a room carrying their name. On the other hand, a medical supply firm might see the $1 million for a criminal justice building as not making sense for it. But for $500,000, a scholarship fund could be named in honor of the company, tying the name permanently to the professionals who will occupy health-care positions in the community.

The same principles work at lower giving levels for smaller

projects. Enlarging a campus art gallery might cost $1 million. The top gift might be $150,000, with other gifts needed at ranges of $10,000–$100,000. If you set the Italian leather sofa gift at $250,000 for the large reception area, no donors may take it, but they might see naming the largest exhibition space for $150,000 as a wonderful way of commemorating a favorite grandparent.

Encouraging Larger Gifts

Of course, the most common major gifts will not be at the very highest level. If you want to raise $4 million, you'll probably need several dozen gifts at $25,000 and even more at $10,000. You'll want to encourage people who have never given more than $1,000 to step up to a new level. Even if you're raising $500,000 for scholarships, you'll need at least 30 gifts of $5,000 to $10,000 to reach your goal and will require a way to encourage people to increase their previous level of giving.

Establishing naming opportunities or gift categories (e.g., Founders, Builders, and Stalwarts) often provides the necessary encouragement. People who have never given major gifts come to the realization that there's a difference with a bigger gift in terms of how you pay it off and what you receive in return. The naming opportunity is one more way of reminding a donor that this is a different kind of gift—one that involves leaving a legacy.

Many colleges have initiated scholarship funds for first-generation students that recognize in perpetuity individual endowments of a specific amount, ranging from $10,000 to $50,000. Such recognition serves two purposes. Initially, it encourages people to think of giving at a higher level than they might, to ensure that they receive permanent recognition. For others, who cannot initially pledge gifts at the threshold level, it serves as an encouragement for them to add to their funds on an ongoing basis. The following are two examples of how initially lower pledge gifts still provided long-term benefits:

- Primo Grill in Tacoma held a small auction to establish an art scholarship in its name. Although it failed to reach the necessary level for permanent recognition during the initial auction, it continued to hold events each year, building up the fund so that it eventually supported two students annually.
- A retro band from Tacoma (Daryl and the Diptones) held benefits to raise funds for a scholarship fund for first-generation students at both Pierce College and Tacoma Community College. Not only was the band able to eventually endow scholarships at each, but also many fans contributed to the funds, allowing each college to further expand scholarship support.

In similar fashion, establishing a minimum level for a donor's name to be placed on a permanent donor wall may encourage people to give more. It defines what a major gift constitutes in a tangible fashion. Setting the minimum level of permanent recognition at $5,000 allows potential donors to understand the difference between a generous gift and a gift that can transform the college.

Alternate Forms of Recognition

For cultural or religious reasons, some communities disapprove of what they perceive as inappropriate or ostentatious displays of wealth. They may find large plaques, named spaces, or named buildings immodest. For community and technical colleges, with their strong roots in less affluent segments of the community, there also might be resistance to anything that varies from an egalitarian approach. In such cases, attaching the names of individuals and businesses to buildings or portions of buildings, or even to programs, may be problematic. This does not change people's desire for recognition, however. It just suggests that recognition should take different forms.

After a campaign, a college might install an attractive fountain at the campus entrance, enhancing the aesthetics of the entire institution and perhaps creating a gathering place for students. The names of all donors above a certain amount might be inscribed at the base of the fountain, providing a lasting legacy of their generosity. This approach puts all donors into a single category and eliminates the perception of the largest donors showing off their generosity. Such an approach recognizes those who made the project possible without calling attention to the amount donated. Another approach is to allow donors of, say, $5,000 or $10,000 to pick an inspirational saying to be inscribed in a "walk of honor" on campus. This depersonalizes the recognition but allows the donor the satisfaction and honor of sharing a favorite sentiment with future students and community members.

The Pros and Cons of Brick Campaigns

At the start of most campaigns, someone will suggest some form of a brick campaign. "We have 100,000 people in town. I'm sure we can get 5,000 of them to pay $100 for a brick—and that's half our campaign right there," they'll say. Neither the assumption nor the arithmetic works. Without massive publicity, tremendous advertising costs, and personal salesmanship, you can never get 5% or 10% of a town or city to do anything. Campaigns that have succeeded in selling thousands of bricks generally have had media sponsors, coupons running in newspapers for months, and other donated (or paid) publicity. Not very many campaigns merit or can afford such an investment. Equally as important is the cost of the actual bricks and inscriptions, which can approach 50% of the donation, which constitutes a poor use of donated funds.

Certainly, there are valid reasons to use such broad-based forms of recognition:

- Your project truly touches almost everyone. If you are raising money for a performing arts center that will host events to which the entire community is invited, a brick campaign is a way to cement the center's relationship to a broad swath of the community.
- You want to make sure that everyone has the chance to be part of the campaign, especially faculty and staff members who would appreciate permanent recognition of their lengthy service to the college.
- You have a huge alumni base and an excellent database that you can reach easily and repeatedly to offer them the chance to buy a brick.
- You think your community would be supportive if they had the opportunity, and you can obtain sponsorship for a broad-based campaign.

Be aware that such a campaign is not an efficient way to raise money; therefore, your motivation for doing a brick or tile campaign has to involve more than a financial goal. Better ways of attracting large numbers of donors will be addressed in chapter 23.

Part 2:
The Campaign

CHAPTER 14

The Essential First Stage: Securing Gifts From the Board

No matter how talented the college president and fundraising staff are, board members are ultimately responsible for the success of the campaign. Board members can't be spectators. They make basic decisions about the campaign, steward the funds spent and received, follow campaign progress, and demand success. They offer the community unrelenting unity and a positive outlook and advocate for the organization and its plans. Initially, however, their commitment comes with dollar signs.

Board gifts set the tone for the entire campaign. Generous board gifts determine how much other community members give. Board members are the people closest to the project and the ones who best understand its significance to the community. If they hold back support, others in the community will sense that board support for the project is tepid, and their response will be equally tepid. Generous, enthusiastic board support will establish a high benchmark for giving.

College trustees also should be expected to support the campaign financially. Many of them were not elected or selected for reasons of personal wealth, but their support is invaluable for informing the community of the campaign's importance. When college trustees make generous gifts, it serves to inspire the foundation board members.

The board's giving will also set the stage for the campaign in a second way. It is essential that board members give only after careful consideration and after being solicited face to face by their peers on the board. Establishing this method of requesting gifts personally, requesting specific amounts, and following effective fundraising approaches will create the base from which the remainder of the campaign will spring.

How Much Should the Board Give?

Board members should give more than you might think. Many consultants quantify the expected board gift by trying to make fixed rules, such as 10% of the total or a pace-setting amount. Although rules can be helpful, they often bear little relevance to reality. The best answer I've ever found to "How much should the board give?" is "an amount that will impress the community and convince them that the board is 100% behind the project."

Board members have to give an amount that is significant to them, ideally the largest charitable gift they have ever made for any project. This shows commitment. Some board members will make excuses as to why this doesn't apply to them, such as "I'm already giving my time" or "No one really will ever ask what the board has given." Forget it. If you don't give when you are closest to the project and have nurtured it from the time it was only an idea, why should anyone else give? How can board members call on the community for support if they haven't made gifts that community members perceive as generous and even ambitious? How can you look a non–board member in the eye and ask them for an extraordinary gift if you haven't done the same yourself?

The first rule, absolutely inviolable, is that every board member must make a gift. The alternative to not giving is leaving the board. Having a non-giving board member advertises to the community that the organization is not unanimous in its support of the project. Many foundations and corporations will not make a gift unless all board members have given.

The second rule is that the board's aggregate gift must be

Examples of Effective Board Gifts

- The Renton Technical College board thought it might give a total of $50,000. After lengthy discussions and soul-searching, the board gave more than $125,000. This level of giving not only got the $1.25 million campaign off to a great start but made board members realize others could give significant gifts as well. They examined their own process of decision making and understood that being exposed to the college's case, having various giving options explained to them, and having the ability to make their gifts over a multi-year period changed their perception of how much they could give. They believed that others would entertain larger gifts than they had initially formulated if they went through the same process.
- South Seattle Community College launched a $1.5 million campaign. The composition of the board reflected that of the community, consisting of some very wealthy people and many longtime residents who had contributed their enthusiasm from the time the college was founded. All members of the board gave the largest gift they had ever made in the community, resulting in a total gift of almost $300,000. This generosity allowed them to expand the scope of their project and eventually raise more than $2 million.
- Midland College in Texas sought to raise $4.75 million for a new science building. The foundation board contributed $127,000 but also paved the way for several significant six- and seven-figure gifts from family foundations. These commitments led to a $1 million challenge gift and state support. The board's generosity and the fact that board members had made gifts that were significant for them personally made it possible for them to ask others for large gifts.

commensurate with the community's perception of the board's wealth. If you're part of a true grassroots board made up of teachers, social workers, community activists, and blue-collar workers, your board's gift will be smaller than that coming from a board in a large city, populated with business owners, doctors, lawyers, and corporate executives. Each board can have a positive effect on community perceptions by exceeding expectations.

Less-than-generous gifts from the board can lead to serious negative consequences for the entire campaign. For example, one board for a large urban system composed of community, social, and business leaders decided that it did not have to make large gifts. Although all board members gave, the total board gift was less than 2% of the campaign goal, with the largest gift being $50,000. The community sensed the lukewarm enthusiasm level of the board, and the campaign languished.

Setting a Board Gift Goal

I still haven't answered the question of how much your board should give or how much you should give. The answer lies in the process. Start by forming a board gifts committee, charged with evaluating the board's ability to give and assigning an aggregate gift goal. The committee should have about one fourth of the board's membership on it, usually including the board chair and other highly respected board members. This group meets and, in a highly confidential and respectful manner, evaluates the ability of colleagues to give. Members should take into account salary, stock holdings (if known), matches from the company at which they work, family wealth, and any other considerations. Past giving history, both to your organization and to others, is also important.

The gifts for which you ask will be provided in the form of a pledge, payable generally over a 3- to 5-year period. Most people will not give the largest possible gift unless they can spread it out over at least 3 years. Five-year pledges allow board members to give even larger gifts.

Gifts to major campaigns are from assets, not from your checkbook. If you want a rule of thumb, most people can donate 1% of their net worth to charity each year. If you assume they're going to provide a substantial portion of that amount to your campaign, you can feel comfortable in asking people for 1%–3% of their net worth in a pledge to be paid over 5 years. If someone is worth $500,000, that translates into a pledge of at least $5,000 and as much as $15,000. If the person's company matches, that could make it a $30,000 total gift. Things add up quickly if you're imaginative! Similarly, the benchmark for giving is that total philanthropic support should be approximately 5% of annual income (half of a tithe). At least half of that should be directed to the college campaign by members of the foundation board in order to demonstrate the high priority the campaign represents to the individual.

Once all members are evaluated, it's time to add up the total. It will invariably surprise you to see what the potential giving amount reaches through this method. Of course, not everyone is going to give at a maximum level. However, some people will make unexpected gifts. If the campaign lasts 3 years, you'll have turnover on the board, with new board members to add to the total. Make certain that you leave room in your total potential gifts goal to accommodate your largest possible gift (if someone can give a $100,000 gift, you don't want to set a $75,000 goal).

The Hierarchy of Giving

The president and board chair should be the first to make their gifts. Who asks? Sometimes they simply make the gift without solicitation, but sometimes they want some guidance. At times, the consultant participates in the request, or sometimes the campaign chair, if it's someone other than the board chair. Sometimes, it's a highly respected former board member.

The Hierarchy of Giving

- College president/CEO
- Board chair
- Board gifts committee members
- Campaign steering committee (cabinet) members
- Board members
- College trustees

Presidents can make or break a campaign with their gifts. College CEOs earning $200,000 annually (or more) have to give a significant gift, probably the equivalent of at least 3% of their total salary over a 5-year period. Although $10,000 might seem to be a generous amount, if it represents only 1% of the CEO's salary, administrators, faculty, board members, and other executives in the community will not perceive that the person in charge is setting the campaign as a priority. And they will find out how much the president gave!

Once the president and board chair make their gifts, and the members of the board gifts committee make their gifts and receive some fundraising training from the consultant or campaign manager, it's time to arrange meetings with individual board members to ask for their gifts. Asking for gifts during a face-to-face meeting not only ensures that board members have an opportunity to get all their questions answered, but also makes it more likely that board members will give generously. Also, because the campaign will depend on asking for every significant gift during face-to-face meetings, these early meetings will provide board members with a model for making solicitations and ensure that they experience what it feels like to be asked for a gift by a peer.

Who's at the meeting? Ideally, two representatives from the college (two board members or a board member and the president) meet with the board member and possibly his or her spouse or partner. This combination guarantees that all questions can be answered and all decision makers are represented. The meeting should be in a quiet, confidential place. It might be in your fellow board member's house or office, an office at the college, or a quiet corner of a restaurant where the tables aren't too close together. You should be able to talk in a normal, conversational tone, with as few distractions as possible, allowing about 45 minutes for the discussion.

This is the time to discuss all potential issues and make certain that your colleagues can enthusiastically support the project in the community, in addition to making a gift. It's also the time to make certain that they have all the facts and are communicating accurately with others in the community. Once you answer all the questions and run out of nice things to say about the college, it's probably time to ask for a gift. One of the easiest ways to ask is to cite your own example: "Natalie and I thought about it for a long time, but we finally decided we could do $25,000 over the next 4 years. I hope you and Felix would consider doing the same."

Another way to ask for a gift is to mention the total goal and place their gift within that context: "We're hoping the board can come together to make a $250,000 gift. To do that, we figure that four of us are going to have to show leadership with gifts at $25,000 each. Three of us have done that, and we're asking that you consider being the fourth."

Asking fellow board members for a gift is easy, because they're already sold on the project, probably know most of the details, and know that they're going to make a gift. You should feel confident that your meetings with other board members will be successful and productive. You will find more information about how to solicit gifts in chapter 15.

Ideally, you should be able to wrap up the board campaign within 6 weeks from when you start. Whatever goal you've reached, you should celebrate and thank everyone. If you've not made your goal, still celebrate, and start making plans as to how you're going to eventually reach it. Think about including former or future board members. Start thinking quietly about whether any board members might have slight misgivings that will disappear as the campaign moves forward, possibly resulting in a second gift. Think about whether any of them might have a windfall coming in over the coming months or years. Is Mr. Y part of an initial public offering? Is Ms. X in the middle of the sale of a house? Don't lower the goal yet. That's a last resort. Instead, be proud of what you have. In all probability, it's the most the board has ever given and will provide the base for moving forward.

The All-Important Internal Campaign

The internal campaign is conducted among three major constituency groups:

- College trustees and foundation directors
- Staff and faculty
- Students and alumni

According to Robin Johnston (2008), "these groups need to give early in the campaign so that you can show internal support when you take the campaign out into the broader community."

What if the Board Campaign Fails?

If you get pledges for less than 50% of the goal you've set for the board campaign, something is wrong. Your board lacks belief in the project or has severe remorse about embarking on the campaign. Now is the time to address these issues. It's one thing to set a board goal of $250,000 and get only $200,000 in pledges. That's a good amount to raise and says that the board cares. As the campaign moves forward, new board members join, and current board members become more invested, you'll probably reach and surpass your board goal.

But if the board members have pledged only $50,000 against the $250,000 goal, you're in trouble. It's almost inconceivable that you were off that much in your evaluation. It shouldn't matter how skilled you were in your requests. Your board members are simply not sold on the project. Their gift doesn't match up with how you (and the outside community) see their capacity. They will be unable to look the collective community in the eye and ask for large gifts. The community will be too likely to ask, "If you don't care, why should we?"

If you reach this point, you should seriously consider putting the campaign on hold, despite the embarrassment (and money) this will cost. You need to delve into why the board campaign failed, perhaps using an outside facilitator (not the consultant). A failed board campaign almost certainly guarantees a failed campaign, so you would be foolhardy to proceed without repairing whatever is wrong. Fortunately, most board campaigns succeed beyond expectations and get the campaign off to a great start. That's when the real fun starts, because you can go out to the community and begin seeing how highly esteemed the college is—and how effectively you can leverage the board's generosity.

CHAPTER 15

Preparing for the Ask

Your mental image of asking for money might entail sitting down with your good friend Martha and, after a glass of wine or two, asking her for $10,000 toward an athletic scholarship fund. You feel nervous tingles in your stomach, you start worrying about what Martha is going to ask *you* for (she's on the board of your church), and you wonder whether you'll ever be as good friends again if she makes the gift. Worse yet, will you remain friends if she turns you down?

The truth is, if you do your job correctly, you'll never have to worry about any of these things, and you'll probably never actually make the request the way you imagine. You simply have to redefine your job. Your job is not to ask for money. It's to deepen the relationship between people you know and the project to which you have committed yourself. You are a matchmaker, a conduit for support to a great project.

As has been mentioned, the majority of Americans regard themselves as charitable, making an effort to support those less fortunate at some time of the year. They give to things they believe in and make large gifts to things that touch them deeply. The main challenge they have is distinguishing among all the competing charitable organizations. They get dozens or even hundreds of appeals annually. How can they tell which organizations are truly worthy of their support?

The answer is, by hearing from people they trust—and that's where you come in. You are involved in your project because you believe in it. You've shown that belief in at least three ways:

- You are serving as a volunteer and providing your time.
- You have made one of the largest financial gifts of your life.
- You're willing to involve other people by asking them to serve and give.

Most importantly, you are approaching them as a peer and a friend, saying that in your best judgment this is a project they might care about. You have nothing personal to gain from their gift, as your only interest is to strengthen your college in a way that will benefit the entire community.

But why won't you actually have to ask for a gift if you do things correctly? Because your goal is to connect people to the cause, not to ask them for money per se. Their gift will follow naturally from that relationship, rather than from your request. If you follow the procedures suggested here, you'll get to the point where your friend will say, "I want to help. What can I do?" At that point, they're prepared to give and simply need guidance. As a trusted friend, you can suggest what would be an appropriate level of support they might consider.

They will agree or suggest another figure. They will establish the payment period and method of payment for their gift. They will be doing it because it makes them feel good and because they have sufficient information to know what their gift will accomplish. Making the gift will help them achieve their most deeply held values. If your project does not correspond to their beliefs and values, you'll never get to the point of talking about a gift. At some point they will have said, "This isn't the project for me. I'm glad you gave me the chance to learn about it, but I have other priorities." You will know that they respect and like you, perhaps even more than before. They will make their decision based on their needs and desires, not yours. This is why basing all fundraising on the donor's needs is so central—it places the focus on them, not you.

Cultivating Meaningful Relationships

Cultivation works on gardens. You plant seeds, carefully keep the soil watered, clear weeds, and stake the plants if necessary. Your care and labor are rewarded by healthy plants and eventually by fruit or flowers. If you just toss the seeds in the ground and return after months of neglect, you're more likely to find a weed-filled, scraggly spot with neither fruit nor flowers.

Dating is another analogy. You usually don't propose on a first date, no matter how wonderful it is. You have to spend time learning about the other person; recognize their interests, strengths, and frailties; permit them to learn about you; and then, after months or years, pop the question. By then, you're assured of agreement.

That's closer to how cultivation works. You introduce people to the project (or perhaps to the entire college). Over time, you provide them with the opportunity to learn about what you're trying to accomplish. You learn about them at the same time—their values, concerns, and hopes. As their relationship to the college and its vision deepens, it becomes obvious that it's time to ask for a significant commitment.

When you have identified people as potential donors, your temptation is always to pour as much information into them as possible.

You love what the college is doing to lead local efforts to improve workforce training and want to inform the world. However, you have to make certain that you always focus on your donors and why they should care about your accomplishments. Always remember that you have to convey the WIIFM for your donor—"What's in it for me?" People want to know what the benefit of your project will be to them. Will it increase their business? Will it attract more workers to the region? Will it help to reduce local unemployment or address the crises in health and human services?

Ways of cultivating relationships are limited only by your imagination. Some, like those listed in Table 15.1, require major

Table 15.1: Opportunities for Cultivating Relationships With Potential Donors

- **Special events.** If people come to your auction, play in your golf tournament, or attend a special concert or lecture, they will see who else supports you. They'll get some information about your mission and programs. It's easy to follow up after the event simply by calling them and inviting them for a tour of the college.
- **College tours.** Tours offer a perfect opportunity to acquaint someone with your mission and vision. Meeting instructors and students, seeing learning in action, hearing testimonials of adults who have returned to school, and other direct contact with your college are perhaps the most effective ways to bring potential donors face to face with what you are doing and what you hope to do.
- **Private meetings.** Meetings, especially those conducted over food, that are set up to introduce prospects to or deepen their knowledge of the college and your project provide excellent cultivation opportunities. Most people are honored to sit down for private time with the president or with the dean of the area they care most about. Such meetings can provide potential donors with an opportunity to get targeted information and answers to questions.
- **Invitations to participate.** Program participation lets people see exactly what you do. Many business programs at community colleges invite local executives to give guest lectures. The executives see the passion and intelligence of the students and grasp the contribution that these students can make to their businesses and the communities in the future. Inviting prospects to serve on a task force, whether it's to help plan your marketing efforts or to get advice on a new program, provides a cultivation opportunity and provides the college with useful expertise.
- **Regular correspondence.** Sending people targeted information after they know a little about you often deepens their interest and answers their questions. An e-mail from the president talking about a major success, a large federal grant, or an award received by a student allows potential donors to feel that they're part of an inner circle.

planning and time. But there are also many simple gestures you can make to remind your donors and prospects that you regard them as individuals and not simply as numbers who write checks. Some are examples are

- Send birthday or anniversary cards.
- Forward interesting news stories about your college and its accomplishments.
- Send a college newsletter that highlights college news for insiders.
- Send a copy of a publication such as a student poetry review or article by a faculty member.
- Send complimentary tickets to student concerts, plays, and other performances.

Forming a Cultivation Team

Remember that you're involved in the campaign because of your community connections, so you are the most effective partner for most potential donors. You need help, however, in talking about the college and its plans. It's always useful to involve the college president, because his or her presence adds weight to any meeting with a prospective donor. The president also demonstrates that the project is in good hands; in addition, the president is generally the primary keeper of the vision for the college and can speak effectively about the project.

The foundation director or vice president for institutional advancement can often be a valuable member of the cultivation team. The person holding this position can provide technical advice about how to give, discuss the details of the campaign, and offer the big-picture view of fundraising. Additionally, the campaign chair or board chair make ideal members of the cultivation team, because their presence carries weight and shows the college's respect for the donor.

Other major donors or high-profile professionals can also be useful additions to a cultivation team. Some people will be impressed by the presence of business or community leaders. Including the mayor, your state representative, or even a local celebrity can make the prospect feel important and lend credibility to the project. Recruiting someone to assist you with cultivation is also a good way to cultivate a relationship with that person.

It is often extremely effective to include a business owner who has hired your students, a student, a grateful alumnus, or another beneficiary of your organization in a meeting with prospective donors. Their testimony on behalf of the organization is powerful because it emanates from direct experience. The men and women who work directly with your students are often the ideal partners for the top volunteer and your college president. A professor, staff member, athletic coach, or other frontline employee can establish a strong link to a donor and ensure that the discussion focuses on the organizational mission.

Consultants can seldom be members of cultivation teams, because they are being paid for campaign services and have a vested interest in the project's success. Consultants will not be working exclusively for your organization. Although they should be involved in creating strategies for each prospect, consultants are seldom the right people to lead cultivation efforts. The only exception may be with institutional donors who wish to know about broader campaign strategy issues and who understand the role of consultants.

Preparing for the Initial Call

There is only one key action needed to move things forward with potential donors: the first phone call. It ensures that everything follows easily and naturally. The call results in an initial meeting that generates follow-up, additional meetings, more follow-up, and eventually a solicitation and a decision. The distance from the first phone call to the gift can be weeks or years, but there's only one initial phone call.

Before you make the phone call, you have to prepare. Why are you calling this person? What major objections might he or she raise? How will you respond to any initial objections?

First, give yourself a pep talk: "This is a terrific project. I've made my gift, so I'm not asking for anything I haven't done myself. We've planned the project to death and there's nothing that ____ can ask that we can't answer. I'm part of a great team."

Although you are part of a fundraising effort, this first meeting is not a request for money. So your next step should be to remind yourself why you're calling:

Table 15.2: Sample Responses to Donors

Donor: "I'm very busy."
Response: "Yes, I know you're busy. When would be a good time for us to get together?"

Donor: "I've given a fortune to the Boy Scouts and don't have money for another gift."
Response: "I'm glad you're supporting the Scouts—it's a great organization. This conversation isn't to ask you for a gift—although you might decide you want to make one once your pledge to the Scouts is paid off."

Donor: "Just send me the info."
Response: "I'll give you the brochure when we meet, but I'd much rather tell you in person why I'm excited about this."

Donor: "You don't need to waste your time. I'll just send you $50."
Response: "I hate to turn down a gift, but it's important that you understand the impact this project is going to have on the whole community."

Donor: "I've heard that the college is in real trouble. How will you possibly raise money for a sinking ship?"
Response: "You're not the first person who's said that. I'd love to have the chance to tell you why that's no longer the case."

- To invite your friend (or acquaintance or business colleague) to meet.

- To share your excitement about, and interest or involvement in, a great college and an important project.
- Because you think this person will be interested in the college, want to hear about it, and have valuable input.

Anticipate what your friend might say and how you might reply. The important thing is to avoid hearing no when your friend is not saying no (see Table 15.2 for some examples).

Then, remind yourself that your goal in this phone call is not to convince, not to correct misconceptions, not to get a gift, and not to get permission to mail a flyer. It's to set up a meeting at which you will talk with the prospect about the project. Your answers will reflect this desire. You're not going to debate, argue, or deny. You'll just focus on the desire to get together and share your excitement for no more than an hour. Possible places to meet include the college, a private club, a conference room at the prospect's place of business, the prospect's home, a golf course, or baseball stadium. Before you call, have your spouse or someone from the fundraising committee listen to what you're planning to say—at least for the first few calls. Make sure your consultant provides some authentic, interactive preparation that includes role-playing.

Assume that your prospect will accept the meeting. An overwhelming percentage of people will agree to meet with you. Why? Because

- They respect you and believe you when you say they'd be interested in something.
- Believe it or not, not very many people are so passionate about a cause that they want to meet in person to tell a friend about it—your friend will be impressed by your enthusiasm.
- They're flattered and honored that you and the president or another luminary would take the time to meet with them in person.
- Most people are charitable and are interested in the best places to put their charitable contributions.

Don't try to hide why you're meeting. Don't say you want to get together to share pictures of your grandkids. If you're proud of what you're doing for the project, the prospect will be happy to meet with you.

Decide beforehand whether you want to meet alone or with the prospect's spouse, business partner, or other joint decision maker as well. It's important that the entire decision-making unit is included in the process, because the chances of getting a large gift are compromised if you've ignored one of the principals. If the meeting is more than a few days away, let the prospect know that you'll e-mail or call with a reminder. In other words, treat this the same way as you would an important business meeting. Your prospect will appreciate the respect.

Preparing for the Actual Meeting

Preparation for making calls is often generic, since you're interested primarily in obtaining a meeting and want to avoid getting into a lengthy conversation about the project. Getting ready for the meeting is another matter. The preparation should be thorough but focused:

- If another person from your team will be present at the meeting, define the role each of you will play. If one of you is closer to the prospect, that person should lead the discussion.
- Determine the minimum and maximum acceptable outcomes for the meeting. The minimum might be for the prospect to agree to take a tour or meet with one of your faculty members. The maximum outcome might be that the prospect expresses enthusiasm and asks for more information about a specific aspect of your campaign.
- Define the three most important ideas you want to convey during the meeting. If, for example, your campaign focuses on expanding your cosmetology program, you should itemize the benefits this will bring: (1) double the number of cosmetology graduates, (2) cut county unemployment costs by $100,000 annually, and (3) ensure that the big salon chain will feel comfortable taking a space at the regional mall because it is certain to have a steady supply of well-trained staff members.
- Prepare yourself to answer prospects' most likely questions. What are their concerns? Do they think you will provide unfair competition with a nearby proprietary college? Are they concerned whether you'll be able to find competent instructors?
- Decide what written materials you want to take. The first meeting is too early to take a proposal, but you might want to take your major gifts brochure as a convenient way to discuss the project. Some prospects might respond to a presentation on a laptop, or they may prefer a formal flip-chart presentation. Do what will be effective for them.
- Spend some time considering what question you most hope they will ask and what question you hope they won't ask. Prepare responses to each.
- Don't prepare a script! Be spontaneous and natural.

No matter how much you tell yourself that it's just a friendly meeting, there's no getting around the fact that a cultivation meeting is somewhat artificial. You and the prospect know why you're there and where this is leading. Small talk seems strained. There's a desire just to get through with the process and get to the point. Resist that urge. People take time to make decisions; they need more information than one meeting can provide, and they don't like to feel pressured.

Start by thanking the prospect for meeting you. Then, talk a little about family, the local baseball or football team, or other common interests. Let your voice relax, and remember that at the base of it all, you're friends or business acquaintances. When you've exhausted small talk, make a definite switch to the subject at hand. Acknowledge why you wanted to meet. You might say something like "I know how important education is to you. We're doing some exciting things at the community college, and I'm glad to have the chance to bring you up to date." Or, "Your daughter got her AA degree at the college 10 years ago, and I know she's gone on to do some great things. We're trying to make sure others have the same opportunity she had, and I'd like to talk about our plans to make that possible."

Ask prospects what they know about the college and whether they have heard about the campaign. Find out their initial reaction. If they give a global response such as "I know the college does a terrific job," then ask what appeals to them most about its programs. If they say, "It's the school of last resort for kids who can't go anywhere else," ask why they think that. This is a good time to talk about the excellence of community college education and the success that its graduates have at 4-year institutions. It's also the time to discuss the additional programs at your college, especially in retraining adults and preparing disadvantaged populations to enter the work force.

These meetings are opportunities for beginning to educate people. And when people criticize the college, your task is to address their concerns, not to make them feel stupid. The following examples illustrate how important these meetings are for providing and clarifying information.

- When Renton Technical College was raising more than $1 million to furnish and equip a technology resource center, a potential donor asked why the college needed 150 workstations in the new building in an age when personal computers are so abundant. The campaign chair was able to explain that more than 50% of the students lacked resources to purchase their own computers and that, currently, there were lines to use the 40 existing terminals. Later, she introduced the prospect to a recent Cambodian refugee who explained that she couldn't get a job without computer skills and that equipment at the college was her lifeline to a new career. The prospect eventually made a $10,000 gift that helped create four stations—his first gift to the college.
- A wealthy developer who was a major supporter of the Washington State's 4-year institutions derided community colleges, saying that they were places where people learn what they avoided in their high school classes. The college president asked him to spend a morning on campus meeting the students and visiting classes. The developer left that visit with his basic assumptions

shaken after seeing students in state-of-the-art facilities learning technical subjects from highly qualified professors. He agreed to consider a $15,000 gift to a scholarship fund.

You must assume that if donors know everything about your project, they'll agree that it deserves support. Your project has to be an open book to your donors. Since you're asking them to give one of the largest gifts of their lives, it's imperative that they have the information they need to make a well-founded decision that makes them feel comfortable.

Your discussion should give you an idea as to the strongest interests of the donor: If your community college is raising money for a performing arts center, you might find a prospective donor whose son had been "a disaster" until he had gotten a job constructing sets at a local theatre company. If the new center supports courses in set design and other theater-related skills, the donor might make a generous gift specifically to support that program.

Frequently, despite your best preparations, a prospect will ask a question you can't answer. It may be a reasonable question, a maddening question, or an off-the-wall question. Your job is to respect the motives of the donor rather than assume that the question either is stupid or denies the project's merits. Never be defensive or imply that the question doesn't deserve an answer. The only proper response is "You know, no one has asked that before. I'm as interested to find out the answer as you are, and I'll get in touch with you as soon as I get the answer." Be grateful when a question leads you to the perfect next step in your cultivation.

Don't leave a meeting without some form of closure. Before the meeting, you'll have established minimum and maximum expectations; now's the time to determine where you are. If there is more than one person making the call, know whose job it is to set the next step into motion. That person must decide whether you're ready to pursue your minimum or maximum expectation, or something in between:

- "Now that you've heard about the changes we're planning to make in our international business program, I'd love to have you meet with one of our instructors who can provide more specifics."
- "It seems as if you'd like some more information on the success of our health information management program graduates. Can we send you some material addressing your concerns and then call you to set up another meeting?"
- "I'm delighted that you've expressed such strong interest in supporting our scholarship program. Why don't we plan to meet again in 2 weeks or so, after you've had the chance to talk to your husband about your level of support?"

When and How to Ask

How do you know when it's time to ask a prospect for a donation to your campaign? It might be after you've answered all the questions. It might be after the prospect attended your annual wine event, had a college tour, studied your materials, and met with your admissions director to determine the need for scholarships. It might be after you've played six or eight different rounds of golf, during which the prospect has moved from skepticism to excitement. It might be when he or she has discussed the project with a financial advisor.

When they are ready to make a decision, most people will neither volunteer a gift nor suggest a number. It's your job to make a formal request. It's time to ask for a gift from prospects when

- You feel that you know their motivation for giving.
- They have indicated enthusiastic support for the project and an interest in being part of it.
- You have provided all the information they need to make an informed decision.
- The conversation has shifted to a discussion of your college's mission and vision rather than focusing on the physical project itself. Prospects may switch from using "you" to talking about "we" or "us." Sometimes, they will simply come out and say, "I know we're here to talk about my gift. What would you ask me to do?"

Important Props to Bring to the Ask

- written proposal
- named gift list
- gift chart
- honor roll
- pledge card

You've reached the moment when it's time to ask, or at least to discuss the gift. Perhaps your heart is beating a bit more quickly than normal. Your throat may be a little dry. But you're prepared. You and your fellow team member (if you have one) have decided who's going to ask—and if it's you, you've stood in front of a mirror and practiced the words. You know three things: the amount you're going to request, whether you will use any props in making the request (the named gift chart or a gift chart), and how you will phrase the request.

How Much to Ask For

Let's start with the first element—that you're going to ask for a specific amount. Before you even met with the prospect, you received an evaluation of what the college hoped he or she would give. As your conversations with the prospect had progressed, you were able to gauge whether that initial target amount was the right level, too high, or too low. The prospect has provided hints, and your staff and consultants have done research to justify the amount for which you're asking.

It may seem awkward or presumptuous to ask for a specific amount. You might think it's easier to either let donors make up their own minds or to negotiate an amount. In fact, more than 100 years of experience in U.S. fundraising (and several thousand before that) show that donors prefer guidance as to what the right size gift might be. People don't want to make too large or too small a gift. They want to know how their gift fits into the entire campaign. Once they have an idea of what is expected, they can decide how much they will give, but the initial guidance is helpful.

Experience has also shown that few people are insulted or put off by a request for more than they feel they can give, as long as the request is made respectfully and after careful preparation. They do not always meet your request amount, but most are secretly flattered that you considered them for such a high level of philanthropy. You should never, however, make a request with the expectation that donors will give one half or one third of what you request. Your request should reflect what you think prospects could give assuming they are as excited and enthusiastic about the project as you think they are. By having a specific amount suggested, donors are actually more comfortable because they are clear about the magnitude of gift you are requesting.

Using Props

All that said, it's sometimes difficult to get the words out when you're asking for a $100,000 gift (or a $10,000 gift) for the first time. There are a number of ways to make it easier. The first is to make certain that you have brought a written, formal proposal to your meeting. Your staff or your consultant should have worked with you to tailor every major proposal. The person with whom you're meeting should feel that he or she is the only person who could possibly receive this specific proposal. Of course, the proposal will include an amount, which obligates you to cite the same figure.

A second prop is the list of potential naming opportunities, whether it's for rooms in a building or designated scholarship funds. If you're asking for $100,000 to establish a named endowment to support accountant education, pointing to that item on a printed form will let donors see where their gift fits in, and they'll see the relative value the gift will have. You don't have to actually say the number if it makes you too uncomfortable—as long as your finger isn't shaking too much when you point.

A third prop is a gift chart illustrating the number of gifts at various sizes needed for you to complete the campaign. It's easy to show prospects that you have 6 gifts at $25,000 already, and that their gift would make 7, against a goal of 10 gifts at that level. Again, with this prop, you can avoid saying the number and let the donor see that others have made gifts at this level already.

A fourth prop can be your honor roll of gifts, on which all donors are listed by name. You can indicate that their friends X, Y, and

Z have each already given at the $10,000 level, and that you're hoping they will give at that same level. If your name is among those who have given at that level or higher, it makes such a request even stronger.

Phrasing the Request

When you finally phrase your request, you should avoid conveying any sense of entitlement ("We know you can do a $100,000 gift, and we're looking forward to listing it on the honor roll"). You should also avoid questions that can be answered yes or no ("You'll make a $10,000 gift, won't you?"). Find a phrase that reflects your relationship with the prospect and shows that you're leaving the decision up to him or her.

Here are two examples:

> "My $50,000 gift to this campaign is the largest I've ever made. I truly hope you'll consider a gift at that same level."

> "You've been a valued supporter of the college for years, and you've often said how grateful you are to have such a fine college in the community. Your gift of $50,000 would help ensure that we can renovate our classrooms so that our students have a better environment in which to learn."

Relating the gift to a specific outcome is also effective, if you know that the prospect has a specific interest:

> "Your past support of the First-Generation Scholarship Fund has allowed many deserving students to attend our college. An endowment gift of $120,000 would fund two full scholarships every year in perpetuity."

You can also use the most simple and straightforward request imaginable:

> "We would be most honored if you and your husband would consider a gift of $35,000 for our campaign."

The response is often some form of hesitation. But, if the prospect says, "Absolutely, I'd love to do that," you know that you've done everything right, and that you've asked for an amount the prospect expected. You can then thank the person effusively and hand over the pledge form. Most of the time, the prospect will say something like, "My God, that's a lot of money!"

Knowing When to Remain Silent

You've just asked for a whole bunch of money, certainly more than the average person earns in a month. Often, it's more than most people earn in a year. Occasionally the gifts are as much or more than many people make in a lifetime.

You made the request in good faith. The prospect has made gifts of this size before. He or she has the assets available to make a gift at this amount, over a 3- to 5-year period. The prospect is excited and interested in your project and believes in your mission.

The prospect has heard the amount. It takes time to absorb a request for a large amount of money. Few people make a habit of giving five-, six-, or seven-figure gifts. The last thing they want is to have someone interrupting their thoughts with a bunch of apologies or fallback positions. Your job is to keep silent unless the prospect says something that requires your response.

Let's say you've requested a $50,000 gift. After an initial gulp, the prospect says, "I just made a big pledge to the library campaign. I can't do this now." At that point you can say, "We're not asking for a gift right now, just a pledge. As long as you can start your payments within the next 3 years, a pledge is just as good as a gift." Or perhaps the prospect will say, "I can't write a check for that much money." Your answer is very simple: "We're not asking that you write a check. Our pledge period goes up to 4 years, so it would only be $12,500 each year, and you can pay against it on a monthly or quarterly basis."

The common thread in these statements and responses is that the

Tips on Making Calls to Prospective Donors

- Focus on the mission—not yourself, not the money, not the capital or endowment projects.
- By far the best way to raise money is to ask for it in a face-to-face situation. The purpose of the call is to get a meeting.
- Don't hear "no" unless they say "no." Almost everyone will offer some resistance.
- You don't have to know everything to talk to people. You can get back to them later with answers.
- There are no magic words. Your commitment and your passion for the project are the most convincing aspects of the solicitation.
- Prepare the two or three major points you want to convey to the prospect.
- Prepare responses to prospects' most likely questions, questions you hope they ask, and questions you most dread.
- Be prepared to listen. People will usually tell you what they want to be asked for.
- If pairing with another volunteer, decide who is going to actually make the request and for how much. Be familiar with all the recognition opportunities including named gifts.
- Be aware of ways to make people's giving easier (e.g., 3-year pledges, appreciated assets, real estate, planned gifts, etc.).
- Don't make people's decisions for them. Let them decide how much they want to give.
- Never contradict or argue. You are building a relationship, not selling a product.
- If people are not ready to make a commitment, treat the call as the first step toward a successful solicitation.
- Never forget that every gift is a good gift.

prospects are not saying no. They are just making a statement that you are duty-bound to agree with. Your task is to reframe the impediment. The worst thing you can do is immediately jump in to say, "Well, it is a lot of money. Do you think you can do $10,000?" The prospect hasn't said no or said the gift is too much. You have to respond to the prospect's concerns rather than assume a refusal when none is intended.

Sometimes people want to give less than what you've requested. You are asking people to consider a gift at a specific amount. Sometimes, for whatever reason, that amount is more than the donor wishes to give. They will usually be clear about this: "I'm sorry, but that's more than I'm prepared to give at this time," or "I wish I could do that, but it's not in the cards." Your response to this should be to leave the decision up to donors. Don't suggest a number, because you're not a mind reader. Instead, ask what amount they would like to donate: "I'm glad you're willing to consider a gift. What level would you be able to make, given a 3-year pledge period?"

And sometimes (although it's very rare when you've been talking with someone for many months and at several meetings), prospects will decline to make any gift: "We've been thinking about it for the past several months, but we just can't make a gift." Your response to a flat refusal must be gracious and immediate: "Thank you so much for allowing me to tell you about the college and our plans. I've enjoyed our conversations and I hope you'll allow us to keep you informed about the progress the project makes. You're an important part of our success."

Never take a refusal personally. Accept it at face value. The prospect has thought hard and can't make a gift or doesn't wish to make one; it's not a personal rejection. Don't guess at motives or question why prospects continued to discuss the project if they weren't going to make a gift. You never know what will make people change their minds in the future: In a non-college example, Claris Poppert, the co-chair for a large campaign at the Oregon Museum of Science and Industry, played golf every week with a wealthy friend, frequently talking about the museum and eventually asking for a gift during one of their rounds. The friend refused the request, but they continued to play

Tony Zeiss's Practical Tips for Fundraising

- See fundraising as training.
- Understand the difference between selling and providing meaningful opportunities.
- Develop and maintain a positive organizational image.
- Trustees, presidents, chancellors, and development officers must collaborate.
- Building and maintaining positive relationships with prospects is essential.
- Profile prospects.
- Make proposal requests for specific purposes.
- Offer opportunities for significant partnerships.
- Partner with businesses and other major community organizations.
- Recognize donors often and loudly, internally and externally.
- Be a donor yourself.
- Be a good steward.

Source: Zeiss (2008)

golf. The co-chair kept up his enthusiastic chatter as the campaign reached 50% of the goal, 70%, and finally 90%. Every few months, he'd repeat his request for a $1 million gift. Finally, the friend agreed, revealing that he had once given a gift to a project that never got built and wanted to be sure this one would really get done.

Sometimes prospects can't give an answer right away. It takes most people time to make a decision about such a large gift. They might have to ask a spouse or partner or discuss the gift with a business partner. Perhaps they need to talk to a financial advisor. Your response to their desire to put off a decision should be matter-of-fact and straightforward, but truthful. Here are some sample responses.

- "We're trying to qualify for a challenge grant, and they're making a decision in 3 weeks. Do you think you might have a decision by then?"
- "Can I provide you with any more information to help you make the decision—are there any unanswered questions?"
- "Do you think 2 weeks from now would be a good time to get back to you?"

Make sure you get a decision date that they agree to, and make clear that it will be your responsibility to call them. If possible, schedule another appointment, whether by phone or in person. You should make sure, however, that you aren't pushing them to make a gift before they're ready. They should make a gift on their schedule, not yours. Although you can mention an upcoming benchmark or challenge that's time-sensitive, that is really your concern, not a motivation for them to rush their decision.

Securing the Gift With a Pledge Form

Pledge forms are required to formally record the amount of the gift and the terms of the gift (restrictions, payment schedule). They may also specify donors' recognition expectations, including a desire to remain anonymous. Pledge forms are considered legally binding and are accepted by banks as evidence of intent to give. Lending institutions require that pledge forms be signed before they will make loans against a fixed percentage of total pledges (often 70%). Donors must sign a pledge form even if they are handing you a check for the full amount on the day they decide their gift. An example of a pledge form is included in Appendix E, but you should design your own and have it reviewed by an attorney.

A donor has not made a pledge until the blanks are filled in and the form is signed. As a cynic once said, "An oral pledge isn't worth the paper it's written on." Have donors fill out and sign the form or fill it out per their instructions, and then give it to them to sign. If they are not ready to make a pledge or gift, do not leave the pledge form with them, because one of three things will happen as a result: (1) They will lose the form, (2) they will fill it out for a much lower amount than you have requested, or (3) they will agree to a gift, sign the form, and mail it back to you.

As former Ohio State University football coach Woody Hayes was reputed to have said about the forward pass, "It can lead to three things, two of which are bad." The third outcome of leaving a pledge form with a donor is by far the rarest. It's easy to say, "I don't want you to worry about the form until we meet again. I'll bring it after you've decided on your gift." It's also respectful, because you're expressing a willingness to make a special trip to meet with the donor again.

Acknowledging Pledges

Every gift is a good gift. Respond with joy to every gift, no matter what size. Never forget that, for donors, this is the largest gift they want to give at this time for this project. Never imply in any way that the gift is too small or give any indication that you're disappointed. Remember that fundraising is about the donor's needs and wants, not yours. If making this gift now makes them happy and provides a sense of satisfaction, avoid anything that interferes with this feeling. Remember that this gift is the start of a deeper, stronger relationship. A small gift now may turn into a huge gift down the line if you meet the donor's expectations. And, as stated previously, no matter how many times you thank a donor, it's not too many.

In addition to formal notes sent by those involved in a solicitation, board members should be informed about any extraordinary gifts, so that they can thank the donor by e-mail, a handwritten note, or in person. Bill Gates, Sr., of the Bill and Melinda Gates Foundation, one of the nation's largest foundations, once remarked to me, "I am so touched when board members take the time to thank me for a gift. You'd be surprised how often we never hear anything except a form letter, even for a million-dollar gift" (personal communication, May, 2001).

The process described here works because you are matching your cause to your friends' values. You are not forcing them to give or manipulating them. You're telling them about a project you support and offering them the opportunity to find the same happiness and satisfaction you have. Although giving is exquisitely personal, it results from following the processes outlined here. You will succeed if you engage in a disciplined and supportive set of activities. If you try to ask for a gift without cultivating prospects, try to rush prospects into making a gift before they have been fully informed, or otherwise ignore the advice contained in this chapter, your results will both disappoint you and deprive your friends of a joyful opportunity.

CHAPTER 16

The College Family Campaign

A recurring theme in this book is that the more fervent the support from the insiders at your college, the better chance you have to attract enthusiastic support from the outside. Because of this, it's important that your college undertakes a campaign to request gifts from its administration, faculty, staff, and retirees early in the process, either simultaneously with the board campaign or shortly after that effort is complete. For the most part, this portion of the campaign will focus on participation rather than total dollars raised. Since the fundraising staff, not you, will coordinate the campaign, you might ask why you have to be concerned. There are four reasons:

- Staff and faculty giving and board and administration giving are synergistic; often the board will see a high response as a challenge and raise its own giving in response. If board members see halfhearted support, they will question why they should be expected to make significant gifts. Board gifts, on the other hand, help validate faculty and staff support.
- For some of these gifts, especially retirees, board members' participation in discussions may be helpful.
- Your staff will spend a great deal of time completing this portion of the fundraising campaign. It is important that you understand its importance to your overall effort and that you avoid unrealistic expectations that may lead to disappointment.
- The retirees' campaign will introduce the element of planned gifts into the campaign. Planned gifts will possibly play a role in future portions of the campaign and are discussed in more detail later in this chapter; this is a chance to familiarize you with how they work.

As was discussed earlier, faculty and staff members frequently feel ambivalent toward fundraising in general. They often fail to see the WIIFMs—what's in it for me?—associated with contributing to the institution where they work. Often, they already are asked to give to various combined campaigns, whether through state combined funds or United Way. Some colleges also have an annual campaign aimed at staff members, with funds going for either special aid funds or professional development. To add a campaign request to these efforts may appear burdensome and meet resistance. This is why the recommended approach to faculty and staff campaigns should follow certain rules:

- There should never be any hint of coercion concerning giving. There should never be a fiat passed on from your president that the staff should step up. Supervisors should not request gifts from employees who report directly to them.
- Giving should be self-directed. The campaign should be organized by department or division. Leadership should come from non-fundraising staff.
- The emphasis should be on participation, with any thermometer displaying the percentage of staff members who have given, rather than the amount raised, unless faculty and staff leaders have set their own specific dollar goal to achieve a definite outcome (e.g., raising $50,000 for a professional development fund).
- When a total or participation percentage is reached, it should be publicized and applauded, whatever it is. The plaudits should be enthusiastic and sincere and never suggest that the campaign was not a success.
- Campus publications should cover the campaign and give public thanks to its leaders.

Faculty and Staff

Before starting the faculty and staff campaign, information about the proposed campaign and its outcomes should be widely and openly discussed with all members of the college community. If you have involved them in your strategic planning, feasibility study, and reconciliation process, you will have an excellent basis for involving them in the campaign. They will understand what you're raising money for and why and be more inclined to be supportive.

Each division and department should receive a briefing on the overall campaign before

> Hudson Valley Community College averaged faculty giving less than 6% until it launched its first capital campaign. Within the first 5 months of the campaign, more than 55% of faculty and staff had participated, generating campuswide excitement. The participation rate continued to climb as the campaign progressed.
>
> *Source: Drew Matonak, president, Hudson Valley Community College*

its members are asked to participate. They should receive materials that explain both the goals of the campaign and your strategies for achieving them. They should understand how the campaign would benefit them even if the funds will not go directly toward their programs.

Your fundraising staff should identify potential staff and faculty leaders to administer the campaign. Although fundraising staff will do all the organization work and prepare all needed materials, it is essential that requests for participation come from peers, not administrators or professional fundraisers. If you're raising money for a new program, it makes sense for faculty and staff for that program to be among the leaders of the faculty and staff campaign. They can speak most passionately about the need for raising money and the benefits that will accrue from a successful campaign.

The first donors, of course, are the key administrative staff. They are the most highly compensated employees and the pacesetters for the college. The president makes the first gift, then the head of the foundation, followed by vice presidents and deans. Solicitations of these gifts should be made by peers, not by board members or the president. Again, it is essential to avoid any hint of coercion.

For active instructors and staff, the most effective campaign is accompanied by a campuswide publicity effort. You might also have a campaign-related reception or picnic to kick off the effort. There should be visible recognition for all those who participate—a pin or ribbon. The campaign should be time-limited, usually a month or so. When it's over, it's over, always treated as a success, always carrying great gratitude to those who gave, and no recrimination toward those who didn't.

If the faculty and staff campaign has been a failure, with only a handful of participants and almost no money raised, you will have learned that the campus has not been adequately engaged in the efforts to that point. They may also be disaffected with the administration or with the direction they perceive the institution to be taking. If the faculty and staff campaign fails, the campaign cabinet, your consultant, and your family campaign leaders need to have a frank discussion to determine whether remedial actions must be taken before proceeding. As was mentioned earlier, support for fundraising must pervade your entire campus if you are to succeed in raising large amounts of money. A successful faculty and staff campaign provides an excellent start to your efforts.

"One of the biggest challenges of moving to an entrepreneurial culture is to get faculty and staff to embrace change, according to Zeiss. "A lot of academics say, 'Well, I'm not an entrepreneur,'" he says. "Yes, you are. Any time you've taught, you're a bit of an entrepreneur because you're selling your ideas or you're selling your concepts or you're selling whatever it is that you're teaching. We just have to learn to take the next step and learn how to better sell our colleges and its needs, so that people and organizations will help us.""

—Bart (2009)

Retirees and Planned Giving

Most community and technical colleges have existed long enough to create a substantial number of retirees, members of the college family who served you for decades before leaving to spend their time on personal projects, travel, or other pursuits. Many of them retain close ties to the college, regarding it as a second family, where they combined friendship, workplace satisfaction, and a reliable livelihood. Depending on where your college is located and the nature of faculty and staff contracts, your retirees have one or two accounts from a variety of pensions. Some belong to TIAA-CREF, the largest private pension fund for educators. Others have state pensions. Some may have also established separate retirement funds.

> Texas's Midland College campaign (the college's third) reached an 82% participation rate for its faculty and staff, reflecting gratitude for previous successful campaigns that helped reshape the campus and provided widespread benefits.
>
> *Source: Eileen Piwetz, executive director of the college foundation*

Most of your retirees own their own homes outright, having been settled in your community for long periods of time. Some have purchased second homes, property in rural areas for recreation, and recreational toys such as RVs and boats. On the other hand, few of them have substantial incomes, because most of them are living off a combination of savings and pension funds. They lack the resources to make large outright gifts.

Help them look to the future. Most of them are at the age when people tend to think about their legacy. They have worked for you for 40 years or more. They have participated in your successes and helped you grow from a single building with a few hundred students to a community resource employing hundreds of people and educating tens of thousands of students annually. Their psyches are closely intertwined with your progress.

This may be where you, as a foundation board member, could participate if you know a specific retiree. As a friend and someone who has already donated to the campaign, you may be able to raise the retiree's sights and provide unexpected ways in which he or she could give something back to the college. This retiree represents a class of repayer donors who may not be able to make outright cash gifts now, but who may nevertheless contribute significantly.

Bequests

There are many types of planned gifts, which is the term applied to gifts that are deferred and often involve assets other than ready cash. Each is important and can help you reach your goals for the campaign. The most common type is a bequest, which is the simple act of naming the college as a beneficiary of a portion of the donor's estate. Donors can leave you the entire estate, a specific amount, or a named percentage of the estate. They can leave you a remainder of their estate after other obligations and promises are kept, or they can arrange for you to receive the bequest after death or after their own and their spouse's death. They can leave you property, a house, a boat, all or part of a pension fund, or virtually anything with readily obtainable cash value.

A bequest cannot be counted in your campaign, according to CASE guidelines, unless it is realized during the time the campaign is ongoing. In addition, there is no tax advantage to donors during their lifetimes. The reason for both of these caveats is that a bequest neither involves a transfer of assets during the donor's lifetime nor guarantees that you will ever receive anything. Donors can change their wills at any time; financial changes can shrink their assets.

Over time, however, bequests will add money to the foundation's assets. If donors inform you that they are making a bequest, you should recognize their intent, thank them, and treat them as if they had made a cash gift. If you don't already have one, you should organize some form of recognition society specifically for those who have left you bequests. The more you publicly recognize the intent to leave a bequest, the greater the likelihood that you will receive bequests in the future.

Gifts of Property

Sometimes retirees have accumulated valuable property, whether in the form of vacation homes, an elegant RV or mobile home, a boat, or other asset. They find that they no longer use it, their children have no interest in it, and they are paying taxes or license fees in return for no benefit to themselves. If you know retirees in

> "Plans to develop a planned giving program need to reflect the setting in which they are to function. There is no boilerplate plan of steps and timeframes that can be adopted. However, following is a checklist of activities and elements that should be included in the plan:
>
> - Policies and procedures that reflect the laws of your state and the organizational structure of your college and foundation;
> - Education of the trustees and the foundation board about the various planned gift opportunities and the responsibility inherent with providing such a program;
> - Workshops for targeted potential donors on various planned giving topics;
> - Continuing education opportunities on charitable estate planning for local allied professionals that provide continuing education credits through their professional organizations;
> - Excellent general college marketing pieces to help make the case, and specific planned giving publications for donor cultivation;
> - Timelines and measurable objectives by which progress can be evaluated. These objectives should be framed in terms of activities to be carried out and gifts closed. The bottom line should be evaluated over time, but there is no way that an organization can predict the mortality of its planned gift donors and a hard dollar goal targeted."
>
> —*Edwards & Hawn (2003)*

this position, you can suggest that they consider giving the asset to the college to use toward the campaign. Such a gift provides them with an immediate tax deduction and gives the college money it can use. While you cannot give them specific tax advice, you can suggest that they meet with an accountant or other advisor unaffiliated with the college.

Trusts

In some cases, retirees are interested in obtaining an immediate tax break as well as guaranteeing ongoing income. They can achieve these ends by setting up one of several types of trusts. The major element of a trust is that the underlying assets are transferred from the donor to your college in an irrevocable manner. This allows the donor to take an immediate tax deduction (and in some cases to receive ongoing tax benefits), as well as allowing the college, as the recipient, to count a portion of the gift as part of your campaign. Many trusts provide that the donor and an heir receive income from the trust until their deaths, often at a guaranteed level better than that of most fixed-income investments. Because there are so many types of trusts, and the rules governing them are so complex, your best advice if retirees (or other potential donors) express interest in this type of gift is to refer them to a specialist in trusts. This can be a specialized consultant, a trust attorney, or an accountant. The college can count the trust in the campaign as prescribed by actuarial expectancies accepted by the IRS. An example would be that a $100,000 trust given by a 92-year-old man is valued at a higher amount than a $100,000 trust donated by a 60-year-old woman.

Charitable Lead Trusts

One type of trust that may be particularly attractive to a retiree with grandchildren is a charitable lead trust. It also has specific positive value for the college. In such a trust, the donor puts money into trust. For a period (usually 10 to 15 years), a percentage (often 6%) of the trust is given to the college for its use. At the end of the trust period, the remaining funds are given to a named beneficiary, such as a grandchild ready to go to college or get married, or to another family member.

The advantage of this arrangement is obvious. The college can count all trust income that is received within its pledge period as gifts to the campaign. It can then count the income received after the campaign has ended as an ongoing donation and use the funds for the desired purposes. The donor gets immediate tax benefits.

Charitable Gift Annuities

For older donors, charitable gift annuities can offer a wonderful solution to their desire to maximize their current income while also providing support for the college. Their purchase of such an annuity guarantees them a fixed rate of return for life, depending on their age at the time of making the gift. Often, this rate is significantly higher than money market or bond rates, especially if the donor is older than 75. In addition, the donor gets an immediate tax deduction, and a portion of the income received is tax-exempt (it is considered recovery of principal). At the donor's death, what money is left in the annuity goes to the college.

Student Support

Most community and technical colleges have student associations that concern themselves both with aspects of student life and with the general excellence of the college. They have particular interests in projects that affect them directly, such as student centers, recreational facilities, and day-care centers. Often they are willing to tax themselves to support these projects; occasionally, they will also be willing to contribute to scholarship funds, new programs they deem important, or even new classroom facilities or campus amenities.

If the student association contributes to the campaign at its onset, they are setting a tone that will carry through the entire campaign. Students, above all other constituents, are strict and influential judges of what is important to the college. They also are often the least affluent constituents. When they choose to support the campaign, it puts a floor under the giving of other groups such as the faculty and staff, while exerting leverage on volunteers and the community.

Part of establishing a solid foundation for your campaign is gaining the support of those closest to you. The faculty and staff campaign (especially if there is also student support for the campaign) helps accomplish this goal. Under ideal circumstances, internal support swells the number of donors, communicates to the community the importance of the campaign, and occasionally unearths unexpectedly large gifts from retirees. Well-run and successful staff and faculty campaigns help establish a climate of success and make all future work easier and more enjoyable.

CHAPTER 17

The Importance of Lead Gifts

Let's go back to the feasibility study, assuming you did one. It indicated that there were several people who would be willing to consider making top gifts to your campaign. For a $10 million campaign, that might mean gifts of $1 million to $1.5 million. For a $5 million campaign, it would suggest a gift of $500,000 to $750,000.

The study indicated that, ideally, there was a person or two willing to consider a gift at the top of your gift chart—that $1.5 million gift for the $10 million campaign, or the $500,000 gift for a $5 million campaign, or the $150,000 gift for a $1 million campaign. Once you've decided to move forward with the campaign, it's time to get serious about making that potential big gift a reality.

In all likelihood, however big your campaign is, it's the largest fundraising effort your organization has ever attempted. You're nervous about reaching your goal, despite the feasibility study and a resolution of support. People in your community are wondering as well. Can you achieve that audacious goal you've set? It's one of the most ambitious projects in the history of your town, or one of the biggest education projects, or the biggest scholarship campaign. There are always skeptics, ready to spread uncertainty and pessimism.

People take your optimism with a grain of salt. They've seen other projects fail. "I'll believe it when I see it," is their attitude toward your goal, whether they say those words or not. No matter what the size of your campaign, it's a steep mountain looming before you and involves hard work, good fortune, and other intangibles if you are to succeed. There's only one thing that will still the chatter and convince everyone that you can climb the mountain and reach your goal: a lead gift, or two or three. Ideally, such gifts come in at the very start of the campaign, offered by those closest to your college. Sometimes, it takes many months to obtain all of your lead gifts, and a very large gift might arrive when you're halfway through the campaign.

The Rule of 12

By now you've noticed that this book isn't much on rules or certainties. I haven't told you that the foundation can only raise three times its annual budget during a campaign or that you need to identify four prospects for every gift you hope to get. I haven't mentioned any of the other ratios that are accepted wisdom in the field. Why? Because rules are often wrong. Many first-time campaigns raise 20 times more than the foundation has ever raised before. One of the distinguishing marks of community and technical college campaigns is that they often represent the first major fundraising efforts by the foundation. At Ivy Tech Community College in Indiana, for example, 66% of all capital campaign gifts had been from first-time donors, a ratio unknown in most other nonprofit sectors (P. Hammond, personal communication, February 3, 2009). In terms of the ratio of prospects to gifts, in smaller communities, where everyone knows everyone else, colleges sometimes reach their goals getting gifts from 85% of their prospects.

But one rule is borne out by experience. Your top 12 gifts will make up more than 50% of your goal. If you're raising $1 million or $50 million, at the end you'll find that a dozen gifts make up at least half of the campaign. In the more than 170 campaigns (for all types of organizations) that I have been part of, the rule has almost never been broken, except when it took fewer than 12 gifts to make up half the campaign. A $180 million campaign had a $35 million gift, another at $15 million, and eight more between $5 million and $15 million, totaling more than $90 million. A $1.2 million campaign had a $250,000 gift, and another 11 gifts between $50,000 and $150,000, totaling $750,000. If you can't get those top 12 gifts, the campaign is in mortal jeopardy.

The Powerful Effect of Lead Gifts

Within your 12 top gifts, there's usually one that calms everyone down and lets them know the project is going to work. Here are two examples.

- Renton Technical College in Washington received a $250,000 gift for a $1.2 million campaign after struggling for months to get fundraising under way. The lead gift inspired volunteers, gave the community confidence in the project, and unleashed several other gifts of $50,000 to $125,000.
- The Seattle Community College system launched a $25 million campaign in difficult economic times after struggling to complete a similar-sized campaign several years before. The community

expressed doubts in its ability to support such a goal—until the Bill and Melinda Gates Foundation made a $5 million challenge grant. That show of confidence demonstrated to the entire community the merits of the college and the campaign.

Sometimes a lead gift comes from a board member, where it has an even greater effect on the campaign. It tells the community how important the campaign is to the board, while also establishing a target for other major donors to aim at. Sometimes it comes from a local foundation or corporation, demonstrating the campaign's importance to the broader community. Occasionally it will be a gift from the public sector that offers a challenge to private donors. Whatever the source, the lead (or pace-setting) gift establishes the validity of the goal and the potential for success.

What does the need for a lead gift do to campaign strategy? Let's assume that you are raising $5 million in a comprehensive campaign. You think that there are five prospects for gifts of $250,000 or more, but only one potential $1 million gift. The potential $1 million donor, the largest corporation in the region, was identified by the community as having the responsibility to step up for the campaign, especially because your college provides it with many workers and also runs training programs for it on an ongoing basis.

The CEO of the corporation has mentioned to a number of people on your steering committee, "We know everyone's looking at us." The range indicated during the feasibility study was the big block on the gift chart that contained possible gifts at $250,000, $500,000, and $1 million. The CEO declined to be more specific, saying, "Our gift will depend on a lot of factors."

This gift and the other four could make up 40% of the campaign, making adherence to the rule of 12 a strong possibility. How do you maximize the amount each donor gives, and make each feel good about his or her gift? Who goes first?

The answer is that you talk to your lead donor first. The corporation will set the level for everyone else. If it gives $250,000, other corporations and foundations, as well as individuals, will give less, because they will feel that since they have less capacity and less to gain from the campaign (their WIIFMs are smaller), they shouldn't be expected to give as much. If the corporation gives $500,000, some of the others will perhaps give half that, others less.

Let's turn it around for a moment and imagine going to one of the $250,000 potential donors first. Imagine how the conversation in the offices of the First Local Bank will go:

Bank president: "Well, our biggest local company hasn't made a gift at all yet and without them in the game, we'll never get to $5 million."
Bank vice president: "Yes, and no one would ever complain if we

made a $50,000 gift. It's still a lot of money."
President: "But we'll never get the campaign done if we don't give more than that."
Vice president: "If they haven't given, why should we?"
President: "I guess you're right. But we can do $100,000, and that'll look better."
Vice president: "If you say so, sir, but I think we could get away with $75,000."

Without the guidance of a lead gift, the bank will probably give a smaller gift and find no joy in giving. It will struggle to do the right thing but will have no real target for its giving. The bank is focusing on the money and not the mission.

Imagine, on the other hand, that you go to the largest company first and suggest that it makes a $500,000 gift, but if other local companies give a total of $1 million, the challenge is widely announced in the community, included in all proposals, and announced at the local Rotary. Now imagine the conversation that the bank's president might have with the bank's vice president:

President: "Can you believe what they're doing? They must really believe in the project. Half a million is a big gift, but $1 million—no one in town has ever heard of a gift that big."
Vice president: "The company's CEO said at Rotary that the gift reflects his belief that our town is ready to grow, and we can't do it without a stronger community college. He really believes in what they're doing out there."
President: "And I also heard that the $5 million goal is really the minimum that's needed. If they could raise more, every penny will be plowed back into more scholarships and new programs."
Vice president: "You know, I was originally thinking about $100,000, but they asked us for $250,000. If we pay it over 5 years, we can do it, and by the time we're done, we'll have a couple of classes of business and finance majors who'll be ready to work for us."

The lead gift has opened up new possibilities for everyone and made it easier for others to make their gifts. Once the $250,000 gifts are made, it becomes easier to go to other prospects. They will also have a reason to consider a larger gift than they might have otherwise.

As shown in the previous example, lead gifts can serve as challenges. They show that the campaign can and will succeed. If a lead gift comes from an unexpected source, it can also very quickly make the campaign seem broader. If a major supporter of a local private college makes a lead gift to a community college, it demonstrates that there's a need for all types of higher education and makes it easier for other donors to join in.

Influencing Prospective Lead Gift Donors

Sometimes prospective lead donors don't make decisions on your schedule. They aren't as close to the organization as you thought or are going through difficult personal times and don't want to think about your project. Perhaps they have taken on responsibilities concerning another campaign. Whatever the reason, there you are with a campaign and no place to go. You can stop the campaign until a prospect is ready, but that kills your momentum and wastes money. There's also no motivation for prospects to make the largest gifts they can.

You can also begin putting together other pieces necessary to influence prospective lead donors:

- Complete the board campaign at an unexpectedly high level.
- Get the editorial endorsement of your local newspaper—making sure the paper is only announcing the campaign, not asking people to give.
- Recruit an all-star chair and steering committee.
- Put together attractive and exciting named giving opportunities.
- Obtain several generous and impressive gifts, probably from foundations or corporations.
- Schedule a series of meetings to ensure that you can be in front of the donor as much as possible.

When the time comes to ask for the lead gift, you'll be prepared. You'll have the right strategy, a completely formed project team, and everything you need to encourage the prospect to make the gift of a lifetime.

Publicizing Lead Gifts

If you've been reading carefully, you've noticed that a lead gift doesn't do much good unless other people know about it. Later on in this book, I'll talk about the issue of publicizing campaigns in general and why the so-called quiet phase of the campaign should actually be pretty noisy. But for lead gifts, there are myriad reasons to spread the word. Most donors give to help the project in any way they can. They're happy to have their gift used in the most productive manner possible.

Determine who has to know about the gift and why. Figure out how to tell them. A campaign insiders' newsletter might tell the few people who really need to know. The regional business journal might be the proper venue for announcing a corporate gift. A special event might be the right place to publicize a special gift. Alternately, an e-mail to the board and steering committee might be the best route to go. Finally, in some cases, the trappings of a major press conference might be the proper response.

Occasionally, lead donors will request anonymity or be reluctant to be featured in any college publicity. There might be other ways to ensure that their gifts are known to those who need to know, as the following example illustrates:

> At Tacoma Community College, an elderly woman preferred not to have her name publicized in connection with the lead gift for an early childhood learning center. However, she later agreed to speak at the groundbreaking for the center, when a hundred close friends of the college, including some prospective donors, were gathered. She talked about her belief in the project and her hope that others would join her in supporting it. Although she never mentioned the size of her gift, those at the event understood that she was there because of her generosity. The fact that the building was named the Annette Weyerhaeuser Early Learning Center allowed attendees to acknowledge her previously anonymous gift.

What if There Is No Lead Gift?

Let's suppose you've started the campaign with the assumption that the board would give $1 million out of a $10 million campaign. You have successfully completed the board campaign, reaching $1.1 million. You go to your first potential lead donor and ask for $1.5 million. She tells you that after careful consideration, she can give you $250,000. You go to your second potential lead donor, a corporation that was evaluated at $1 million, and request a gift at that level. "I'm sorry, but business is terrible. I've thought about it and would be happy to give $150,000," the CEO responds. You go to your third and final lead gift prospect, a prospect who was not quite as close to the project but was perceived as having the ability to make a $1 million gift. He indicates that he'd need some time to consider the amount of his gift, but it would be no more than $250,000.

So there you are with three wonderful, generous gifts that represent a total of $650,000 from three prospects rated at $2.5 million. And no lead gift. What next? Remember the rule of 12. Assuming that your largest board gift was $500,000, with another at $250,000, and four more at $100,000, you now have nine gifts totaling $1,800,000. Three more gifts of $250,000 would still put you at only $2,550,000. This projects to a total campaign amount of about $5 million—half of your goal. Your choices are clear:

- Analyze whether there are any prospects for gifts, either from those who have already given or those on whom you have yet to call, which would allow your top 12 to increase, thereby increasing your potential giving total. Remember that lead gifts still have the same effect even if they arrive later in the campaign.

- Redo your project plan (after consulting your donors) to fit the new, revised campaign goal.
- Consider whether any of your current donors might increase their gifts if certain considerations were met.

If none of these choices works, you really have only a single choice—take a break in the campaign, determine why your feasibility study missed the mark so badly, and decide whether the campaign can be salvaged. It may be time to change consultants, volunteer leadership, or both. Clearly, whatever was in place has not done the job. In general, it appears that campaigns fail less than 10% of the time. Whether as cause or symptom, failure to meet the rule of 12 provides the telltale sign that failure is imminent.

CHAPTER 18

Pursuing Institutional Gifts

As a board member or college president, it's tempting to look to your staff to bring in money through writing grants without your involvement. After all, there are all these institutional donors (corporations and foundations) out there just waiting for your application to come in. They have procedures. You submit grant applications. They review them. If your grant writers know what they're doing, your grant will be funded most of the time. You won't have to worry about talking to anyone or cultivating a stranger. All you need is the application form and a computer.

This all sounds great in theory, but it's based on faulty assumptions. The truth is, the best grant writing in the world won't succeed if you don't do your job as a board member, campaign volunteer, or president! The first thing you have to remember is that you shouldn't necessarily expect grants to yield the majority of your campaign total. When you assemble your campaign plan (as covered in chapter 8), corporate and foundation gifts shouldn't be the largest segments on the gift chart, unless your feasibility study has indicated a likelihood of gaining the majority of your gifts from such sources.

Corporations and foundations often provide considerably less than half of your campaign total. This is still a much higher percentage than what other nonprofits receive from institutional donors. Of all the money given away in the United States, only about 5.1% comes from corporations and 12.6% from foundations (Hrywna, 2008). For major campaigns, the figures are higher (since church-related giving, almost all by individuals, skews the numbers sharply), but still account for less than half of all funds.

The Status of Corporate and Foundation Giving

Corporate giving in the United States has been on a downward slide for decades, with small undulations. There are several major reasons for this.

- For most publicly held companies, stockholders do not value charitable giving, because it is not perceived as increasing profitability.
- Most corporations have gravitated toward funding programs and projects from which they will derive the maximum publicity and goodwill and often spend as much money publicizing the gift as they do on the gift itself.
- Over the past 5 years, corporate profits have been relatively low for the most part, discouraging large gifts. In the economic climate that has developed since 2007, this has become even more pronounced. Some of the largest corporate donors in the United States have simply disappeared (e.g., Washington Mutual and Shearson Lehman Brothers).
- More and more previously local companies have merged and acquired themselves out of local markets, so they don't feel tied to major projects in specific communities.
- Many new economy technology corporations allow their giving to be employee-directed. They match employee gifts (usually on a one-to-one basis), which results in generous total giving, but limits the potential for targeted, large-campaign gifts.

Foundation giving has grown over the past decades, with the arrival of thousands of family foundations resulting from the new wealth of software, Internet, and other industries. Starting with the Packard Foundation and continuing with the Bill and Melinda Gates Foundation, pioneers in technology have placed their wealth into charitable foundations and trusts. In addition, many local and national foundations support community colleges. The Kresge Foundation, one of the nation's most prestigious and largest funders of capital campaigns, recently made community colleges eligible for their challenge grants.

Which Foundations Give the Most?

The Bill & Melinda Gates Foundation is currently ranked #1, giving more than $2 billion. Which community foundations give the most? Silicon Valley Community Foundation is the largest in terms of total community foundation giving. See a list of top funders in both categories on the Foundation Center Web site: www.foundationcenter.org.

Well-managed foundations rode the stock market boom of the 1990s to huge gains, which many of them consolidated before the crash of 2000–2001. All of these elements have helped push up the total amount of foundation giving, but it's still only slightly more than 12% of all funds provided to charities in the United States (Hrywna, 2008). The stock market implosion of 2008 reduced the endowments of most foundations, but the long-term effects of this shrinkage of assets are not yet apparent.

Approaching Corporations and Foundations

Once you accept the fact that you may not be able to base your campaign solely, or even primarily, on corporate and foundation gifts, there's an even bigger change in attitude required. Writing grant proposals is not, in itself, the way to get gifts from corporations and foundations. There's a magic ingredient that separates successful applications from rejected ones—you. Sure, your grant writer has to fill out the application. It has to be well-written, with excellent grammar and correct punctuation and spelling. Neatness counts. You have to put forward the project in the most positive way possible and demonstrate that your goals meet the guidelines of the organization. Recognition may be important.

At the same time, you should remember that institutional donors aren't faceless. Human beings are reading your grant applications. They have likes and dislikes. They're subject to the same emotions as everyone else. They help people they care about and reject those with whom they have no connection. This translates into the same basic lesson that lies at the base of all successful fundraising: People give to people and projects they know and respect. They respond to those applicants who take the time to establish relationships with them and who succeed in putting a real face on an otherwise anonymous grant application.

Table 18.1: Guidelines for Approaching Potential Funders

- If there is a sufficient number of institutional donors to warrant a separate committee, establish one to undertake the majority of tasks outlined in this chapter. If you have a smaller number of prospects, assign them to members of the steering committee or the major gifts committee.
- Determine who the decision maker is.
- Determine the best way to influence a positive decision. In a corporation, if there is a director of corporate giving, you should never go over that person's head unless you have talked to him or her first. Make the corporate giving officer your ally in approaching the CEO—don't act as if the officer is only a gatekeeper.
- Share the list of decision makers with your fellow board members and volunteers, and see who has connections. Don't forget, many foundations only require one board member to support a project to make sure it is considered.
- Make certain your college fits the organization's guidelines, even if it takes a bit of explaining or special pleading.
- Arrange a meeting with the decision maker, ideally bringing along a college volunteer (trustee or foundation board member) who knows him or her, along with your college's president.
- Decide on your positioning and create talking points (see chapter 15).
- Follow up all meetings with a phone call. After thanking the person who met with you, the best question to ask is always "What did you think?"
- Have your grant writer prepare the application, making certain that it is tailored to the funding source and reflects your conversation with the decision makers.
- Before the application is submitted, contact your connection (e-mail or a phone message is fine) to say that you incorporated his or her ideas into the application and that it should arrive soon.

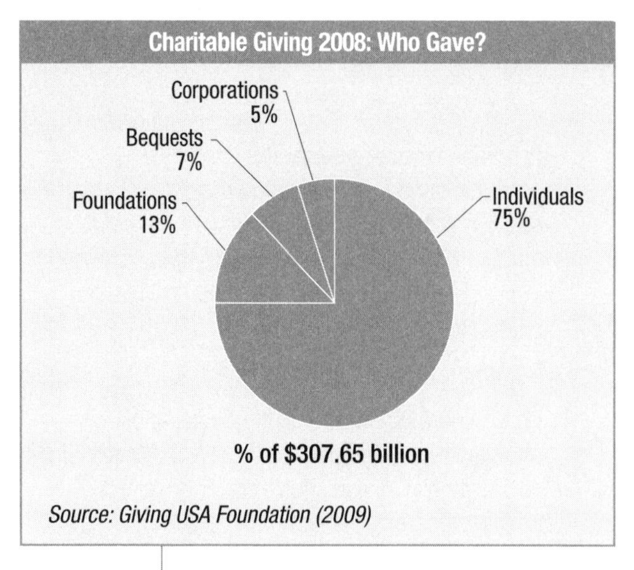

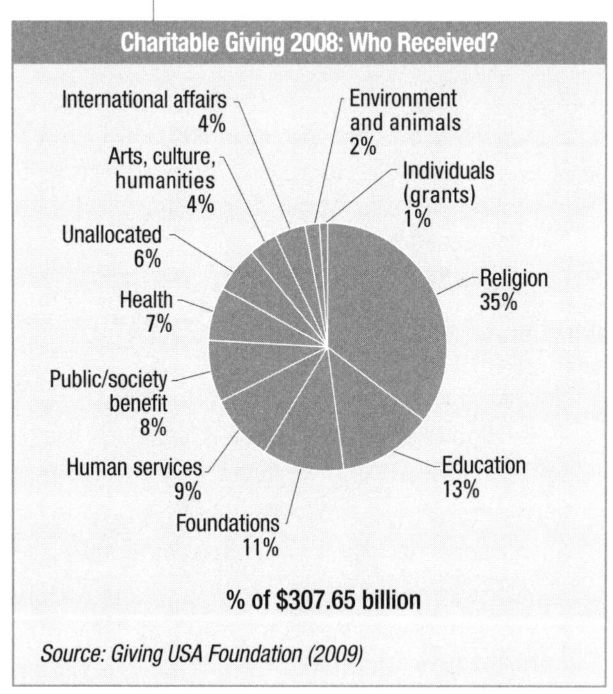

Most corporations and foundations receive far more applications than they can conceivably fund. They look for reasons to eliminate organizations so that they can winnow down the applications for serious consideration. Think how much easier it is to toss your application into the rejected pile if they've never met you, never talked with you, and know none of your board members or volunteers.

Foundations and corporations need the same attention as individuals. They are governed by human beings playing roles as executives, administrators, board members, and sometimes, even as volunteer site visitors. You have many opportunities to interact with those who make the ultimate decision—before the completed form hits their desk. Here are two examples of colleges that made themselves known in advance:

- Renton Technical College was launching a campaign and made an early call on the local bank, which had never made a charitable gift of more than $25,000. During the course of the conversation, a bank board member remarked that the longtime bank president was retiring soon and that they had been thinking of a proper way to honor him. The foundation board chair had the perfect response to that remark, and the result was eventually a $250,000 grant that named a public space on campus for the retiring president.
- During the feasibility study, Tacoma Community College discovered that most of the local CEOs did not differentiate among the four community and technical colleges in the county. Over the next 6 months, foundation board members and the college president met with more than 40 business and foundation leaders, making their case for support. More than 30 corporate

and foundation grants resulted, many of them following repeated past rejections.

Some guidelines for approaching corporate and foundation funders are presented in Table 18.1. Using these approaches will greatly increase your chances for success in your grant applications. It will also establish relations with the funders to prepare for future support.

Following Up on Grant Applications

Follow-up is essential once the grant application has actually been delivered to the funder. Again, volunteers should participate. You should share both good and bad news, obeying the rules of transparency laid out earlier in this book. If you've received several substantial gifts from other corporations, let them know that they'll have company in their giving. If you told a foundation that you hoped to receive a $500,000 gift from another funder but received only $100,000 (or nothing), tell them. You never know how they will react. Perhaps, as often happens, they will be convinced that you really need their gift, and they will be impressed with your openness.

Often, the funder will ask for additional information or updates. Although staff is responsible for preparing those, a call or e-mail from you can help at this stage. If you've gotten gifts that bring you to 80% of your goal, a short message saying "We're almost there. Your gift will get us within $100,000" will carry a lot of weight when paired with the sober analysis submitted by staff.

You've worked very hard to ensure that the corporation or foundation views you as an individual with whom they have a relationship. You've tried to show them that you care about their needs and concerns. You've told them how important they are to your success. Now's the time to prove that you mean it. As soon as you receive an answer, respond. Call your contact and thank him or her, even if your application was rejected. Your contact has met with you, talked with you, read the application, and given your project consideration. While giving thanks, you can also ask what more you might have done to get support or whether you can reapply in the future.

A formal thank you is not enough. Everyone involved in the request should contact the granting agency directly, preferably through a handwritten note. All of your board members should be put on alert so that they

"The first step is to educate oneself about the foundation field. Do you know the difference among a family foundation, a public charity and a corporate giving program, for example? What are the trends for gift size, type of grant, subject area, or geographic area? How many foundations are in the United States? How many foundations are located in your community—and who are the people behind them? What are the application differences between a federal agency and a private foundation, a larger foundation and a smaller foundation?"

—Kennedy (2004)

will thank any of the funder's board or staff members when they see them. The situation is no different from that with any other donor. Personal attention goes a long way toward making people want to give you a future gift—and glad that they've given you the first one.

Even if a gift is less than what you requested, thank donors profusely. They've given you as much as they think the corporation could and should. To them, it's a generous gift. Again, don't ever fall prey to a sense of entitlement.

"Gifts-in-kind might include such items as equipment, software, printed materials, food or other items used for hosting dinners, etc. Gifts-in-kind usually (although not always) come from companies, corporations, or vendors, in contrast to individuals, who typically give personal property."

—CASE (2009)

Don't Neglect Possibilities for In-Kind Gifts

Your college has many opportunities to receive in-kind gifts from your local and regional businesses (and individuals). These will take many forms and can have value to you ranging from a few hundred dollars to more than a million dollars. Your local mall may be willing to provide space either for free or at a reduced rate for a new workforce-training center. A local piano dealer may provide an excellent instrument for your music department. A restaurant supply firm may provide equipment for an expanded culinary arts center.

Your local hospitals have a strong interest in ensuring that your health-care professionals graduate with experience in using modern equipment. They are often willing either to donate sophisticated and expensive equipment or help you in approaching the manufacturer to obtain it free or at reduced cost. Similarly, if you have a specialized industrial applications program, the businesses that hire your graduates may be willing to supply equipment or help you obtain it from the supplier or manufacturer.

Capital projects offer opportunities for donated labor or materials. A local paving contractor may be willing to surface your parking lots as a contribution in place of cash. Your roofing contractor may donate all or a portion of the labor and materials for a new roof. A major corporation may provide you with an experienced, professional construction manager to help oversee the project.

Before submitting a request to a corporation, always consider what will allow it to make the maximum possible contribution. For many firms, cash gifts are difficult, despite their desire to support the campaign. Consider whether they can make an in-kind gift that benefits the college without requiring them to use scarce cash (see chapter 13). Requests for in-kind gifts should be treated the same as requests for cash. They ordinarily require a well-crafted proposal or grant application, personal follow-up by staff members and you as a volunteer, and ongoing stewardship of the requests.

CHAPTER 19

Getting the Word Out

One of the few things that most people think they know about fundraising campaigns is that you don't make a public announcement until you've reached 50% of your goal. Or is it 75%? Or 90%? They know that the period during which you're amassing board and staff gifts, lead gifts, and assembling your various committees is known as the silent phase or quiet campaign. During that stretch of 6 months to 2 years or more, only the inner circle is supposed to know about the campaign, with details shrouded in secrecy for all but a privileged few. They believe that if you share the news, several bad things will happen:

- You'll have egg on your face if things go wrong down the road and you don't make your goal.
- People will get bored hearing about the campaign.
- Talking about the campaign in its embryonic phase destroys the pleasure of surprising people about your success when you've reached a critical benchmark.

All of these things are true—but they aren't quite on target. If you remain secretive about the campaign until you reach a preset point, you run the risk of losing support, disappointing early donors, alienating potential donors, and missing the opportunity to build excitement about your project.

Telling as many people as possible about the campaign is good, as long as you don't ask them to do anything! If your college is planning a new building, how can you not share the good news with the entire community? If you plan to launch an entirely new EMT training program, how can you maintain that as a secret to all except a select group? If your college is planning to open a new center in a suburb and is raising funds to equip the building, why not tell the entire community, and let the excitement build? When you've just received the first million-dollar gift in the college's history, why wouldn't you trumpet the news as loudly as possible?

A campaign is a great opportunity to build public awareness, and let your potential constituency know what you do. Most organizations reach only a tiny portion of their possible supporters. Community and technical colleges often enroll up to 10% of their local populations within a given year in credit and noncredit courses yet receive philanthropic support from only a tiny portion of these students. Many community and technical colleges take an almost perverse pride in defining themselves as the city's best-kept secret. The foundation boards of these colleges bemoan the fact that the colleges do great things for the community, provide extensive educational and training services, stage wonderful cultural offerings, and spur economic development—but nobody knows them.

Yet these same colleges, when it comes time to launch a campaign, think they should keep the news under wraps until they've reached 50% or more of their goal. This makes no sense. If people don't know about you, why are they going to give you large amounts of money? If there isn't a groundswell of support for your cause, why should the local bank, grocery chain, or department store make a gift?

Leveraging the Media

Few donors make gifts only because they've seen a news spot about your college or read an article in your local newspaper. If they've seen a spate of such coverage, however, they notice and begin to think that maybe you're worthy of further investigation. You can help this process. When your newspaper publishes a feature on how you've helped retrain workers who lost their jobs at a local factory that closed, you can send it to your top 50 potential donors with a personal note. If your local newspaper has a Web edition, you can put a link to the article on your Web site. You can send out an e-mail to your top donors to alert them of upcoming TV coverage. Even if they don't watch the piece, they'll know that you're drawing attention to your good works.

If you are especially interested in generating corporate support, you have a variety of ways of reaching out to those decision makers. Most large cities have weekly or monthly business publications that are always looking for good stories. Contacting them and encouraging them to cover your activities and plans ensures your ability to reach their subscriber base. Many cities also have a more nuts-and-bolts publication, such as a journal of commerce that runs public notices of contracts to let, records leases, and carries stories on pending major construction projects. If you're planning to build one of the biggest new facilities in your district, the journal of commerce will want to know about it. The readership (contractors, attorneys, accountants, and others who are connected to the construction industry) will be interested in your plans.

A detailed article will provide you with a great tool for explaining your project to potential donors. You'll be able to hand them copies of the newspaper piece, so they can see drawings, read specifications, and be impressed that your project is important enough to be in a major business publication. Press clippings excite your board and your steering committee. Everyone likes to see his or her name in lights. It validates your investment in a project and gives you hope that the broader community shares your enthusiasm.

Seeing a headline touting your college cannot but help build enthusiasm among your board. They no longer feel like a voice in the wilderness, crying to no one but themselves. It's easier for them to start conversations with potential donors: "Did you see the great article about our new welding program in yesterday's paper? I'd love to introduce you to the faculty member they featured," is an easy way to introduce people to your organization, especially if they own a business that employs welders. Equally important, there's something magical about having a print or broadcast reporter say something positive about your college. Media personalities have the credibility that will get your acquaintances to see that your passion for the technical college is merited.

Publicity Within the College

Publicity should not be limited to broadly disseminated media. It should start with those closest to you. Keeping in mind the need for absolute transparency, you should commit yourself to keeping anyone associated with your college well informed about the project. Most colleges have weekly or other newspapers or newsletters, usually separate ones for faculty and staff, and students. Including information about the campaign and its progress in these publications is an important way to lay the groundwork for internal fundraising and to ensure that your college family knows as much as possible about your plans. It's also a good way to recruit spokespeople for your campaign. If you want to establish a speakers' bureau to support a scholarship campaign, an all-campus publication is the ideal venue in which to ask for volunteers.

Putting out a periodic insiders' newsletter is another means of ensuring effective internal communications. Such a newsletter can be distributed in hard copy or through e-mail, but in all cases it should be separate and distinct, punchy, upbeat, and focused on all the good things happening within the campaign. It should allow readers to follow the project's development and success, with a special focus on your volunteer leadership. The audience should include all those people whom you want to play major roles in the campaign as donors and volunteers.

But won't all this publicity make people feel left out if they're not asked to give? Campaigns generally go from the top down. If you keep everyone within your community informed about the campaign, some may feel that you don't think of them as important enough to ask for a gift early in the process. For the most part, you can address this in the newsletter itself, explaining that you are approaching the board, the college staff, and the key prospects first, and that you'll be talking to everyone eventually. Your basic message should be, "Your time will come."

You can also avoid discussions of a campaign and instead focus on the outcomes. You can talk about a new program or facility and mention large gifts but emphasize how the community that the publication is reaching will benefit. People can share in the excitement of knowing that your college will have an expanded computer sciences program without connecting it to their role as donors—at least not until you want them to.

If people are adamant about being among the first to give, don't refuse their gifts, but make certain that they at least have the opportunity to consider a gift at the appropriate level. Preemptive gifts can cripple a campaign if they come in well below projected levels. Generally, however, publicizing the campaign actually lessens the risk of people making unsolicited gifts. They're more likely to wait until they're asked if they know there's a defined campaign structure and schedule. If everything is rumor, they're more likely to send in an unbidden (and usually small) check.

So what's the difference between the quiet phase and the public phase? The quiet phase focuses on carefully chosen audiences. It aims to bring the campaign to the fail-safe point, where success is absolutely assured. If you refer to the rule of 12, you'll remember that a small number of gifts get you to the halfway point. If you add board support to those gifts, you'll be at the 60% level by the time you complete the lead gifts phase of the campaign.

The campaign then spreads out somewhat, encompassing gifts from corporations and foundations, as well as from individuals with the interest and ability to give the next level of gifts. The size of these gifts varies according to the campaign goal. For a $1 million campaign, you probably want to meet with any donor who can give $5,000 or more; for a $10 million campaign, the figure may be $25,000.

The public campaign starts when you've already met with and requested gifts from most of these donors. You may be at the 60% mark at this point or the 85% mark, but the theory is the same—going fully public means you're inviting everyone to give, whether they're personally solicited or not. Going public also means that you're telling the community that you've succeeded and that your project will be completed. You've progressed to the point where there is no way you can fail. At this point, there's no risk in giving and you're hoping that everyone will jump on your bandwagon.

In chapter 23, I will discuss the public phase of the campaign. For now, just remember that getting the community involved in the last 10% or 20% of the campaign will be a lot easier if you haven't kept the project a secret during the first 80% or 90%.

CHAPTER 20

Forming Additional Solicitation Committees

Most campaigns proceed based on big gifts first, then medium-size gifts, and then smaller gifts. If you're working on a campaign with a goal of $5 million or more, to complete your gift chart you'll have more than 150 prospects for gifts of between $10,000 and $100,000. In larger campaigns (those for up to $25 million), you may have as many as 500 prospects. Your staff and consultant will huddle together and determine how the list of prospects should be distributed. They'll figure out the right mixture of volunteers and activities. Then they'll present you with a plan. The types and responsibilities of solicitation committees were discussed in chapter 10. The purpose of this chapter is to encourage you to listen to the recommendations made by your staff and consultants and to remember three things about committees:

- Most campaigns need committees to ensure proper organization and implementation of gift cultivation and solicitation. It may seem that you don't, that if people just did what they're supposed to, you'd never have to meet. However, few individuals are as effective on their own as in committees. Those people provide great examples to inspire the rest of the committee—but only if the committee meets.
- Committees have to meet, because the best way to get things done is through shared responsibility.
- Committees can't be allowed to quietly peter out; they need to be held to goals and benchmarks and to dissolve only after their job is done.

Determining How Many Committees Are Needed

How many committees you need depends on at least three factors:

- How many identifiable layers of gifts you have between the lead gifts and the community campaign.
- How big your campaign is and how many prospects you have.
- How many distinct constituencies you've identified as providing the basis for gifts.

During the course of a campaign, most people will be able to establish relationships and request gifts from no more than five people. Perry Hammond, executive director at Ivy Tech Community College in Indiana and leader of several campaigns, limits most volunteers to three calls. While your campaign may have the super volunteer who completes 30 calls, it's seldom something you can count on. Most volunteers, faced with a 10-name call sheet, feel only paralysis.

In a $1 million campaign, you may have a total of 40 gifts of $10,000 or more. The first $500,000 will come from the top 10 gifts, while the next $400,000 will come from perhaps 30 gifts. A 15-member steering committee can reach each of these donors. In a $5 million campaign, the numbers change. You'll have 150 prospects for 100 gifts at $10,000 or more, once you've secured the 10 to 12 gifts that make up the initial $2.5 million. In all probability, an additional committee made up of 15 people can reach those prospects. If your campaign goal is substantially greater than $5 million, you'll need more committees, because you may have scores of prospects at $25,000 to $100,000, and hundreds more at $10,000 to $25,000. This translates into forming both a major and a special gifts committee, each of which will have 15 to 20 members willing to make face-to-face calls.

The Special Case of Multicampus Campaigns

The figures cited in the previous section apply to campaigns for single-campus colleges, where everyone is raising money for the same set of initiatives. Although you might have an additional committee for a specific initiative, the majority of your face-to-face fundraising outside the college family will be done by the steering committee and perhaps a major gifts group. Multicampus campaigns call for individual committees, since each campus serves a discrete community and individual volunteers have strong ties to potential donors within the campus service area. The steering committee takes on the largest gifts by donors with an interest in the entire system; it would also serve as a sounding board to help determine which campus might have first call on specific other large donors. Each of the campuses would have its own major gifts committee, which would seek campus-specific gifts.

The following examples illustrate how different sizes and configurations of campaigns correspond to special circumstances surrounding the effort.

- Tacoma Community College had a $7 million goal for a comprehensive campaign covering several separate initiatives. The great majority of gifts were acquired by the steering committee, with some successes among the major gifts committee. An exception was a separate committee assembled to raise funds for a Japanese garden. This group had a goal of $300,000, which was reached primarily through the efforts of the highly motivated and successful chair, Griselda "Babe" Lehrer, and a small number of her colleagues on the committee. In return, the Japanese garden was named in honor of her and her late husband.
- Midland College in Texas raised about $5 million for a new building, relying solely on its board to function as a committee on behalf of the whole campaign. Board members made contacts, engaged in cultivation, and represented the campaign in the community. The campaign got its funds from a relatively small number of donors outside of family gifts. This approach is a rare exception and depends on the college having a significant number of previous donors and supporters.
- Ivy Tech Community College in Indiana uses a 45- to 60-member campaign cabinet for each of its campaigns (it includes 14 regions and has run one or more campaigns each year for the past decade). Each cabinet member is expected to solicit three to five major gifts ($25,000+ over an 18-month period). Although there are sometimes subcommittees, they are perceived as offshoots of the cabinet.
- The Seattle Community College system had four campuses, each with a separate foundation and specific campaign initiatives. In addition to an overarching campaign steering committee, each of the campuses formed its own committee responsible for seeking support for its goals. The college development office was responsible for ensuring that campuses did not make competing requests, while also taking charge of large requests for systemwide goals.

In a $30 million campaign, you're probably not going to be able to have personal, one-on-one meetings with donors from whom you'll request less than $25,000. You'll still need committees to reach donors at the $10,000 level, but they will focus on discovering ways of meeting with prospects in groups. House parties, cocktail parties, hosted parties at your college, and regional alumni gatherings are all approaches that allow you to invite prospects at this level to consider gifts to the campaign.

> "Identifiable similarities of giving among diverse populations are:
>
> - Convergence of wealth accumulation, education, career growth and increased earning capacity allows many to become philanthropists.
> - For many cultures, philanthropy is seen in the broadest sense—gifts of time, talent and treasure—and revolves around family, church and education.
> - Most groups are highly influenced by leaders—religious, community, professional, social and family.
> - There is direct and informal support to children, elderly, community members.
> - Level of immediate need is important to the potential benefactor.
> - Planned giving is seldom a priority.
> - There is some distrust of traditional nonprofits.
> - Much philanthropy is focused outside of the United States, with no concern for tax benefits.
> - Generosity is often extended through networks and to those who are part of the donor's personal world.
> - Reciprocity is an accepted concept. Helping those in ways they themselves were helped often motivates giving in diverse populations."
>
> —*Wagner (2007)*

In extremely large campaigns, gifts of $5,000 to $10,000 may be solicited by telephone after careful cultivation by mail and other means. Prospects might not give at the level they could, but by the time you solicit them, enough large gifts are in place for them to understand how their gift contributes to the goal. There are so many possibilities that you have to rely on your staff and consultants to determine the best way to proceed. The fast-food outlets that let you build your own burger brag about the number of possibilities available to you. Campaigns are no different. If you have hundreds of potential donors, dozens of volunteers, scores of different methodologies to reach the donors, and eight or ten different structures to choose from, the permutations are endless.

You might disagree with the approaches outlined by your staff or consultants, and disagreements should be heard and discussed. In the end, you and your staff and consultants should make a decision that reflects the following concerns:

- If you believe every donor deserves individual attention, you'll need more committees.
- If you are seeking to reach people in multiple communities, you'll need more committees than if you're focusing on a small service area.
- If you have a strong advisory committee program, you'll need a separate committee to ensure that specific supporters can contribute to the campaign and receive the respect embodied by a personal request.
- Because you should plan on future volunteer-based fundraising, this is the opportunity to train several cohorts of committed volunteers.

You'll be raising money from the top down, but it's like a relay race. For you to move smoothly from one level of the campaign to the next, the lower level has to be in motion when it receives the handoff. The chair has to be in place, the members chosen and at least partially trained in how to cultivate and solicit gifts, and an evaluated prospect list in place. You'll be finishing the work of one committee when the next starts. Your lead donors will take months to make decisions. At the next level, major gifts donors can be asked for their gifts as long as enough lead gifts are in place to demonstrate strong support for the campaign. Campaign progress is important, as you've seen in many of these chapters. The worst thing is for months to go by without new solicitations. Overlapping committees help avoid a major gap between soliciting gifts at one level and the next.

CHAPTER 21

Seeking Public Funding to Gain Private Money

Because CASE's focus is on private philanthropy, *CASE Reporting Standards* does not recommend counting money from government entities (public funds) as part of your total. CASE acknowledges, however, that government funds are important to help institutions achieve their goals and can help colleges leverage private support. Often, the public funds you receive during your campaign are only vaguely related to the initiatives on which you're focusing. Nonetheless, your campaign ignores the potential for public funds at its peril, since money from all levels of government can strengthen your institution, provide a needed boost to your fundraising, and constitute a building block for a successful comprehensive campaign. In terms of the goals you set for the campaign, you should include public funds as a potential source.

Three types of government funding exist, usually at all levels of jurisdictions (federal, state, county, and municipal):

- Earmarks, which are funds from the general fund or a large section of the general fund, that are garnered by elected representatives on your behalf. Although much negative press has been aimed at earmarks, they allow your representatives to ensure that a portion of your taxes is returned to your district for important, publicly oriented projects.
- Competitive grant programs, again at all levels of government (depending on the part of the country you're in), which offer pots of money for specified areas pertaining to your activities. Funds are available from federal agencies such as the National Science Foundation and the National Endowments for the Arts and Humanities or from the state for historic preservation, arts, workforce training, or myriad other programs. What all of these programs have in common is requiring an application that

demonstrates that your project falls within the fund's guidelines and is worthwhile.

- Large pots of appropriated money for specific purposes that often require you to raise matching funds. Many states have scholarship and endowed professorship-matching funds available to qualifying institutions that raise a specific amount of private funds for the prescribed purpose. If an endowed professorship requires a $500,000 fund, a state might provide half that amount if the college can raise the other half.

The Public Funding Task Force

Your college already has relationships with government officials and engages in government relations at multiple levels. Depending on where your funding comes from, you have close contact with state, county, or local officials. You probably also have ongoing relations with your federal representative and perhaps with your U.S. senators. You work through the national office of the American Association of Community Colleges or the Association of Community College Trustees to lobby appropriate officials.

None of this is new. Your college president, government relations officer, hired lobbyist, grants coordinator, and perhaps other staff members follow funding opportunities on an ongoing basis. Your existing resources provide an excellent foundation for a concerted effort to gain funds specifically tied to your campaign.

Forming a task force with members who have strong ties to individual layers of public funding sources helps you gain the support you need. Is there a local businessperson who is a major donor to your federal legislator? Do you have politically perceptive allies who have served as campaign managers or finance chairs for state or county executives and legislators? Is the former mayor a strong partisan of your college? The goal is to bring together people whose phone calls to legislative and executive offices will be accepted and answered. You need people with political influence and a willingness to use it on your behalf.

This is where foundation board members enter the picture, since many of you possess precisely those attributes. You are well connected, know who your elected officials will listen to, and can recruit those people to the task force. In many cases, your foundation board will provide half or more of the task force.

Depending on which type of funding you're seeking, task force members have different functions. If you're looking for an earmark, you need contacts with legislators and other officials who can gain access to available funds. You need the ability to influence members of appropriations committees at the state and federal level, as well as the information as to where the funds for an earmark might originate.

Even in challenging economic times, there will be funds for projects with strong political support. If your mayor or city manager makes your project a major municipal priority and instructs his or her lobbyist to seek federal or state funds, you multiply your chances for success. Often, legislators have staff people whose primary focus is finding specific locations of funds available to projects in their district. Making certain that they make your project a priority helps you find where the money is and how to pursue it most effectively.

For competitive grants, it is counterproductive to seek political influence over decision making. Independent, highly qualified staff members administer most competitive grant programs. They respond negatively when they receive pressure from either the executive or the legislative branch to fund specific initiatives. However, legislative staff members often can help you steer toward appropriate grant opportunities, and then your staff (including the president) can begin cultivating relationships with the granting agency.

Large amounts of money for matching or challenge purposes provide an attractive target for community and technical colleges. If you can qualify for such a match, it can often double the amount you have available for scholarships or for faculty support. Task force members with close ties to state legislators can use their ties to identify opportunities and ensure that you're not missing funding because the source is not well publicized.

You can observe that seeking government funding resembles the model you have developed throughout your campaign. It is highly dependent on personal relationships with decision makers; the most effective ambassadors for the college are frequently volunteers such as foundation board members or campaign committee members.

"Having all the fundraising functions at the college working together does much more than keeping each other informed. It ensures that no money is left on the table. Working together, grant developers (public and private) and staff who cultivate donors can leverage each other's success. A prime example might be matching grants with donor derived funds. Pooling public and private investment in a project raise donor interest and increase the likelihood of success in reaching the goal."

—Steven Budd, president, River Valley Community College

Leveraging Public Funds Effectively

Public money can play an important role in your campaign's structure, because it usually depends on raising private funds. The types of interrelationships can include the following:

- The public money is a direct match to private funds. In Washington and Oregon, as well as many other states, there are increments of scholarship funds that have to be matched by private money.

- There is a threshold before you qualify for public funds. Many jurisdictions require that you reach 50% or more of your private goal before they will consider your college for a grant or other funding.
- There is an informal expectation of significant private support before public money can be considered. This is frequently the case with local funds, where the city or county will indicate, "We'll consider supporting your project when you can show us that our constituents care."
- Public money is the last money in. Often, while public funds are approved for your project, the money will not be transferred unless you have all other required funds pledged (supported by signed pledge cards).

Each of these stipulations offers the opportunity to encourage both asking and giving. Matching gifts of any sort provide an irresistible impetus to fundraising. If you can obtain $500,000 by raising $250,000, you also realize that each dollar you don't raise costs you two. The thought of losing money that is waiting for you motivates you to make your calls and provides an added reason for donors to contribute. Interestingly, it almost never results in a donor halving a gift.

Public funding that relies on a threshold level is also an extremely effective factor in stimulating committee activity. If your state has a program that requires you to be at 50% of your total before applying for a specific grant, the application date for the grant becomes a deadline for acquiring gifts. It can be used as a benchmark for your fundraising committees that they can then share with prospects. For example, "You know, we're at $675,000 now. If we can get to $850,000 by the end of next month, we'll qualify to apply for a $200,000 state grant. If there's any way you could make your decision by then, it could potentially help us get a really big boost."

The expectation of private money coming in before public money becomes available inspires both volunteers and donors. You can't sit back waiting for a big public sector gift to jumpstart your campaign. It's an effective rationale for successful board and family campaigns, as well as for the lead gift phase. Your campaign chairs can tell the early givers, "Your gifts will perform double duty. Not only will they show the community that we really care, but it'll convince the people in the statehouse that this is a priority. If we're going to get a special appropriation, our legislators need to know that their constituents care about it."

Public gifts that cap a campaign offer an excellent carrot when you're approaching the end of the campaign. The last 5% or 10% of your campaign is waiting there for you to claim it if you can only raise the rest of the initial 90% or 95%. If you're engaging in a community campaign, this incentive allows people to feel that even a small gift is meaningful. You can say, "Our goal is $2 million, and we've raised

$1.8 million. But of that, $100,000 is in county money that won't come to us until we get the entire $2 million, which is $200,000 from now. If we don't get to $2 million, we lose that $100,000. So now's the time to give, with so much at stake. We don't want to lose that money from the county."

It's important to note that public money with strings performs two important functions:

- It provides concrete goals, benchmarks, and deadlines to your volunteers, ensuring that they are constantly focused on raising funds and meeting expectations.
- It defines a framework within which you can talk easily to donors, because you can truthfully tell them that their gift will be multiplied by public money, or that you will lose the chance to pursue public funding if you don't meet the requirements. Challenges motivate asking and giving throughout the campaign.

On balance, seeking and obtaining public funding for campaigns yields positive results. There are, however, a number of issues that you must be aware of in seeking these funds. Accepting federal money ordinarily means that you will fall under the Department of Labor's Davis-Bacon Act guidelines, which mandate you to pay prevailing wages for any labor involved in a building project. This may increase your costs, depending on the region of the country in which your college is located. Public money may also carry the expectation of a broader bid process on capital projects rather than a negotiated contract with one or more preferred contractors.

Pursuing state funds may have the effect of contorting your campaign schedule, because so many states operate on a biennial budget. If you start just after the appropriation cycle has ended, you may have to wait almost 2 years before requesting support—an awkward circumstance if you're planning an 18-month campaign.

Some public money may tempt you because it's available, although it applies to programs that your college doesn't now offer or that fall outside your mission. Such funds might actually cost you more than their initial value. It is important to avoid chasing money if it leads you away from your strategic plan and vision. Public funds also usually require periodic, detailed reporting. You should make certain that the college has the staff members available to comply with these requirements because it can cause embarrassment if you fail to turn in reports in a timely and accurate fashion.

"Bismarck State College's National Energy Center of Excellence (NECE) anchors the Bismarck, ND, community college from a hillside overlooking the Missouri River. Partnerships ... were key in completion of the spacious 106,200 square-foot national center of education and training for the energy industry. Sources of funding for the $18.3 million building include industry partners; local, state and federal government agencies; and individual and Bismarck State College employee donations."

—Conrad (2009)

With these elements in mind, public funding remains an important part of most community and technical college campaigns. The funds depend on your ability to use your contacts as well-placed individuals within your community to make the needed connections. Elected and appointed officials and government staff members respond to the same approaches that any other prospect does—they pay attention to those they know and respect.

CHAPTER 22

Keeping the Campaign Going

Community and technical college campaigns typically last between 18 months and 3 years. Sometimes they last even longer. Volunteers get tired, staff members wear down, and consultants find themselves out of fresh ideas. It's easy to get discouraged and wonder whether you'll ever complete the campaign. You expect the campaign to progress in a straight line, always moving forward. In fact, campaigns move in steps, from plateau to plateau. You work hard; money comes in. You continue to work hard and see few results. Then after a few more months, more gifts arrive, followed by another dry spell. At the end of the campaign, you can look back and see steady progress. But at the time, it seems like a stop and start process.

Campaigns seem long because you never see the end until it's there. You slog uphill and are always hoping to see over the crest, but you just see the mountain rising in front of you. Part of the problem is that you don't feel safe until you reach the goal, because if you fall short, everyone feels the campaign has failed. It's often an all-or-nothing feeling, with 99% representing disappointment and relief arriving only at 100%.

One way to keep campaigns fresh is to break them up into manageable pieces. First you have the board campaign, with a specific goal and timeline. Then you have the family campaign of faculty and staff, followed by the lead gifts campaign. There may be a corporate and a major gifts campaign and perhaps a public funding campaign. At the end, you may have an all-encompassing community campaign. Each campaign has a goal and a timeline, often with separate committees and volunteers and at times even different staff members.

Breaking the campaign down using separate volunteer committees and working with discrete goals and timelines all help keep the campaign moving and prevent burnout. But no matter how you try, the steering committee, the executive director, staff members, and consultants all are constantly looking at the totality of the campaign. The overall goal seems to stay tantalizingly out of reach, with progress measurable only in tiny increments. Tempers can fray if overall timelines slip or gifts don't come in as quickly as predicted. Everyone is anxious and concerned when prospects refuse to make decisions or say no. When things don't go according to plan, the plan comes under scrutiny—sometimes with very testy questions.

Maintaining a Positive Attitude

During a campaign, the community has you in its crosshairs, and some people may be hoping you'll fail. Others are deciding on gifts according to whether they think you'll succeed or not or may be unwilling to make a really big gift unless they see others doing the same. Your leaders are there for a reason. The community looks to them for signals and wants them to broadcast a uniform, consistent belief that the campaign will succeed. When your leaders express doubt, the entire community casts a negative eye on your campaign. They find reasons to put off appointments with your volunteers. They temper their enthusiasm about giving. They spread the word rapidly that the college's campaign is in trouble. Problems emerge when concerns leak out into the community and affect the broader perception of the campaign.

The first rule of campaigns is that outside of the innermost circle, the campaign must project an unshakable optimism. There is never any advantage to sharing doubts about the campaign with anyone outside the steering committee. You can't be a Pollyanna, acting happy even when a major donor turns you down. You do, however, have to respond positively—except within the deepest inner sanctums of the campaign.

When you get bad news, you have to ask what happened and why. You have to be willing to ask the hardest, most probing questions and be honest in your answers. Staff and consultants must be totally frank and unsparing in their discussions. It is often helpful for the consultant to provide a confidential scorecard to the board and steering committee each month to ensure that the campaign never loses its moorings. The scorecard can enumerate requests made, gifts received, the number of declines, and the number of pending requests, helping your college to gauge its progress. But all of this remains in house, under the assumption that the campaign will find a way to succeed and surmount all obstacles. You can be honest within your board and steering committee, but your goal is to design better strategies for success. You can't compromise your potential for success by admitting doubts.

The same rules apply to making decisions. During the course of preparing and implementing a campaign, an organization makes difficult and often contentious decisions. Debate will be hot, tempers will flare, and some people will walk away without getting their way. But everyone has to agree from the start on one incontrovertible rule: Once you make a decision, the debate is over, and the organization speaks with a single voice. Backbiting, second-guessing, and ongoing questioning are the surest path to failure. It is not easy to admit you've lost, but you have to accept the collective wisdom—and the collective wisdom is 50% of your decision-making body, plus one.

The Role of the Consultant When Challenges Arise

In most campaigns, this relentless optimism pays off. You overcome doubts and questions, you get past disappointments, and, more or less on schedule, you complete the campaign. However, almost every campaign will find itself in a position where failure seems as likely as success. How do you decide what to do? This is one of the reasons you hire consultants. They have done dozens or perhaps hundreds of campaigns and can assess your position from an objective, experienced point of view.

Throughout the campaign, consultants should have been acting as the navigator of the ship, making small course corrections as needed, but generally sticking to the chosen path. If they see that the winds have changed, the ship has veered off course, or a storm is brewing, they must feel free to share that with the college. You are responsible for considering the analysis and determining what to do. Generally, consultants will provide you with recommendations or choices such as the following:

- raising the goal (the most common major change)
- altering the project
- reducing the budget
- taking on debt
- changing staff
- adding more volunteers
- abandoning the campaign

Consultants also will provide advice on how to relay this news to the rest of the organization and to the community to minimize negative fallout. Most of the time, the response from the community will be positive, because you'll be saying what it will take to get the project done. You'll obey the rule established early in this book concerning total transparency.

Jumpstarting Stalled Campaigns

Sometimes a campaign stops dead in its tracks. Your volunteers stop making calls. You have no more prospects. You haven't received any substantial gifts in several months. Your staff seems at a loss as to what to do next. Your consultant is repeating the same messages again and again. The board is worried.

Usually, this point comes when you're through with the board campaign but have not yet completed the lead gifts portion. More rarely, it occurs when you've had a fairly successful lead gifts campaign, but the next level of donors is not responding as well as you had hoped. Generally, you're finding that prospects are less prepared to support you than you had thought. They either make token gifts or refuse to make decisions. Your volunteers feel as if they are unable to inspire their friends and colleagues to give.

Don't panic. If you think you're stalled, take a moment or two to analyze your position. Consider whether you're just on a plateau that will serve as a springboard to success. Are there gifts in the pipeline, but your prospects are just taking longer than you hoped to make decisions? Have most gifts come in at the hoped-for levels but taken more time to develop than you expected? Have a few prospects delayed decisions but remained interested and engaged in discussions? If the answer is yes to any of these questions, then you're probably not really stalled. You might reconsider your schedule and determine whether you can make up for lost time. You might check to make certain that you're still on a path to success. In all probability, you'll recover and catch up to your schedule.

On the other hand, if your situation doesn't look as if it's going to get better any time soon, you have to face reality. Have you remained at the same level for more than 3 months (or 2 months for smaller campaigns)? Are you unable to see where the gifts needed to complete the campaign will come from? If a single big gift falls through, will it kill the campaign? Then it's time for a summit meeting. You have to gather the key players in your campaign, probably the same people that decided to embark on the campaign in the first place:

- campaign chair
- college president
- foundation executive or chief development officer
- board chair
- campaign director
- consultant
- chair of the major campaign committees

The meeting should be at a time and place where you won't be interrupted and where you are guaranteed absolute privacy and confidentiality—perhaps even secrecy. This is the one time when rules of transparency and openness don't apply. You have to have the total freedom to express yourself, vent, fret, show your fear and concern—even get angry. You're truly at a crisis point, and you can't deny it or keep it concealed. However, it's not a time to affix blame. Your purpose at this meeting is to find solutions and a path to success. If the plans you hatch here fail, then you can worry about blame—but be certain, there'll be more than enough to go around.

Using Generative Thinking

Volunteer groups exist as more than sounding boards to ratify staff members' ideas. They exist to generate new ideas and solutions (for an excellent discussion of generative thinking, see Chait, Ryan, & Taylor, 2004, pp. 79–100). Your summit meeting is the perfect place to put this approach into practice. To succeed, you need to frame the issue in a way that makes it easy to follow the right path. You want to ask the questions in a way that results in productive, forward-looking discussion rather than self-questioning and pessimism. Rather than ask "Where did we go wrong?" or spend fruitless time discussing whether you can ever recover momentum, ask "What strategies and actions will move us forward?"

Framing questions correctly means that you focus on the process, not the people. You've gotten as far as you have by relying on best practices and proven approaches, by taking things in the proper order, and by allowing gifts to unfold according to their inner dynamic, not your panic. This is no time to abandon those best practices. Instead, you have to find new ways to apply them. There are a number of productive framing questions:

- Is there any one gift that could turn the campaign around and ensure its success?
- Is there involvement by any one or two people that would jumpstart the campaign?
- What hidden pockets of support have you been ignoring, and how can you reach them?
- Is it time to alter the order in which you're undertaking the campaign? Would your major givers respond more enthusiastically if they knew that 500 community members had contributed?
- Are there people who gave early in the campaign who might either connect you to their friends or consider a larger gift?

If you've reached 60% or more of your goal, you can find a way to complete the campaign successfully. To have reached that point means that your project is solid, it has support from people who care, and those who have invested will help you reach your goal. It might take you longer than you'd hoped, but you'll get there eventually: The Fred Hutchinson Cancer Research Center in Seattle, Washington, had reached about 50% of its $11 million campaign goal when the gifts stopped coming in. A summit identified several possible new leaders and one key donor. It also determined a path to a potential large donor who had been resistant to meeting. The campaign recruited new leaders, secured the key donation, and made a connection to the large donor. The campaign eventually exceeded its goal by more than $3 million, although it took 6 months longer than leaders had hoped.

Your summit has to be totally honest and all-encompassing. No sacred cows can go unexamined. Does the plan need changing? What more should the board chair do to inspire board members? Is the consultant providing appropriate and sufficient guidance? Is anything standing in the way of volunteers making their calls? Again, the purpose in asking these questions cannot be to skewer a guilty party. It has to be to find ways to fix the process and position the campaign for success. Sometimes the answer can be as simple as finding the right challenge grant that can be broadly publicized to attract new gifts. Sometimes it's getting a donor to step up to an unexpected level and give the campaign an extraordinary boost. Sometimes, the two can be combined.

Pursuing Easy Victories

Campaigns are always balanced on a razor's edge. When a few gifts come in, and calls go well, optimism pervades the entire apparatus. When you get several denials in a short time, your volunteers are having trouble getting appointments, and your foundation director seems depressed, doubts inevitably arise. One way of reviving a stalled campaign is to look for easy victories. Are there a few businesses that you know are going to give, but you have delayed approaching them because their gifts won't be very large? If a donor told you to "come back if you're close to your goal," now's the time to come back. Did a newspaper reporter offer to write a story about the campaign when the time was right? Well, the time is right.

CHAPTER 23

The Community Campaign

Community campaigns play an important role in many successful campaigns. They increase your college's donor base, convey a sense of community ownership to participants, and provide your volunteers with a sense of accomplishment, because for several months your campaign becomes the talk of the town. It's important not to confuse running a community campaign with actually raising a substantial portion of your campaign's goal; it is extremely rare for a community campaign to raise more than 10% of the entire campaign goal. The real purpose of the community campaign is to heighten community involvement and acquire new donors for the future.

The community campaign should be part of your initial campaign plan (see chapter 8). You should know from the start whether you're going to include a community phase, what percentage of your total goal you expect to derive from it, and what methods you'll be using to raise those funds. If you're going to take 2 years to raise $4 million, you'll probably kick off your community campaign around 18 months into the campaign. If you're taking 3 years to raise $25 million, you'll wait until about month 28 to kick it off. However, working backward from the actual start of the campaign, you'll need 6 months to a full year to get everything in place. You'll need printed and media materials. You may have to hire outside vendors to perform telemarketing services. You'll need to rent halls for special events, hire entertainment for concerts, or acquire underwriting for major special events.

The community campaign should have its own plan, developed by staff and your volunteers, and then presented to and approved by the steering committee. You should be sure that the community campaign doesn't absorb too much time from the volunteers, who are pursuing large gifts, or from the president, who has to maintain his or her focus on larger gifts. The community campaign is meant to bring you sprinting over the finish line on a high note, not staggering over exhausted and on your last legs.

The Value of the Community Campaign

Twenty years ago, it was a commonplace assumption that 80% of the money came from 20% of the donors. That seemed extreme, and many board members doubted it. Now we know that the number is wrong, but on the low side. Over the past decade in campaigns managed by consulting firms throughout the country, the ratios are closer to 95 to 5—that is, 95% of the money comes from 5% of the donors. The remaining 5% comes from the other 95% of the people who now support you or who can be attracted by the campaign.

> *"Take credit for nothing!*
> *The trustees did it.*
> *The foundation board did it.*
> *The faculty did it.*
> *The students did it.*
> *The donors did it.*
> *Hey, if it ain't fun, get another job!"*
>
> —Daniel (2002)

Incomes in the United States have become skewed over the past several decades; the number of millionaires and multimillionaires has skyrocketed, while the willingness and desire of people to make transformational gifts has increased. Twenty years ago, a list of the top 50 gifts given in the United States included donations at the $250,000 level. In 2008, a similar list's lower level is 100 times that, with top gifts at more than $1 billion (a list of the top gifts in the United States is compiled four times annually and available at www.slate.com). At the same time, competition in fundraising has increased. Donors are more selective in their giving. Although most people still give to multiple organizations, responses to traditional fundraising techniques such as direct mail have declined.

Depending on your college and the definitions you use for the community campaign, setting a goal of between 5% and 10% of the entire campaign is usually a realistic goal. Fewer than 5% brings into question whether it's worth the effort. More than 10% is probably unrealistic except in exceptional circumstances. If you're seeking $1 million to remodel your library, it is likely that you'll get at least 90% of those funds through gifts that require individual approaches. You will have cherry-picked your supporters to request larger gifts from those with passion and capacity. It's unlikely that there's an untapped set of donors in the community that you haven't already considered. If you can get $100,000 in smaller donations from community members, students and former students, and perhaps some sort of an event (e.g., a reading by a well-known regional author), you will be doing well.

Community campaigns are expensive. It costs more to raise a dollar during a community campaign than during any other portion of your effort. It is more labor-intensive, involves more events, requires proportionally more expensive recognition (such as bricks and plaques), and requires approaching people with little previous attachment. Community campaigns seek to attract new donors who have not given to you before. They will give smaller gifts after receiving more information than your longtime supporters receive. You may have to use direct mail, telephone solicitation in combination with direct mail, or other techniques to gain their contributions. All of these methods are more expensive per dollar than direct, face-to-face solicitation of people you already know.

Many community campaigns will cost as much as 40 cents for each dollar raised—that is, in a $1 million campaign, it will cost $40,000 to raise the last $100,000. You may have spent only $80,000 to raise the first $900,000. Why is it worth another 50% to raise the last 10% of your goal?

The answer is that you will gain 90% of your donors while raising the last 10% of your goal. An extraordinary benefit of the community campaign will be to broaden and deepen your donor base. These new donors represent your foundation's future. They will, if properly stewarded, become your future annual donors, event attendees, and, over time, your major donors. In 7 to 10 years, when you're conducting another campaign to meet community demand, those donors may be prepared to make significant gifts to support your efforts. You shouldn't think in the short term in relation to the cost of community campaign gifts. You will be amortizing the cost of obtaining these donors over the next decade or longer and decreasing future fundraising expenses.

Examples of Community Campaign Activities

In almost every campaign, colleges find new types of events, new ways to involve more people, and new types of challenges. There is an unlimited number of ideas. Have a brainstorming session with your most imaginative volunteers. List all their ideas, and then have the community campaign committee evaluate them. They should choose the best opportunities to increase your donor pool, raise money, and prepare you for the future. They should also evaluate the amount of work required and ensure that the ideas can be implemented without draining the organization. Table 23.1 lists some ways to reach others through your community campaign. The list is not meant to be exhaustive but to get your creative juices flowing in thinking about how your college can attract new donors and complete your campaign.

Table 23.1: Typical Community Campaign Activities

- Send direct mail or e-mail to your already existing constituencies, especially current adult students and alumni.
- Conduct a telephone solicitation of current adult students, alumni, area high school teachers, or other close-in constituencies that have not already made larger gifts to the campaign. There are firms that do sophisticated work in this discipline. Their fees tend to be fairly high, but they reach people you cannot otherwise solicit.
- Organize well-publicized challenge grants that allow you to invite donors to give with the knowledge that their gift will leverage funds from an individual, corporation, or foundation.
- Form corporate partnerships (sometimes referred to as cause-related marketing) that involve a portion of funds spent on goods or services to be donated to the campaign. A grocery store might donate 5 cents every time a customer purchases its proprietary brands. A bank might donate $25 for every new account that's opened during a 6-month period.
- Host special events tied specifically to the campaign. For example, if an alumnus who is now a well-known author or singer lives nearby, you might have a lecture or performance, preceded by a reception for people willing to donate $100 to mingle with the alumnus.
- Schedule dinner parties hosted by committee members, either with an admission fee that goes to the campaign or with a solicitation. In either event, the attendees have the opportunity to visit the host's house, the host is seen as charitable, and the college gains considerable money.
- Sell bricks, pavers, or other tokens of permanent recognition. This has been a popular activity in the past but may be less so now because of the low return on investment (see chapter 13). The challenge is setting the price high enough to cover the costs of inscribing the bricks and marketing the opportunity.

Building Public Awareness

You want absolute maximum media coverage during the community campaign. Although publicity should target your best prospects, you shouldn't be concerned about getting coverage that's too broad. If you're in a small town and a metropolitan TV station wants to cover you, let it. It won't hurt for people in the big city to hear about you. The community campaign is the time to bring in a media sponsor who'll run your ads for free; tell their readers, listeners, or viewers about your campaign; and even help sell your mementos. They can advertise your events and feature interviews with your staff and students.

The community campaign is the right occasion to install a well-known chairperson willing to ask for money exclusively for your campaign. Your local baseball star who played on the college team, an anchorwoman who got her start after returning to school as an adult, an author who got her first encouragement in a course at your college, can lend credibility to the campaign and attract others to the effort. Their presence at a special event can increase attendance, and their signatures on a direct mail appeal can attract attention. A celebrity's face on a billboard or a television ad can ensure that your message is seen and heard.

If you wish to recruit celebrities as campaign spokespeople or chairs, there are a few things to make certain they agree to:

- Like other leaders, they have to make gifts to demonstrate that this really is something they care about.
- They have to project the right image for your organization.
- They have to be clear about what they're agreeing to in terms of use of their name and image, tasks to be performed, and events to attend.
- They have to be clear about the amount of time they're willing to commit and the types of activities they're willing to undertake.

For many organizations, a well-known, highly respected citizen is an ideal community campaign chair. Perhaps you have a retired faculty member who's been active in a variety of community activities and is highly regarded by much of the community. Or if you have a retired president who's still active in Rotary and has headed up United Way campaigns since retirement, she's perfect as well. Such people convey the concept that you're credible and connected to the community. They're believable because they walk the walk of community service. They're also accessible and just plain folks, sending out a positive message about how your organization regards its grassroots supporters.

The Fun Factor

The initial phases of your campaign are seldom vehicles for true fun. You're talking to people about their deepest values and helping them make decisions that are sometimes life changing. Although you can feel joyful about the process in which you're engaged, you're not very often having fun in the normal sense of the word. Donors are looking deep into their own souls, often in private or with the help of a trusted counselor. Eventually they'll celebrate and rejoice in their gift, but ordinarily not while they're thinking about it.

The community campaign is different. You are trying to attract new people to your organization. Part of the reason they'll decide to join you is that you represent an enjoyable group of people who understand that fundraising is not always a life-or-death situation. They are the type of donors labeled social donors in *The Seven Faces of Philanthropy*, those who get involved in a campaign because they want to interact with people they like and respect.

During the community campaign, only a fraction of the gifts are of the variety that requires either deep thought or deep conviction. They're gifts from the heart, rather than emanating from reason. Donors love the idea of helping the underdog, ensuring that new immigrants can get the education they crave, or that others in the community get a second chance.

Community campaign donors make gifts that they can pay off with relative ease, often by writing a check or charging it. The majority of community campaign gifts are $250 or less, a size that falls into ongoing discretionary expenditures, rather than a gift from assets. In return, you offer a sense of satisfaction and enjoyment. If donors attend an event, the emphasis should be on fun. If they are invited to buy something, there should be a sense of playfulness and fun in the invitation.

The committees involved in raising money during the community campaign should focus on fun as well. Make the meetings more like parties than the serious, straight-laced gatherings that governed the lead gift efforts. Serve some wine, meet at people's houses or clubs, and spend some social time around each meeting. During this phase, you'll touch the most potential donors and volunteers. You'll be laying the foundation for long-term financial health based on an expanded support base. Make sure that your community campaign volunteers and donors are left with a good feeling and the desire to come back for more.

Part 3:
After the Campaign

CHAPTER 24

Ending the Campaign

At some point, you have to say "done" and mark completion. Whether you're at goal, $150,000 away from it, or $500,000 beyond it with money pouring in, there's a point at which the campaign is over. There are two reasons campaigns must come to a clearly defined close:

- Your volunteers have signed up for a limited commitment, not a life sentence.
- The community heard you set a goal and a timeframe. They want you done so the next project can take center stage. When your campaign drags on, you're violating a trust that you've established with your supporters. You're putting into question your willingness to play by the rules.

When is the campaign over? If you've raised enough money to complete your project (whether you've reached your goal or not) and volunteers' energy is flagging, it's time to stop. If you've reached your goal, even before the campaign is scheduled to end, it's probably time to stop unless you have a very good, mission-based reason to continue. If raising more money will allow you to increase services by cutting debt service, it might be a reason to continue until you're scheduled to end. But raising money after your goal is reached makes you appear greedy in the eyes of the community and puts you in a position of hogging the wealth.

It's time to stop if you've reached your goal and the campaign time has run out, even if you think you could raise more. As is the case in show business, it's always good to leave them wanting more, rather than wearing out your welcome. Just be sure you continue to talk to the prospective donors you haven't yet reached. It will give you a head start on your next campaign—and there will be a next campaign.

How to Celebrate

Start with an internal celebration for the folks who made it happen—you, your board colleagues, your president and staff, your committee members, the consultants, architects, and everyone else who made your success possible. Use the celebration to achieve closure, thank them, acknowledge their hard work, and give thanks for your success. This celebration is the smallest and can be the most intimate and enjoyable, because you can let your hair down. You can roast the campaign chair, share horror stories of the campaign, and admit your fears and concerns. You've won. Your only concern is that everyone who was a part of the campaign feels appreciated for his or her work. This celebration should be the first and should allow those involved in the campaign to have the first full appreciation of the finished project.

This group should be treated as the ultimate insiders and be given a behind-the-scenes tour if you built a new facility. They should meet with scholarship recipients if they raised funds for an expanded scholarship fund. If they raised money for a new program, they should get to meet your new faculty or have the curriculum shared at the celebration.

A second celebration includes your donors, your staff, and volunteers. It's a time to thank everyone who's gotten you to the point where you can open the doors to your new facility, start drawing money from a larger endowment, or begin offering important new programs. Your volunteers should meet the donors and thank them for their monetary contribution. The donors should meet your faculty, staff, and administration so that they understand who's responsible for making sure their investment is used well.

The third celebration is for everyone—the entire community. This celebration should feature a very short program to thank those who made the successful campaign possible, followed by a celebration of this great gift to your community. The point is not that Mrs. X is a generous patron of education, it's that your campus can now offer an improved science program. The celebration is not for demonstrating that Mr. Y showed great leadership during the campaign, but rather that your students now have a child-care center that eases their lives.

The celebration should be all-encompassing, involving as many people as possible. Campuses have attractive outdoor spaces, large gathering places, and enough parking to invite the whole community. Such a celebration brings in new people and introduces them to your campus, your offerings, your faculty and staff, and your students. In nice weather, you can host an open house that allows visitors to experience your entire campus. You can prepare special exhibits for them (the prizewinners from the welding rodeo, a student art exhibition, outdoor music or drama presentations, demonstrations of emergency medical techniques, or blood pressure screenings). An event like this gives the board and your other volunteers the chance to bask in the community's admiration. It also marks the moment when the campaign is absolutely done and you can start preparing for the next one.

Gala Occasions

The celebrations described so far are a legitimate part of the fundraising campaign, and the cost should be absorbed by the campaign. Usually your college food service can provide catering and keep costs low. You stage a gala when you've created something special that in itself is going to be an attraction in the future. Whether it's a performing arts center that will be used by the entire community, a campus art gallery, or a new dining room attached to your culinary arts center, you want to bring in interested community members.

You can charge for this, because you're giving people a first look at your new building and an insider's glimpse of what all the hoopla has been about. The gala can be for people who'll pay for the privilege of a first look or who want a unique experience. Here are examples of two colleges in Washington that decided to have a gala after a campaign.

- South Puget Sound Community College opened a spacious, state-of-the-art performing arts center. It invited the community to a celebration, at which a dozen regional acts performed.
- South Seattle Community College renovated its dining room and installed a demonstration kitchen as part of its culinary arts fundraising campaign. At the completion of the campaign, the college staged a dinner in which each course was prepared by a different chef from a well-known restaurant, all of whom had graduated from the culinary program over the past decades. The funds raised from this $100-a-plate dinner (all food and wine were donated) added to the campaign total and led to an ongoing event that supports scholarships.

If you're going to the trouble of staging a gala, with Klieg lights, musicians, good food, fancy wine, and perhaps a well-known entertainer, you're going to have to spend a lot. Get underwriters to cover your costs—they'll want to be associated with a winner, and it's a good way to attract some corporations that want high visibility but aren't especially charitable. Charge enough to make a tidy profit—maybe enough for an endowed scholarship or a professional development fund for a year. People love a party, and having it at a gleaming new site that the entire community has come together to build is a good thing. Using the opening to raise more money is simply icing on the cake.

CHAPTER 25

STEWARDSHIP FOR THE FUTURE

The campaign is over. You've celebrated, reveled, and relaxed. You wake up in the morning, and you no longer have to ask yourself, "Will we make it?" You've reached your goal, the building is built or nearly so, the endowment is invested with policies in place, and the new program will start in a few months. The entire campus has breathed a sigh of relief.

But, from the point of view of your donors, the campaign has really just begun. Depending on the size of your campaign, between a few dozen and several hundred people have just made one of the largest gifts of their lives. They have made those gifts in the belief that they would achieve a goal of importance to them. Their gifts reflected their most deeply held personal values. They believe in the education your college offers to the community. They believe in the need for more trained employees in medical technology, computer science, or auto maintenance.

Many of your donors will pay off their pledges over a multiyear period. Although pledge fulfillment rates for campaign gifts are extremely high (usually close to 100%), you must help ensure this high rate of fulfillment by exercising excellent stewardship of your donors. If they feel as if they know how their gift is being used, are made to feel like an insider, and continue to receive attention from you on a regular basis, the chances of them completing their obligation are increased.

Remember that they haven't given to a building, an endowment, or anything concrete or financial. They've given to something more precious—the ability to achieve change in your community. They will continue to support your mission and protect their investment as long as they are convinced that you bring their ideals and values to life. If you maintain and improve the quality of education at your college, offer relevant programs with great teachers, and help invigorate the community, they will continue to support you financially and to act as your advocates in the community. Some will join your board. Some will join your advisory committees. Some will talk about you at the Rotary Club or at their golf club. Some will help you gain access to other leaders. But none of this will happen unless you are accountable.

The third ethical principle discussed in chapter 3 is accountability. Accountability means many things to donors. It means that you should report to them how the campaign has gone. Did you reach your goal? Stay under budget? If not, why not? It also means that they want to know you're protecting their investment. If you've established an endowment, how is it being invested? What sort of return will you get? What are the fees charged?

Most of all, accountability is about your ability to deliver your mission. You promised that your campaign would allow you to reach more people, serve them better, and perhaps offer new courses or programs. Has that happened? How can you demonstrate that you are reaching more people in more effective ways? Did you establish evaluation procedures and standards?

You have to be willing to share your outcomes with your donors. You made projections about your enrollment and your quality of instruction. You should share your results with your donors. That's what they've paid for.

Sustaining Lifelong Relationships With Donors

The worst mistake that you can make is to assume that someone's gift to your campaign is his or her final gift to you. Would you buy a new house and then stop putting money into it for maintenance and modernization? No—it would remain the biggest recipient of your expenditures for housing. Your college is no different. You've spent months or years developing a relationship with a donor. This relationship was not based on a single gift—it was based on creating an ongoing commitment and partnership that would ensure that both you and the donor feel gratified by the progress your college is making. Midland College in Texas received a million-dollar gift from a new donor, recognized by naming a building for his wife. In the ensuing years, the man was made part of the college family, brought in to celebrate his own and the college's milestones. Although he had graduated from a nationally prominent research university, he came to feel closer to his hometown college than to his alma mater. At his death, he left his significant estate to the college.

As time goes on, your major donors should deepen their relationship with you, not abandon it. They should feel that they are part of your family, are entitled to frequent reports on your progress, and be privy to your family secrets. Your major donors are fully aware that in most cases you can't survive without ongoing support. They should be part of your future celebrations and successes, as well as your confidants when things are not going well.

As I mentioned in the discussion of ethical fundraising earlier in the book, you have to be open and honest about your organization. You can't hide the bad or mask disappointments. Your donors deserve an honest, complete report. They have your best interests at heart and will not try to apportion blame—if they're not surprised.

More and more, major donors see themselves as actively involved in the organizations they support. They don't want to meddle in the organization, but they want to feel useful. Unless they know your challenges, they can't help you. By denying them that opportunity, you are missing an opportunity, as well as implying a lack of trust in their fidelity to you.

"The early part of each working day I write letters to donors—yes, long hand and personal. They deserve that kind of attention from the president. They are friends of the college, thus my friends."

—Daniel (2002)

Good and bad things happen to everyone. Your donors are attracted to you because they feel needed, but also because they know you're willing to take chances. They will forgive you for failures and mistakes, as long as you show a willingness to learn from them.

Always expect your donors to support you in hard times if they have the opportunity. Don't spare them bad news or save them for when you really need them. Let them be part of your college on an ongoing basis, so that they are never surprised or feel that they're the last to know about major developments.

Currently, with state budgets shrinking, many colleges find themselves having to lay off staff, close doors to qualified students, and curtail important but unprofitable programs. This is news that will be in your local newspapers, in blogs, and on TV. Your donors deserve to be the first to know what you are doing to meet these challenges and how you will be affected. You can't expect them to believe that you'll escape unscathed. In most cases, such honesty and demonstration of need will translate into renewed generosity on their part.

Share good news as well. Your faithful donors and board members should be the first to know when you receive a big grant. They should be in the lead position to thank the donor and tell others about your success. They should know when your students place highly in national competitions or your faculty members publish books or win awards.

The Cost of Good Stewardship

The point of this chapter is that when the campaign is over, contacts with donors must go on. Your college needs to remain in close touch with them, to ensure that they will continue to be your first line of support in the future. That takes staff time, materials, and technology infrastructure.

You have to have an interactive Web site and frequent e-mails, phone calls, and notes from the college. The foundation should pay for a financial audit and include its major findings in a printed annual report. You need to gather your important donors for advisory meetings and updates, show them the new laboratory, introduce them to the new dean of student affairs, and invite them to your conference championship in basketball.

In general, if you have an active, ongoing fundraising program that follows on a capital campaign, you need to retain a full-time staff person for every 200 major donors you wish to retain contact with. Professional development staff will not only pay for themselves but also generate increased revenue over time. Their contribution will be quantifiable and predictable, assuming you and your fellow board members perform your tasks. Often, this means retaining your campaign manager, who already has relationships with these donors and has a track record of success.

When the campaign is over, your job starts again. As a foundation board member, you are responsible for maintaining the relationships you generated during the course of the campaign. Your staff members can support these activities, but if one of your friends has made a $50,000 gift to the scholarship fund, you have to make certain that person remains connected to that gift. Make sure the donor comes to the annual scholarship banquet and meets the recipient of the scholarship. If the donor has contributed to an EMT program, arrange for him or her to ride along with a crew one night, ideally in an ambulance that includes one of your college's graduates in its crew. You are the donor's peer. No matter how mature and skilled your foundation staff members are, they cannot take your place. All of the same reasons why you had to be part of all campaign requests factor into why you provide the lead during stewardship efforts. Donors to your first campaign, at whatever level, are the best prospects as donors to your next one.

REFERENCES

American Association of Community Colleges. (2009a). *Community colleges past and present.* Retrieved from the AACC Web site: http://www.aacc.nche.edu/AboutCC/history/Pages/pasttopresent.aspx

American Association of Community Colleges. (2009b). *Fast facts.* Available from http://www.aacc.nche.edu/AboutCC/Pages/fastfacts.aspx

American Association of Fund-Raising Counsel, Association for Healthcare Philanthropy, Council for Advancement and Support of Education, and the Association of Fundraising Professionals. (1993). *Donor bill of rights.* Washington, DC: CASE. Available from the CASE Web site: www.case.org

American Association of University Professors. (2009, April 13). AAUP rating scale. *Chronicle of Higher Education, 55*(32). Retrieved from http://chronicle.com/stats/aaup/ratingscale/2009aaupratingscale.htm

Angelo, M. A. (2005, October). A fundraising boost: community corteges are learning about alumni in the quest for more financial support. *University Business.* Available from findarticles.com

Association of Community College Trustees. (2009). *Guide to trustee roles and responsibilities.* Retrieved from http://www.acct.org/resources/center/roles-responsibilities.php

Bart, M. (2009, January 26). Fundraising strategies for community colleges. *Faculty Focus.* Retrieved from http://www.facultyfocus.com/articles/trends-in-higher-education/fundraising-strategies-for-community-colleges/

Bloom, A. (2009, May 31). Maricopa Community Colleges seeking more funds. *The Arizona Republic.* Retrieved from http://www.azcentral.com/community/mesa/articles/2009/05/31/20090531collegetaxes0531.html?&wiredi

Budd, S. G. (2006). *Community colleges: Empowering people—Enhancing communities. The case for private philanthropic support* (New Century Resource Paper #4, 2nd ed.). Washington, DC: Council for Resource Development.

Center on Philanthropy at Indiana University and American Express. (2007, November). *American Express charitable gift survey.* Indianapolis, IN: Center on Philanthropy at Indiana University. Retrieved from http://www.philanthropy.iupui.edu/Research/amex_gift_survey.pdf

Center on Philanthropy at Indiana University. (2009, March). *The 2008 study of high net worth philanthropy: Issues driving charitable activities among affluent households.* Indianapolis, IN: Author. Retrieved from http://www.philanthropy.iupui.edu/Research/docs/2008BAC_HighNetWorthPhilanthropy.pdf

Chait, R. P., Ryan, W. P., & Taylor, B. E. (2004). *Governance as leadership: Reframing the work of nonprofit boards.* New York: Wiley.

Clements Group, L.C. (2009). *A summary: "The feasibility study: A road map to success."* Retrieved June 30, 2009, from http://www.clmgroup.com/whitepaper-feasibilitystudy.htm

Community College of Vermont. (2009). *Mission, vision, and values.* Retrieved from http://www.ccv.edu/about/mission.html

Conrad, J. (2009, Winter). Partnerships key to National Energy Center of Excellence. *Dispatch.* Available from the Council for Resource Development Web site: www.crdnet.org

Council for Advancement and Support of Education. (2009). *CASE reporting standards and management guidelines for educational fundraising* (4th ed.). Washington, DC: Author.

Culp, K., LeRoy, M. L., & Armistead, L. P. (2008). *The feasibility study: A road map to success* (New Century Resource Paper #16). Washington, DC: Council for Resource Development.

Daniel, D. (2002, January). *Our time has come. Fundraising in the community college: A president's perspective* (New Century Resource Paper #3). Washington, DC: Council for Resource Development.

Donor Advising, Research and Educational Services. (2009). *Philanthropy facts.* Retrieved June 30, 2009, from http://www.donoradvising.com/press_facts.php

Edwards, J., & Hawn, S. (2003). *Timing right for developing a planned giving program* (New Century Resource Paper #5). Washington, DC: Council for Resource Development.

Farrell, A. (2008, March 13). Millionaire population growth slows. *Forbes.com.*

Galford, R. M., & Maruca, R. F. (2006). *Your leadership legacy: Why looking toward the future will make you a better leader today.* Boston, MA: Harvard Business School Press.

Giving Institute. (2007). *Standards of practice and code of ethics.* Retrieved from http://www.givinginstitute.org/code/index.cfm?pg=Code_of_ethics.cfm

Giving USA Foundation. (2009, July). *Giving USA 2009: The annual report for the year 2008.* Available from the Giving USA Foundation Web site: http://www.givingusa.org

Grant, K. A. (2008, Fall). Technology and the foundation: What every president should consider. *Dispatch.* Available from the Council for Resource Development Web site: www.crdnet.org

Hrywna, M. (2008, July 1). *Giving USA* shows bequests, foundations boosted otherwise flat giving to $306 billion. *The Nonprofit Times.* Retrieved from http://www.nptimes.com/08July/7-1%20Special%20Report.pdf

Ilisagvik College. (2006). *About us.* Retrieved June 30, 2009, from http://webspace.ilisagvik.cc/index.php?option=com_content&task=view&id=19&Itemid=63

Ivy Tech Community College. (2009). *April in Paris 2009.* Retrieved from http://www.ivytech.edu/indianapolis/ivybay

Kennedy, J. L. (2004, Winter). Foundation fundraising 101: Introduction to the world of private foundations. *Dispatch.* Available from the Council for Resource Development Web site: www.crdnet.org

Kentucky Community & Technical Community College System. (2009, June 5). *BGTC hosts chef camp 2009 for kids.* Retrieved June 30, 2009, from http://www.kctcs.edu/News_and_Events/News_Articles/Bowling_Green/BGTC_hosts_Chef_Camp_2009_for_Kids.aspx

Lanning, P. (2008a, January 8). The true state of fund-raising at two-year colleges. *Community College Times.* Retrieved from http://www.communitycollegetimes.com/article.cfm?ArticleId=710

Lanning, P. (2008b, October 31). Reaching critical mass: Why community colleges need to increase private funding. *Chronicle of Higher Education.*

López-Rivera, M. (2009, February 27). Pay of senior administrators still beats inflation, even in sluggish economy. *The Chronicle of Higher Education.* Retrieved from http://chronicle.com/weekly/v55/i25/25a02201.htm#table

Maister, D. H., Green, C. H., & Galford, R. M. (2001). *The trusted advisor.* New York: Simon & Schuster.

Maricopa Community Colleges. (2009). *Vision, mission and values.* Retrieved from http://maricopa.edu/academic/AARO/Accreditation/Vision.html

Miami Dade College. (2009a). *About Miami Dade College.* Retrieved from http://www.mdc.edu/main/about

Miami Dade College. (2009b). *Mission & vision.* Retrieved from http://www.mdc.edu/main/about/mission_vision.asp

Network for Good. (2008, July 29). *Ephilanthropy code of ethics.* Retrieved from http://www.fundraising123.org/article/ephilanthropy-code-ethics

Perkins, J. (2007, July 24). *Is it worth it? An ROI calculator for social network campaigns.* Retrieved from http://www.frogloop.com/social-network-calculator

Prince, R. A., & File, K. M. (2001). *The seven faces of philanthropy.* San Francisco: Jossey-Bass.

Spectrem Group. (2009, March 11). *U.S. millionaires shrink 27% to lowest level since 2003* [Press release]. Retrieved from http://www.spectrem.com/custom.aspx?id=93

Renton Technical College. (2005). *TRC—Technical Resource Center.* Retrieved from http://www.rtc.edu/Foundation/TRC

Tacoma Community College. (2006, February 2). *Primo Grill supports art at TCC.* Retrieved from http://www.tacomacc.edu/advantage/story.aspx?storyid=52

Tacoma Community College. (2009). *Mission, vision & strategic plan.* Retrieved from http://www.tacomacc.edu/abouttcc/missionvisionandstrategicplan.aspx

Wagner, L. (2007, Spring/Summer). Embracing diversity in community college fundraising. *Dispatch.* Available from the Council for Resource Development Web site: www.crdnet.org

Webber, A. M. (2009). *Rules of Thumb: 52 truths for winning at business without losing your self.* New York, NY: HarperBusiness.

Wicker, L. (2005, Winter). Internal campaign: Success story of 100% participation. *Dispatch.* Available from the Council for Resource Development Web site: www.crdnet.org

Zeiss, T. (2008). *Resource development for community colleges* [CD]. Madison, WI: Magna Publications. Available from www.magnapubs.com (Online seminar originally aired May 28, 2008)

Resources

Web Sites

Fundraising and Philanthropy

Association of Fundraising Professionals (www.afpnet.org)
The sanctioning organization for professional fundraisers in the United States and most of the world. Offers useful information, reviews of publications, and other how-to advice. For specific documents on ethics codes and guidelines and donors' rights, go to www.afpnet.org/ethics.

BoardSource (www.Boardsource.org)
Offers advice to boards in every area discussed in this book. Produces many helpful books, papers, and electronic tools that offer guidance and instruction.

The Center on Philanthropy at Indiana University (http://www.philanthropy.iupui.edu)
Good source of research of interest to nonprofit professionals and training programs for fundraisers.

Certified Fund Raising Executive International (http://www.cfre.org/)
Establishes and administers a voluntary certification process based on current and valid standards that measure competency in the practice of philanthropic fundraising.

Chronicle of Philanthropy (www.philanthropy.com)
Information about the state of philanthropy, new techniques and trends, and periodic surveys. Indispensible for every development shop.

The Clements Group, L.C. (www.clmgroup.com)
Focuses on managing major gift and other campaigns for community colleges; has stories of recent campaigns and links to clients' Web sites.

The Collins Group (www.collinsgroup.com)
Resources for fundraising campaigns, including detailed templates for developing case statements and a how-to-ask toolbox.

Council for Advancement and Support of Education (www.case.org)
See page 227.

Council for Resource Development (www.crdnet.org)
See page 228.

The Foundation Center (www.foundationcenter.org)
A national nonprofit service organization recognized as the nation's leading authority on organized philanthropy, connecting nonprofits and the grantmakers supporting them to tools and information they can trust.

National Center for Charitable Statistics (http://nccs.urban.org)
National clearinghouse of data on the nonprofit sector in the United States.

Fundraising and Social Networking

Dosh Dosh (www.doshdosh.com)
Managed by a philosophy student in Toronto, blog offers Internet marketing and blogging tips and social media strategies for bloggers, entrepreneurs, Web publishers, marketers, freelancers, and small business owners.

Frogloop (www.frogloop.com)
Care2's online nonprofit marketing blog.

Meyer Memorial Trust Weblog (www.mmt.org/weblog/)
"This is a forum for discussion of all things related to our mission of investing in people, places and efforts that deliver significant social benefit to Oregon and southwest Washington."

NPTech Blog (http://nptech.info)
A resource aggregating nonprofit technology information from across the Internet.

General Works on Fundraising and Advancement

Angelica, E. (2001). *The Fieldstone Alliance guide to crafting effective mission and vision statements.* St. Paul, MN: Fieldstone Alliance. —Offers advice on involving constituencies in creating mission and vision statements that convey your uniqueness and value.

Briscoe, M. G. (1994). *Ethics in fundraising: Putting values into practice.* San Francisco: Jossey-Bass.
—Offers insight into ensuring your organization that your fundraising practices meet all applicable ethical guidelines.

Burk, P. (2003). *Donor-centered fundraising.* Chicago: Cygnus Applied Research.
—A research-based approach to attracting and keeping donors; especially valuable for its focus on donor stewardship.

Chait, R. P., Ryan, W. P, & Taylor, B. E. (2005). *Governance as leadership: Reframing the work of nonprofit boards.* Hoboken, NJ: Wiley.
—Invaluable resource for foundation board members as they seek ways to spend their time as productively as possible for the benefit of the college. Takes board membership beyond policy creation and fiscal management to the more challenging realms of truly shaping (and reshaping) the organization.

Chronicle of Philanthropy. (2009, June 26). *The philanthropy 50: Americans who gave the most in 2008.* Retrieved from http://philanthropy.com/topdonors/gifts.php?view=topdonors&year=2008&sort=rank&page=2
—From an annual database, lists the largest givers during 2008, with the smallest being $50 million and the largest $5.2 billion.

Council for Aid to Education. (2009, June 18). *A current overview of philanthropy and the economy.* Retrieved from http://www.ccsfundraising.com/about-philanthropy/forum

Grace, K. S. (2004). *Fundraising mistakes that bedevil all boards (and staff too): A 1-hour guide to identifying and overcoming obstacles to your success.* Medfield, MA: Emerson and Church.
—Offers a quick guide to fundraising for the nonprofessional and practical advice to help boards avoid wasted effort.

Grace, K. S. (2005). *Beyond fundraising: New strategies for nonprofit innovation and investment* (2nd ed.). New York: Wiley.
—This seminal work helped change the philosophy of fundraising from just asking for money to a more holistic approach that results in long-lasting, meaningful relationships that translate into maximum support for your organization.

Hammond, S. H., & Mayfield, A. B. (1998). *The thin book of appreciate inquiry* (2nd ed.). Plano, TX: Thin Book.
—Provides a brief introduction to learning how to use what you are doing right to guide you toward a more successful future, rather than focusing on what you are doing wrong. An indispensible aid in strategic planning.

Hammond, S. H., & Mayfield, A. B. (2004). *The thin book of naming elephants: How to surface undiscussables for great organizational success.* Plano, TX: Thin Book.
—Explains how to discuss the most difficult topics and ensure that you don't ignore your elephants.

La Piana, D. (2008). The nonprofit strategy revolution: Real-time strategic planning in a rapid-response world. St. Paul, MN: Fieldstone Alliance.
—Offers detailed advice on strategic planning for nonprofit organizations.

Maister, D. H., Green, C. H., & Galford, R. M. (2001). *The trusted advisor*. New York: Simon & Schuster.
—Written for a general audience, especially for those in personal service industries such as consulting and accounting, but helps explain what it takes for volunteer fundraisers to effectively influence decisions made by peers.

Prince, R. A., & File, K. M. (2001). *The seven faces of philanthropy.* San Francisco: Jossey-Bass.
—Offers a useful and provocative typology of donors and their motivations for giving. Although some assertions rely on questionable stereotypes, the work is helpful in helping board members determine why their friends might wish to support a community college.

Sternberg, D. (2008). *Fearless fundraising for nonprofit boards* (2nd ed.). Washington, DC: BoardSource.
—Offers ways to motivate and empower boards to get involved in fundraising. Explains the roles that CEOs, development professionals, and board members play in the fundraising process.

Sturtevant, W. T. (2004). *The artful journey: Cultivating and soliciting the major gift* (2nd ed.). New York, NY: Institutions Press.
—Remains the best work on major gift fundraising in higher education. Sturtevant writes in an engaging style to describe the process by which a college can transform someone from a prospect into a lifelong donor.

Warwick, M. Hart, T., & Allen, N. (Eds.). (2008). *Fundraising on the Internet: The ephilanthropyfoundation.org's guide to success online.* San Francisco: Jossey-Bass.
—A collection of recent resources, as well as guidelines on how to keep up to date in an ever-changing field.

Wolverton, B. (2008, February 29). Private donations to colleges rise for 4th consecutive year. *Chronicle of Higher Education.*

Works Focusing on Fundraising Campaigns

Bancel, M. (2008). *Preparing your capital campaign.* San Francisco: Jossey-Bass.
—Offers an extremely useful and user-friendly workbook for organizations considering launching a campaign.

Grover, S. R. (2006). *Capital campaigns: A guide for board members and others who aren't professional fundraisers but who will be the heroes who create a better community.* Lincoln, NE: iUniverse, Inc.

Novom, M. (2007). *The fundraising feasibility study: It's not about the money.* New York: Wiley.
—Offers more information than you will ever need about conducting a feasibility study, including best practices in all facets of this important phase of a campaign.

Schumacher, E. C., & Seiler, T. L. (2008). *Building your endowment.* San Francisco: Jossey-Bass.
—Introduction to raising funds for endowments.

Seiler, T. L. (2008). *Developing your case for support.* San Francisco: Jossey-Bass.
—A detailed workbook to guide organizations through the production of an effective case for support.

Worth, M. J. (2002). Elements of the Development Program. In *New strategies for educational fund raising.* Westport, CT: American Council on Education/Praeger.

Works Focusing on Community Colleges

From the Community College Times *and* Community College Journal

CC Times. (2007, October 26). The state of fund-raising at community colleges. *Community College Times.* Retrieved from http://www.communitycollegetimes.com/article.cfm?TopicId=8&ArticleId=580
—A critical look at community college fundraising and suggestions to improve results.

Chappell, C. (2009, April 15a). Colleges get better at soliciting funds. *Community College Times.*
—The Council for Aid to Education recently announced that contributions to all colleges and universities are up 6.2%, reaching $31.60 billion, the most ever reported.

Chappell, C. (2009, April 15b). Fund-raising challenges in a down economy. *Community College Times.*
—As public funds become more unreliable in the current economy, fundraising is becoming even more critical for community colleges.

Community College Journal. (2008, January/February). Fund raising from the top. *Community College Journal, 78*(4), 30–31.

Dembicki, M. (2008, April 22). Salt Lake Community College tops fundraising list. *Community College Times.*
—Salt Lake Community College in Utah is well known for its biotechnology and entrepreneurship programs. Now it can add fundraising to the list.

Dembicki, M. (2009, February 2). Investments are down, but donations are up. *Community College Times.*
—Investment portfolios of most community college foundations have taken it on the chin over the past year. But, despite the recession, many two-year college foundations are seeing a spike in do-

nations, from small, individual contributions to grants from companies and foundations.

Halliday, S. (2009, May 26). "Affinity marketing" can improve fund raising. *Community College Times.*
—Times are tough for nonprofits, including institutions of higher education. But some colleges and universities are maintaining strong levels of contributions.

Halligan, T. (2008, February/March). Growing your donor base. *Community College Journal, 78*(4), 27–29.
— Explains how to create strategic and effective fundraising campaigns for community colleges to attract new donors. Calls for top-down commitment from college leaders, investment in software applications to manage annual campaigns and gifts, and use of Web site as a forum to promote the effects of special gifts.

Morley, R. H., & Gaudette, M. (2009, January/February). Gift planning: You can't afford not to. *Community College Journal, 79*(4), 32–35.
—Excerpt from a CRD report, describes need for planning and types of gifts.

Piwetz, E. (2007, October 26). Fund raising is about community ties, personal touch. *Community College Times.*
—"Friendraising" and subsequent fundraising at Midland College has been not only rewarding and fun but also relatively easy.

Pulley, J. (2008, November 7). Fund raising a priority during economic slump. *Community College Times.*
—A sharp decline in the value of the endowment at Montgomery County Community College in Pennsylvania will force the institution to cut financial aid next year. One in every five scholarships could vanish.

Viniar, B. (2008, February 4). Mind your Ps in fund raising. *Community College Times.*
—The speakers at the Institute for Community College Development's recent "Growing Giving" program were corporate and private donors, development professionals, trustees, foundation board members, college presidents, and authors. Their perspectives were diverse, but their messages were consistent: If you want to succeed in increasing private support for your community college, mind your Ps—pride, professionalism, personal relationships, partnerships, philanthropy, and perseverance.

Books and Articles

Angelo, J. M. (2005, October). A fundraising boost: Community colleges are learning about alumni in the quest for more financial support. *University Business.* Retrieved from http://www.universitybusiness.com/viewarticle.aspx?articleid=156
—Excellent article includes case study of alumni giving at Monroe Community College.

Babitz, B. (2007). *Growing giving: A Guide to securing private support for your community college.* Washington, DC: CASE Books.
—Provides specific recommendations to enhance the productivity, effectiveness, and bottom-line returns of community college advancement efforts.

Boice, B. P. (2008, November/December). A collaborative effort. *Advancing Philanthropy.* Available at http://www.afpnet.org/content_documents/a_collaborative_effort.pdf
—A history of the fundraising success enjoyed by the Kentucky community college system in tandem with multiple campaigns using the same consulting firm.

Chen, G. (2009, January 20). How community colleges fundraise to improve campuses. *Community College Review.* Retrieved from http://www.communitycollegereview.com/articles/73
—Outlines ways in which community colleges can increase fundraising to meet vital needs.

Cohen, T. (2008, March 17). Johnston Community College retools fundraising, *Philanthropy Journal.* Retrieved from http://www.philanthropyjournal.org/nc/ncnews/johnston-community-college-retools-fundraising.
—A case study of how a rural community college revitalized its fundraising and quadrupled its endowment.

Craft, W. M., & Guy, K. E. (2005, September). *Knowing where you're going: Strategic planning and community college fundraising* (New Century Resource Paper #6. Washington, DC: Council for Resource Development.

Foxwell, E., & Myers, J. (1986, June). Winning tickets: Capital campaign strategies that helped rally support for seven community colleges. *Currents, 12*(6), 40–45.
—Describes strategies that helped rally support for Bishop State Junior College (AL), College of the Desert (CA), Frontier Community College (IL), Kalamazoo Valley Community College (MI), Lorain County Community College (OH), Rancho Santiago Community College (CA), and Somerset County College, NJ.

Gose, B. (2006, October 27). At a growing number of community colleges, fund raising is no longer optional. *Chronicle of Higher Education, 53*(10), p. B5.
—Discusses community college fundraising programs, including several capital campaigns. Colleges highlighted include Rockingham Community College (NC), Valencia Community College (FL), Queensborough Community College (NY), Dallas County Community College District, Trident Technical College (SC), Ivy Tech Community College system (IN), Arkansas State University at Mountain Home, and Cape Cod Community College (MA).

Henderson Community College. (2007, November 9). *HCC surpasses campaign goal.* Retrieved from http://www.henderson.kctcs.edu/news/news_detail.asp?newsid=157

—A summary of a Kentucky community college campaign that exceeded its $3.5 million goal by almost 50%.
Lyons, N. L. (2007). The advancement myths of community colleges. *Currents, November/December.*
Meaders, S. J., Carrier, S. M., & Keener, B. J. (2003). *A study of resource development at community colleges* (New Century Resource Paper #7). Washington, DC: Council for Resource Development.
Wilmington College. (2006, January 20). *WC exceeds $17 million goal as fundraising campaign concludes* [News release]. Retrieved from http://www.wilmington.edu/about/news.cfm?news_id=64&archive=no
—Provides an exciting summary of a successful campaign by Wilmington College in Delaware. The brief article illustrates most of the elements discussed in this book.

Strategic Plans

California Community Colleges
http://strategicplan.cccco.edu/Default.aspx?tabid=56
Davidson County Community College (NC)
http://www.davidsonccc.edu/pdfs/StrategicPlanningSummary.pdf
Tacoma Community College (WA)
http://www.tacomacc.edu/abouttcc/missionvisionandstrategicplan/

Campaign Case Statements

Blue Ridge Community College: "Securing Our Future" Endowment Campaign http://www.brcc.edu/EdFound/support/sofec.htm
Ivy Tech Community College: "Building Communities. Changing Lives." Vision Campaign http://www.ivytech.edu/kokomo/about/give/Annual_update08.pdf
Mount Wachusett Community College: "Where Learning Never Ends" Campaign http://www.mwcc.edu/PDFs/CapitolCampaign.pdf

Webinars

Coulter, E., & Marti, E. (Presenters). (2007). *Building and enhancing fundraising efforts for community colleges* [CD]. Washington, DC: Council for Advancement and Support of Education. Available from www.case.org (Online seminar originally aired April 26, 2007)
—Offers new perspectives on the importance of advancement for community colleges and provides tools to boost fundraising activity while enhancing marketing efforts. Also helps in identifying and building new donor constituents.

Hawn, S. (Presenter). (2007). *Establishing and developing a planned giving program* [CD]. Washington, DC: Council for Advancement and Support of Education. Available from www.case.org (Online seminar originally aired December 5, 2007)
—Gives a detailed overview of the steps to initiating a planned giving program—or reigniting a dormant one—that can become a source of long-term private support for your community college.

Johnston, R. (2008). *Zero to $60,000: Fundraising for community colleges* [CD]. Madison, WI: Magna Publications. Available from www.magnapubs.com (Online seminar originally aired November 19, 2008)
—Addressed to directors of development, vice presidents, executive directors of foundations, and directors of institutional advancement. Johnston shares insights gained from a highly successful development campaign at Randolph Community College.

Kirtland, S. (Presenter). (2009). *The easy way to develop a strategic marketing communications plan* [CD]. Washington, DC: Council for Advancement and Support of Education. Available from www.case.org (Online seminar originally aired March 26, 2009)
—Gives a step-by-step approach to developing a strategic marketing plan and provides sample documents from a college communications plan that used this successful approach. Especially valuable for community colleges and small colleges in navigating internal politics and marketing subjectivity.

Starace, M. (Presenter). (2008). *Building and growing your community college alumni program* [CD]. Washington, DC: Council for Advancement and Support of Education. Available from www.case.org (Online seminar originally aired March 26, 2009)
—Learn techniques that can help move your alumni program forward and build brand loyalty. Get practical information on how to develop and maintain a useful database, define your alumni and build internal support for your program. Review best practices from a community college that has been involved in alumni programming for more than 20 years and learn what it takes to ensure long-term success.

Zeiss, T. (2008). *Resource development for community colleges* [CD]. Madison, WI: Magna Publications. Available from www.magnapubs.com (Online seminar originally aired May 28, 2008)
—President of Central Piedmont Community College encourages participants to create a culture of entrepreneurialism and provides specific examples of how to maximize primary and alternative revenue sources.

APPENDIX A

Fundraising Campaign Budget Worksheet

Budget Category	Amount
Construction—Soft Costs	
Project planning fees	
Architectural design fees	
Architectural consultants (e.g., interior design, acoustical)	
Engineering fees	
Redesign fees (if applicable)	
Land acquisition costs	
Exhibit design (if applicable)	
Site survey/site preparation	
Project administration—internal (additional staff)	
Project financing (% interest plus fees on $ million for years)	
Other	
Subtotal	$
Construction—Hard Costs	
Construction: sq. ft. @ $ per sq. ft.	
General contractor construction	
Sales tax	
Construction/structural testing	
Demolition	
Telephone/computer networking system	
Furniture, fixtures, equipment	
Landscaping	
Permanent donor recognition (e.g., donor wall, plaques)	
Construction contingency @ %/yr. through midpoint of construction	
Other	
Subtotal	$

Budget Category	Amount
Project—Soft Costs	
Permits/fees	
Hook-up fees/utilities	
Construction and liability insurance	
Performance bond	
Relocation costs (including transition)	
Real estate property taxes during construction	
Appraisal (for construction loan)	
Owner's representative/project management	
Legal closing costs	
Title insurance	
Environmental assessment	
Closing costs	
Lender's inspection	
Project contingency (miscellaneous)	
Other	
Subtotal	$
Fundraising Costs	
Campaign personnel	
Infrastructure/resources	
Professional fees	
Materials	
Campaign meetings/events	
Donor recognition	
Other	
Subtotal	$
Budget Summary	
Construction—soft costs	$
Construction—hard costs	$
Project—soft costs	$
Fundraising costs	$
Total Projected Budget	$

APPENDIX B

SAMPLE GIFT CHARTS

Profile of Gifts Needed to Raise $1,500,000				
Gift Size	**# Needed**	**Category Total**	**Running Total**	**% of Total**
		Keystone Gift		
$300,000	1	$300,000	$300,000	20%
		Lead Gifts		
$150,000	2	$300,000	$600,000	
$100,000	3	$300,000	$900,000	
$50,000	5	$250,000	$1,150,000	77%
		Major Gifts		
$25,000	6	$150,000	$1,300,000	
$10,000	8	$80,000	$1,380,000	92%
		Community Gifts		
$5,00	15	$75,000	$1,455,000	
$1,000	25	$25,000	$1,480,000	
<$1,000	many	$20,000	$1,500,000	
TOTAL	**125+**	**TOTAL**	**$1,500,000**	**100%**

Profile of Gifts Needed to Raise $5,000,000				
Gift Size	**# Needed**	**Category Total**	**Running Total**	**% of Total**
		Keystone Gift		
$1,000,000	1	$1,000,000	$1,000,000	20%
		Lead Gifts		
$500,000	2	$1,000,000	$2,000,000	
$250,000	4	$1,000,000	$3,000,000	
$100,000	8	$800,000	$3,800,000	76%
		Major Gifts		
$50,000	10	$500,000	$4,300,000	
$25,000	12	$300,000	$4,600,000	
$10,000	18	$180,000	$4,780,000	96%
		Community Gifts		
$5000	30	$150,000	$4,930,000	
$1,000	60	$60,000	$4,990,000	
<$1,000	many	$10,000	$5,000,000	
TOTAL	**260+**	**TOTAL**	**$5,000,000**	**100%**

Profile of Gifts Needed to Raise $10,000,000				
Gift Size	**# Needed**	**Category Total**	**Running Total**	**% of Total**
		Keystone Gift		
$2,000,000	1	$2,000,000	$2,000,000	20%
		Lead Gifts		
$1,000,000	2	$2,000,000	$4,000,000	
$500,000	2	$2,000,000	$6,000,000	
$250,000	6	$1,500,000	$7,500,000	
$100,000	8	$800,000	$8,300,000	83%
		Major Gifts		
$50,000	12	$600,000	$8,390,000	
$25,000	20	$500,000	$9,400,000	
$10,000	25	$250,000	$9,650,000	97%
		Community Gifts		
$5,000	35	$175,000	$9,825,000	
$1,000	100	$100,000	$9,925,000	
<$1,000	many	$75,000	$10,000,000	
TOTAL	**325+**	**TOTAL**	**$10,000,000**	**100%**

Marketing Materials Worksheet

Item	Date Needed	Quantity	Total Cost
Stationery			
Letterhead			
Second sheets			
#10 envelopes			
Thank you cards/envelopes			
Pledge cards (triplicate)			
Return envelopes			
Other			
		Subtotal	$
Major Gifts Materials			
View books			
Press packets			
Presentation folders			
Other			
		Subtotal	$
Brochures and Newsletter			
Major donor			
Community campaign			
Newsletter (# issues/yr.)			
		Subtotal	$
Donor Recognition Materials			
Pins			
Pavers			
Plaques			
Other			
		Subtotal	$
Electronic Media			
Video			
Web site creation			
Web site redesign/enhancement			
Web site maintenance			
Donor/gifts database			
Training			
		Subtotal	$
		Total Marketing Materials Cost	**$**

APPENDIX D

JOB DESCRIPTIONS

CAMPAIGN CHAIR

Tenure: Duration of the campaign

Role: Works with staff, fundraising counsel, and community volunteers to lead the campaign.

Tasks:

- Chairs meetings of the steering committee.
- Helps establish and monitor campaign policies and progress.
- Maintains frequent contact with staff and campaign counsel to preserve momentum, reviews strategy, and implements decisions.
- Recruits and solicits additional campaign leaders.
- Works with all committees to assist in identifying prospects and tailoring strategies.
- Identifies potential donors and approaches peers for campaign gifts (initial focus on pledges of $50K+).
- Encourages campaign workers at all levels.
- Serves as key spokesperson at events and in news stories and is a constant, positive representative for the campaign.
- Makes a campaign gift that is personally significant.

Time Commitment: Approximately 3–5 hours a month is required for monthly steering committee meetings, overseeing subcampaign chairs, and making fundraising calls. Occasionally, a separate co-chair briefing may be scheduled for discussing specific strategies or issues that need to be addressed.

Board Gifts Task Force Member

Tenure: Approximately 2–3 months, until all board gifts are determined

Role: Works in concert with staff and the consultant to provides leadership for the board campaign, setting the tone and expectations for the overall campaign.

Tasks:

- Shapes board campaign to establish stretch goal and 100% participation.
- Identifies appropriate, respectful request levels for board members to reach that goal.
- Makes stretch campaign gifts that are personally significant.
- Approaches board peers for stretch campaign gifts.
- Is a constant, positive representative for the campaign.

Membership: The full task force consists of the chair plus 2–4 additional trustees.

Time Commitment: Two to three task force meetings, plus personal and team solicitations of board members.

Campaign Steering Committee Member

Tenure: Duration of the campaign

Role: Works with 2–3 co-chairs, staff, fundraising counsel, and community volunteers to lead the capital campaign.

Tasks:

- Helps establish and monitor campaign policies and progress.
- Identifies and recruits additional campaign leaders.
- Plays a key role in a campaign subcommittee or task force.
- Identifies potential donors or approach peers for campaign gifts.
- Makes a campaign gift that is personally significant.
- Maintains regular contact with staff and counsel to preserve momentum.
- Is a constant, positive representative for the campaign.

Membership: The full steering committee consists of 15–20 volunteer leaders, supported by a subcommittee of 25–50 volunteers.

Time Commitment: The full steering committee meets monthly. Approximately 1.5–3 hours per month is required plus fundraising calls.

Sample Pledge Form

Insert Logo

CAPITAL CAMPAIGN GIFT
[Insert Project Description]

Donor Information

Name ______________________________

Address ______________________________

City ______________________________ State_____ ZIP __________

Phone (Hm.) ____________________ Phone (Bus.) __________________ FAX ______________
E-mail ______________________________

Pledge Information

In consideration of the gifts of others, I (we) hereby contribute cash and/or assets to [Organization Name].

I (we) pledge a total of $ ______________ enclosed $ ______________ pledged $______________

Please bill me beginning _______ and thereafter ❑ monthly ❑ quarterly ❑ yearly ❑ other _______

I (we) wish to have this donation spread over ❑ 1 yr. ❑ 2 yrs. ❑ 3 yrs. ❑ other ____________

My gift will be matched by ______________________________ company/foundation/family.

❑ Form enclosed ❑ Form will be forwarded

❑ I (we) would like information on including [Organization Name] in my (our) will/estate planning.

Contribution Form

I (we) plan to make my (our) contribution in the form of ❑ cash ❑ check ❑ charge ❑ stock ❑ property ❑ other______________________

Please charge my credit card (check one) ❑ VISA ❑ MC number ____________________________
exp. date __________________________

Authorized signature ______________________________

Listing

(Donors will be recognized in campaign materials unless an anonymous gift is requested).
Please use the following names(s) in all acknowledgments ______________________________

Signature(s)______________________________ Date______________

Please make checks, corporate matches, and stock transfers payable to: [Organization Name]
Donations are tax-deductible to the extent allowed by the law.
Mail your pledge to: [address]
For more information, contact [Contact Name], [Title]

Phone [#] • fax [#] • [e-mail] • [Web site]

Index

Aa

Bb

Cc

Dd

Ee

Ff

Gg

Hh

Ii

Jj

Kk

Ll

Mm

Nn

Oo

Pp

Qq

Rr

Ss

Tt

Vv

Ww

Zz

About CASE and CRD

Headquartered in Washington, DC, with offices in London and Singapore, the Council for Advancement and Support of Education (CASE) is the professional organization for advancement professionals at all levels who work in alumni relations, communications, fundraising, marketing, and other areas. Today CASE's membership includes more than 3,400 colleges, universities, independent elementary and secondary schools, and educational associates in 61 countries around the world. This makes CASE one of the largest nonprofit education associations in terms of institutional membership. CASE serves more than 60,000 advancement professionals on the staffs of member institutions and has more than 22,500 professional members on its roster.

CASE helps its members build stronger relationships with their alumni and donors, raise funds for campus projects, produce recruitment materials, market their institutions to prospective students, diversify the profession, and foster public support of education. CASE also offers a variety of advancement products and services, provides standards and an ethical framework for the profession, and works with other organizations to respond to public issues of concern while promoting the importance of education worldwide.

Underscoring its commitment to community colleges, CASE has developed a number of resources specifically for community college advancement professionals, who may also take advantage of the full range of CASE resources: books, conferences, networking opportunities, the award-winning *CURRENTS* magazine, awards programs, the InfoCenter, webinars, and an online member directory.

Visit www.case.org to learn more about CASE and CASE membership.

The Council for Resource Development (CRD) is the essential education and networking choice for all community college resource development professionals. CRD connects, educates, supports, strengthens, and celebrates community college development professionals, serving over 1,500 members at more than 700 two-year institutions. Members include foundation directors; grant developers; grant managers; alumni officers; planned giving and major gifts officers; and community college presidents, administrators, faculty, and staff. CRD offers its members access to a wealth of resources and a network of colleagues all over the country and Canada who are willing to share their expertise, solutions, and innovations in fundraising.

CRD member benefits include

- Federal Funding to Two-Year Colleges Report: Members can not only access the report online but also download copies.
- *Dispatch* Newsletter: This publication reports trends, issues, activities, advice, and practices in seeking grants and fundraising to enable CRD members to better serve their colleges.
- Resource Papers: A collection of current research and resource papers directly related to community college fundraising, with new works published annually.
- CRD Electronic Mailing List: The CRD list includes over 500 active participants who discuss resource development issues.
- Member's-Only Online Access to Resources: The CRD Web site contains numerous resources in the area of grant development, foundation development, and alumni development.

Visit www.crdnet.org to learn more about CRD and CRD membership.

About the Author

Stuart R. Grover received his doctorate in history from the University of Wisconsin in 1971. He taught at University of California (Santa Barbara), Vanderbilt University, Wittenberg University, and Ohio State University over the following decade. He also directed marketing efforts for the for-credit continuing education department at Ohio State University before founding and publishing a community newspaper in Columbus, Ohio.

In 1982, he moved to the Northwest, where he founded a fundraising consulting firm, Stuart Grover and Associates. In 1990, his firm merged with The Collins Group, which grew to be the largest consulting firm in the region. During the period when he owned The Collins Group, he oversaw more than 140 capital campaigns that raised more than $1 billion. Community and technical college campaigns became a particular passion for him, primarily because of the importance of their mission and their service to their communities.

He sold the firm to his employees in 2004, although he has continued consulting. In 2006, he published *Capital Campaigns: A Guide for Board Members,* which has been used by organizations nationwide to help plan their campaigns. He wrote a chapter on feasibility studies for Lord and Lord's *The Manual of Museum Planning* and an article on community and technical college campaigns for the *Community College Journal.* He has published widely in local, regional, and national publications on a variety of topics and is a frequent speaker at fundraising conferences and workshops.